LEICESTERSHIRE
FIELDWORKERS
Bringing archaeology to life

The Medieval Earthworks of South and South-East Leicestershire Harborough District

Lutterworth
Market Harborough
Billesdon

by Robert F. Hartley

Foreword by Christopher Dyer

**Editing and layout by Kathleen Elkin
on behalf of Leicestershire Fieldworkers**

Monograph No 4
2018

Published by Leicestershire Fieldworkers, Leicester 2018

Cover Design:
A graphic representation of part of the Whatborough Map by Dan Haas, Media 4D, Market Harborough.

Printed by 4Word, Bristol

Leicestershire Fieldworkers

Leicestershire Fieldworkers is an active county archaeology society that supports individuals and local groups to investigate the remains of past human activity by practical investigation, research and small-scale excavation. It provides a forum for interested individuals to come together to hear the results of the latest research both locally and nationally and provides assistance to professional archaeologists both in the field and by reporting fieldwork results to the county Heritage and Environment Record (HER).

CONTENTS

INTRODUCTION AND ACKNOWLEDGEMENTS

Kathleen Elkin

In 1979 I and others from our archaeology course at Leicester University were sent for a week at Easter to learn landscape surveying with the Leicestershire Archaeological Survey Team comprising Peter Liddle and Robert 'Fred' Hartley (see also photographs page xiii). It was my first introduction to the medieval earthwork remains in the Leicestershire countryside and I had, of course, no idea that 40 years later I would still be in the county and publishing these last plans in Fred Hartley's Earthworks series. Most of the surveys were done pre-1995 though some have been produced or reviewed since then. They were produced to provide a baseline for earthwork survival in the fields, allowing these sites to be managed through the planning process and then for work with the Countryside Stewardship scheme with which Fred was also involved.

The importance of these surveys cannot be understated. When thinking about this Introduction I asked Richard Clark, Principal Archaeologist with the Planning Service at Leicestershire County Council, what the influence of these surveys has been for the county. He replied:

I am more than happy to confirm that Fred's work - most especially his medieval earthworks series - contributes significantly to the work of the section here, they are a regular resource and point of reference, and sit next to me as I type! Interestingly, in respect of his field work, given the elapse of time between the surveys (sometimes undertaken more than 25 years ago), and the present day, we have on a number of occasions had reason to revisit the earthworks, applying modern digital survey techniques to the recording process. In many cases the results show an on-going process of erosion particularly of those sites lacking statutory protection or designation (e.g. Scheduled Monuments or Registered Parks), most commonly within the agricultural environment, where the mechanisms of the planning process can't readily be applied.

In that context Fred's work stands as a hugely valuable point–in-time reference to the former and current earthwork landscapes of the county, a comment on the positive and negative effects of change in the agricultural environment, most especially a feature of the post-war period. In other circumstances where earthworks survive in, or close to the condition Fred recorded them, a regular feature of note is how accurate his survey has been (every bit as good as modern survey techniques), and furthermore how helpful the interpretation and knowledge he brought/ brings to each site is in informing current management. I would also note, alongside the moats, shrunken and deserted village earthworks, the country house gardens and parks, that Fred has also recorded the ordinary landscapes of medieval and early post-medieval industry and agriculture, the latter the 'Champion' landscapes of the Midland Open field system studied by Howard Gray and most recently David Hall. If anything this confirms Fred's credentials as a landscape archaeologist, a labour beyond anything I could contemplate, and represents an outstanding example of the integrated relationship of settlement and landscape, and the communities who lived and worked there. (Gray 1915, Hall 2014). (Richard Clark, pers comm.)

The Earthworks series began publication in 1983 with Rutland and continued soon after with North-West Leicestershire in 1984, North-East Leicestershire (Melton District) in 1987 and Central Leicestershire (Charnwood, Leicester City, Oadby and Wigston and Blaby) in 1989. All of these volumes were originally published by Leicestershire Museums, Arts and Records Service. Departmental and council reorganisations in both county and city then meant there was then a gap of nearly 20 years until Leicestershire Fieldworkers underwrote the cost of the next publication. The Earthworks of South-West Leicestershire (Hinckley and Bosworth) was published by them in 2008 and was the first digital version (albeit using word processing software), previous volumes having been produced by the offset litho process at County Hall. See overleaf for a plan of Leicestershire districts and the areas covered.

*Districts of
Leicestershire
and Rutland*

This current volume on the Harborough District is thus the final one in the Earthworks series and was originally intended to be three smaller books in line with the original publications. Each one of these covered a district of Market Harborough (Lutterworth, Market Harborough, Billesdon) prior to their merging in 1974 to form Harborough District. However as all three areas had been completed it was decided to publish as one volume, hence the larger size. It is clear from comments made by professional and amateur archaeologists that it is eagerly awaited 'to complete the set'. Not only that but this area of Leicestershire holds some of the most 'iconic' and widely known deserted medieval settlements (DMVs), selected by the great landscape historian W G Hoskins in the 1940s as examples for his early work. It is hoped that today's landscape historians will take these plans as a starting point for their further research.

Kathy Elkin
Leicestershire Fieldworkers

Acknowledgements

The author would like to thank Emeritus Professor Chris Dyer, of the University of Leicester Department of History, Centre for English Local History, for writing the Foreword; Bob Rutland, Peter Liddle, Anne Graf, Richard Knox and Richard Clark from the County's archaeological staff, and the work of amateur fieldworkers, especially Mick Harding and the late Arthur Hurst. Thanks are due to Leicestershire Fieldworkers for taking on the cost and final publication of this volume and Kathy Elkin for layout and editing of the original manuscripts and digitised drawings.

The editor would like to thank Richard Clark and team for their help, Dan Haas of Media 4D for his design for the cover, Maureen Hallahan for additional artwork, Nick Fothergill and Julian Pooley for illustrations, and John Roost and staff of 4word, Bristol, for final volume consolidation and printing.

ROBERT F HARTLEY - ABOUT THE AUTHOR

Robert F Hartley (Fred) was born in Glossop, Derbyshire but grew up in Stalybridge and went to Stockport Grammar School. He remembers the diesel trains freezing up in the winter of 1967 and the service reverting to steam for the duration which probably started his love of trains and industrial heritage. Taking an historically-focused Combined Studies degree at Leicester University Fred then worked for a year at Newarke Houses Museum which included cataloguing the collections for Bob Rutland. He was an archaeology site assistant for Patrick Clay at the Sproxton Barrow site and followed this up by post-excavation experience at Humberstone Store, Leicester. When a vacancy came up under the job creation programme in 1979 which had to be filled quickly Fred was in the right place at the right time to become Assistant Archaeological Survey Officer working for Peter Liddle at Jewry Wall Museum.

Although Peter and Fred worked together on some of the earthwork surveys their duties soon diverged with Peter concentrating on fieldwalking and identification and Fred specialising in earthwork survey and aerial photography (the latter with Jim Pickering). Most of the earthworks surveys were carried out alone which he now finds preferable as it allows him to work quickly carrying a mental 'map' of the shape of the field as he surveys it.

In the early 1990's Fred gained his Diploma in Museum Studies and became a very busy Curator at Harborough Museum before local government reorganisation in 1997 brought him back to County Hall as a Curator splitting up the collections of the County and City. He thus found that the card indexing done all those years ago at Newarke Houses was incredibly useful! After taking on the Curatorship of Snibston Museum for short time in 2001 Fred became Curator for the Social History collections of the County Museum Service until 2012, when he officially retired although he continued to assist with collections research until 2014. Now finally retired he has found time to join local history and gardening societies in Nottinghamshire as well as pull together and revise the plans for this final volume of the earthwork surveys. Fred has a special interest in the history of coalmining (publishing a paper on this in the Leicestershire Fieldworkers 'Medieval Leicestershire' book) and has published research on the life of George Stephenson. His latest published paper is in the Journal of the Railway and Canal Historical Society about the S. W. A. Newton Collection of photographs which record the building of the Great Central Railway (preserved at the Record Office for Leicester, Leicestershire and Rutland).

FOREWORD

Christopher Dyer
Centre for English Local History, University of Leicester

Fred Hartley's series of surveys of medieval earthworks in Leicestershire and Rutland began in the 1980s and are now completed by this volume covering south and south-east Leicestershire. The word 'earthworks' makes us think of those great mounds and embankments deliberately dug in the industrial revolution in the course of building canals and railways, and in more recent times as part of large scale road schemes. Some of the earthworks of the middle ages were created on the orders of kings, earls, abbots and landed gentry, particularly as defences, in the form of castle mounds, or as banks and ditches or moats around castles, towns and high-status houses. Earth was also moved to make dams or leats to control the flow of water, often in connection with moats, fish ponds and water mills. Documents sometimes tell us of the great expense involved in such projects in hiring itinerant gangs of labourers, not unlike the navvies of modern times. Defensive earthworks in particular were surveyed and described by pioneers of field archaeology, even as early as the eighteenth century as noticed by Fred Hartley, but especially around 1900 by such observant scholars as Hadrian Allcroft.

Another type of earthwork was beginning to be recognised by Allcroft and the researchers of his day, and these were more difficult to discover and plan: the everyday lives of medieval settlements left indelible traces. The passage of wheeled vehicles and the hooves of animals churned up the earth which was then eroded by rain, leaving holloways to mark the sites of roads and tracks. Yards where animals had been penned are visible because their trampling and the periodic removal of manure mixed with earth left rectangular hollows. The boundaries of each plot which once contained houses and farm buildings (often called a toft in the middle ages) can be identified as ditches, mounds or scarps depending on the fence, hedge or other barrier used by the villagers. The heaping of earth from the digging of ditches around houses and the accumulation of building materials and occupation debris created building platforms. Occasionally the stone foundations of the houses are visible as grass-covered walls, and we can even identify the likely site of the doors and internal partitions, but much of Leicestershire lacked abundant stone, so these remnants of ruined houses occur only occasionally, most notably at Whatborough. Beyond the edge of the settlements ridge and furrow was formed in the routine process of ploughing arable fields in narrow strips, as each year a small quantity of soil was added to the height of the ridges. So these earthworks were not executed at the direction of some aristocrat, but developed gradually by the piecemeal actions of dozens of people managing their domestic and farming operations. These relatively slight but very distinctive patterns left in pasture fields tell us where ordinary villagers had once lived and farmed, and most of Fred Hartley's work has been to record these precious indications of medieval settlement and cultivation.

Fred Hartley's publications on different parts of the county add up to a remarkable achievement in terms of the great skill required to observe the earthworks and then to transfer the perceptions on to paper. Air photography helped with deciphering the settlement earthworks, but the plans that feature on almost every page of this publication had to be drawn at ground level, by the expert observer walking over the 'humps and bumps' and assessing their size, shape and eventually their meaning. Producing these plans needed physical stamina, a practised eye, accuracy in deploying some basic surveying equipment, and powers of intellect to identify, classify and understand the patterns of the past.

One reason for admiring Fred Hartley and the Leicestershire Museums Archaeological Survey Team's ambition was that they took on a county with a high level of preservation of medieval earthworks, so to make a complete record Fred Hartley had to plot many thousands of acres of ridge and furrow from air photographs, and hundreds of acres of settlement earthworks. These many sites, often on the edge of existing villages, represented the surviving visible remains of manor houses, monastic granges, monastic sites and above all the houses, streets and boundaries of village settlements. To these can be added the features often on the edge of the settlements, such as windmill mounds, fishponds and rabbit warrens. The amount of work required to visit and record earthworks in every village and town in a large county took up Fred Hartley's time for many years. The only counties which have a similar level of recording were those surveyed in the heyday of the Royal Commission on Historical Monuments of England, of which Northamptonshire is the best example. The Royal Commission could deploy a team of fieldworkers, whereas Fred Hartley did much of the work on his own, with Peter Liddle, or with a few helpers or a single assistant.

As this addition to the series of earthwork surveys confirms, a great deal survives of the physical residues of medieval settlement and agriculture. Although those researching Leicestershire, or simply enjoying its countryside, should be grateful for the way that damage has not been inflicted on the same scale as in Northamptonshire or Warwickshire, there is no reason for complacency as Richard Clark has previously indicated in the Introduction. Fred Hartley has published an instructive series of maps of the parish of Theddingworth. The map of 1696 shows that its open fields were still functioning, with furlongs and strips covering almost the whole territory. There were only a few small areas on its western and eastern edges which had been enclosed: one field is helpfully called 'Old Close'. If the evidence of the vertical photographs taken by the RAF after the Second World War is plotted, a high proportion of the land planned as open field in 1696 was circa 1950 covered with ridge and furrow; the strips on the map were marked by the earthwork ridges. The 'old enclosures' had abundant ridge and furrow, so they had been arable before 1696. The only major destruction of the remains of medieval or early modern cultivation was in the middle of the parish, probably by some improving farmer encouraged by the wartime Ministry of Agriculture. But by 2014 most ridge and furrow had been cleared away for modern farming, leaving scarcely a sixth of the parish with the remnants of the medieval field system. A thousand years of history had been largely swept away in a few decades, and throughout the county and beyond the destruction of ridge and furrow still continues. Inevitably sites planned by Fred Hartley in the 1980s and 1990s no longer exist in the form that he saw them. The records that he made were intended to be included in the early Sites and Monuments Record maintained by the County Council, where they could be used in the planning process, and also to inform the Countryside Stewardship Scheme. His plans of earthworks have therefore played a part in conserving these important parts of the heritage.

Fred Hartley shares with other landscape historians a regard for the pioneers of the subject of the eighteenth century. In these pages he celebrates as he moves from one part of Leicestershire to another the topographers and antiquarians who were his precursors in describing and sometimes drawing plans of earthworks. In these pages we find little known figures such as Sir Thomas Cave of Stanford Hall, or John Tailby of Slawston who identified the Bush where the Hundred of Gartree met at Shangton. However the most valuable products of Fred Hartley's industry are the scientific depictions of the earthworks which he has seen and has interpreted. We can go into the countryside, Hartley in hand, knowing exactly what to expect. Sometimes there are few surprises, as sites such as Ingarsby are well known and have been photographed, planned and interpreted in the past. But there are some fresh discoveries and novelties. I am sure that I am not the only landscape historian to walk southwards from Kimcote to see the site of Poultney village, which one would expect to see next to Great Poultney Farm, only to be disappointed. Hartley approached the problem more systematically, and found the site further south, near Glenfield Farm, not near the centre of the parish, but on its edge. The remains of Poultney are on quite a small scale, but one cannot fail to be impressed by Hartley's courage and tenacity in tackling some very large sites, such as the extensive earthworks at Carlton Curlieu and Lowesby. He is not overawed by the sites on a massive scale with challenging banks and ditches, such as the castle at Sauvey in Withcote, which deserves to be much better known. Hartley offers convincing explanations of the sites that he plans and describes, but he is also honest about his puzzlement and doubts, which is comforting for those of us who are less practised than him: we also cannot explain everything that we observe. One problem that constantly prevents us arriving at a definite conclusion is the presence in many places of the remains of large and complex gardens, often of the sixteenth to eighteenth centuries. Abandoned gardens bear an uncanny resemblance to the earthworks of deserted settlements, and of course both are often found near large country houses or their sites.

Any piece of research when completed gives us a sense of satisfaction at a job well done, but we have also reached a starting point for the next stage. Fred Hartley has been very thorough, but there are still a few sites to be identified and planned. He has indicated what the earthworks represent, but no doubt other scholars will offer alternatives, in the way that Brown and Everson have their own explanations of Hamilton, Ingarsby and Knaptoft. There is also a need for the comparison and classification of the full range of sites now that they are all available. Further research on individual villages will include more research in the documents. Test pitting programmes, both in the surviving and the abandoned parts of settlements can provide a chronological dimension which must remain uncertain if the earthworks are the only source of evidence.

These surveys will provide raw material for future scholars seeking to understand the origins and early growth of villages. The earthworks are undateable but their shape and layout suggests sometimes an uncoordinated coming together of settlers, clustered around some point of attraction such as a road junction, while others invite by their neatness and regularity the conclusion that they were planned, either by an authority such as a lord, or by agreement among the community. This simple distinction has recently been doubted because it is argued that new settlers could have been accommodated by adding their houses at the end of a row, with their houses built on the strips in the open field. The other great historical problem which these surveys illuminate is of course the abandonment of medieval settlement. The abundance of earthworks in south-east Leicestershire resulting from both the desertion of villages and the reduction in size of a greater number of settlements presents us with numerous questions about the events and trends of the period 1300 to 1700, when most of the losses of houses occurred. The population fell dramatically from its peak around 1300, but we have not done enough on the chronology of that decline, or the reason for the differences in the severity of the depopulation. Any such enquiry would now need to combine the landscape evidence in Hartley's work with the documents.

Finally, a point must be made about the potential of Hartley's maps of ridge and furrow, now completed for the whole of Leicestershire. A great opportunity has arisen for a systematic study of the origin, growth, development and shrinkage of cultivated fields, using the physical remains in combination with early maps and documents. England, and more particularly the east midland counties, have an important resource, unparalleled in Europe, and yet we do not take advantage of these excellent and accessible materials.

This publication, and the others in the series have opened doors into exploring new dimensions of Leicestershire's past.

Christopher Dyer
Leicester 2018

INTRODUCTION TO HARBOROUGH DISTRICT

Robert F Hartley

This volume is a survey of earthwork evidence of Medieval and post-Medieval landscape features in south and south-east Leicestershire. It is one of a series of publications on this aspect of the landscape history of the counties of Leicestershire and Rutland. Most of the survey work was carried out between 1979 and 1995, when the author was a member of the Leicestershire Museums Archaeological Survey Team. At that time Rutland and the City of Leicester were included in Leicestershire for administrative purposes, but they were given unitary status in 1997.

Simple surveys of earthwork sites, using hachures to indicate slopes, were at that time a convenient and relatively easy way of making a map record of such sites and allowing a start to be made on interpreting it. Having set out a straight line across the site using ranging rods, a simple sighting device called a crosshead (below, top left) was used to set out survey lines at right angles and at 45 degrees to the base line. With measuring tapes laid along these lines it is possible to measure the distances to the top and bottom of any slope which is intersected, and to mark this on a plan set out with a scale version (usually 1:1000) of the grid of lines set out across the field.

Leicester University students surveying course Easter 1979

With practice it is possible to draw up quite a detailed picture of the earthworks and show how they relate to each other. Typical features include sunken roadways, the characteristic ridges and furrows of Medieval cultivation systems, rectangular platforms where buildings once stood, fish ponds, and moats. The primary purpose of the surveys was to build up knowledge of the extent and likely importance of surviving Medieval earthworks to help with planning the future conservation of these aspects of the historic landscape and to make as complete a record as possible of their surface appearance. At the very least they increased the recorded information on sites which were subsequently ploughed flat or destroyed by modern developments.

The Harborough district was formed in 1974 under the Local Government Act 1972, by the merging of the urban district of Market Harborough, Market Harborough Rural District, Billesdon Rural District and Lutterworth Rural District.

The landscape of Harborough district comprises both pastoral and upland characters. Generally the A6 Market Harborough to Leicester Road forms the boundary between the undulating upland landscape of High Leicestershire to the east and the lower pastoral landscapes of South Leicestershire to the west of the A6, areas characterised now as the Welland Valley, Laughton Hills, Lutterworth Lowlands and a small area of the Upper Soar. In the south low hills swell out of shallow valleys and villages are pinpointed by church spires peeping above dark spinneys. Near Foxton and Gumley the Laughton Hills tumble down to the Grand Union Canal and Welland Valley, forming one of the best landscapes in this part of the district.

High Leicestershire consists of the tract of land between Market Harborough, Tilton On The Hill and towards Melton Mowbray and forms some of the loneliest countryside in the Midlands. Many villages were deserted centuries ago and remote hills such as Robin-a-Tiptoe in the parish of Tilton peer out over pastures and the occasional farmhouse.

The infant River Avon and River Welland form the southern border of the district with Northamptonshire with sources at Naseby and Sibbertoft respectively.

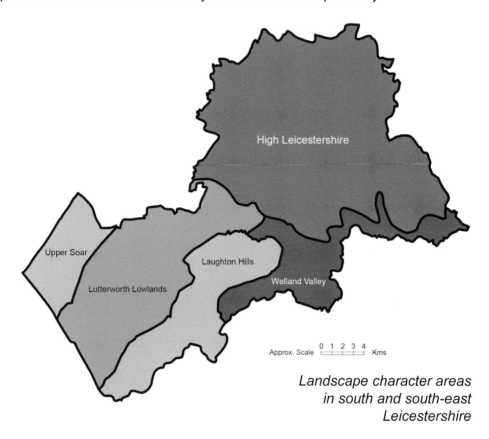

Landscape character areas in south and south-east Leicestershire

THE SURVEY

There are two types of survey reproduced here. At the end of each Part is a map of the whole area with earthwork features sketched out (initially at a scale of 1:10560) from vertical air photographs, mainly the RAF photographs taken in the mid-late 1940s, before the large scale conversion of pasture to ploughland in the second half of the 20th century.

In the main gazetteer for each Area are more detailed surveys, done initially at a scale of 1:1000, by measurement in the field using measuring tapes and a crosshead. Additional information, for example ridge and furrow, or features no longer in existence, have been plotted from aerial photographs. The original field surveys are kept by the Historic Environment Record Centre (formerly the Sites & Monuments Record) at County Hall, Glenfield, Leicestershire.

THE MAP BASE

All of the plans are drawn up on a base of the Ordnance Survey First Series large-scale maps, surveyed in the mid-1880s.

THE PARISHES

The parishes are the Civil Parishes defined on the O.S First Series maps in about 1885. These largely follow the medieval boundaries, and in most cases within this area the same boundaries have been maintained to the present day.

TYPES OF EARTHWORK

This survey in concerned with earthwork features created in the landscape between late Anglo-Saxon times and the 18th century. Most of them are elements of the Medieval arable farming landscape which was converted to pasture land (and enclosed with hedges) as part of a slow and patchwork process between the 14th and 19th centuries. Because the former arable fields, villages and other features were simply allowed to grass over, a huge amount of evidence remained visible as undulations or earthworks. This was particularly the case up to the 1960s, and it is fortunate that we have the RAF vertical air photographs to record the appearance of these features in the 1940s and 1950s.

1. Open-field Earthworks

The area was intensively cultivated during the Medieval period, with no major woodlands or open wastes. Most of the population lived in compact "nucleated" villages, surrounded by the arable fields which provided most of their food. Usually a village had three large "open fields", divided into roughly rectangular blocks called furlongs, each of which was further subdivided into cultivation strips or "lands". The strips are generally about 9 metres in width, with the soil mounded up to form long, narrow ridges. A huge amount of physical work, ploughing and digging year after year, must have gone into creating them, and the pattern of them survived long enough over the great majority of this area to be recorded as "ridge and furrow" on aerial photographs. The exact process of ridge and furrow creation is still a subject for debate.

Because the fields were farmed in common, with the villagers being allocated different strips each year, the boundaries of the strips and the furlongs would have been carefully marked with posts or stones. Each furlong had a name, and in the case of some villages there are detailed maps made before the system was dismantled. Where we have both maps and surviving Medieval documents it is possible to find out a great deal about the ownership and management of the farming landscape. The area does not have any particularly well-documented parishes, but the Record Office for Leicester, Leicestershire and Rutland (ROLLR) holds an incomplete open-field map of Lutterworth, dated 1790, and John Nichols published an interesting 1638 Terrier of the fields and village of Claybrooke (Nichols 1810, 1067-1071).

2. Settlement Earthworks

The abandonment of the open-field system of cultivation was accompanied by a reduction in the population and a process of migration within village sites or between villages. As a result most villages locally have some evidence of areas where houses, outbuildings and their related small fields have been abandoned. In some cases there may now only be a single farm, and the sites have been described as "Deserted Villages" though they may also be hamlets rather than villages. The process of desertion is much debated and probably differs from settlement to settlement and area to area in England. For a discussion about this see Richard Jones 'Contrasting patterns of village and hamlet desertion in England' (Jones 2010, 8-27).

3. Watermills

Watermills existed before the Norman conquest and continued in use in many cases into the early 20th century. Related earthworks include dams for the millpond, supply channels (leets or lades) and tailrace channels. Watermills were developed and repaired over many years, and the surviving surface evidence is more likely to be post-Medieval rather than earlier.

4. Windmills

Windmills were introduced to this area during the Medieval period. Often they were built on existing or newly-constructed earth mounds to gain extra height, and in many cases these mounds survive as earthworks.

5. Castles

The Normans built castles in the period after 1066 to subjugate the local English population. The most prominent feature was usually a conical mound or "motte". For a gazetteer of castle sites in Leicestershire see Richard Knox 'The medieval fortified sites of Leicestershire and Rutland' (Knox 2015). The castle sites of Sauvey and Hallaton are particularly picturesque.

6. Manorial Sites

Most villages had one or more large houses for the lords of the manors. In many cases there will still be a "Manor Farm" on the site. Manorial sites often had fishponds, enclosures, and gardens, as well as substantial buildings, and in many cases these features, having gone out of use, can still be identified as earthworks. In the 15th and 16th centuries particularly there was a fashion for surrounding manor houses and some other buildings with water-filled "moats", generally rectangular in plan.

7. Monastic Sites

Until their suppression by Henry VIII in the 1530s, there were monastic houses of varying size and wealth in most parts of England and several occur in the the Harborough District.

8. Ponds

Within the Leicestershire landscape, which has only small rivers and no natural lakes, ponds have long been created for fish rearing and to provide water for livestock. Ponds, whether full or drained, quite often survive as features forming part of a manorial site, park or garden.

9. Formal Gardens and Amenity Parks

During the 16th century the suppression of the monastic houses, and the gradual enclosure of the open-fields, provided opportunities for wealthy and powerful men to create mansion houses, surrounded by gardens and parks. Sometimes they would build their mansion on a new site, but more often they enlarged an existing manor house, clearing away the cottages of the poorer villagers to create space and privacy for the exclusive use of their family.

Around the house would be levelled parterres with ornate flower beds, raised terraces to walk along and view the gardens, and ornamental fishponds and moats. Avenues of trees were laid out, radiating from the mansion towards the horizon, and plantations of trees were created to add variety to the view. The creation of these formal gardens involved much movement of earth, and earthwork evidence now often survives, long after the flowers and trees have gone.

10. Negative Evidence

Despite the extent and diversity of the recorded earthwork evidence, there are many areas which appear never to have had earthwork features. Around the Lutterworth area these are mainly the low-lying areas alongside streams, which were used a hay meadows in summer and pasture land after the hay crop had been taken. Some of the more remote upland areas, such as Walton Holt, seem also to have a long history as pasture land, and perhaps in early Medieval times as woodland.

11. Access and Further Information

The sites described in this volume are on private land, and while many are crossed by rights of way, they should not be explored further without first seeking the permission of the land owner. Anyone interested in further research should in the first instance contact the Heritage and Environment Records section of Leicestershire County Council.

Robert F Hartley
The Green
Elston
Newark
Nottinghamshire

The Medieval Earthworks of South & South-East Leicestershire Part I

Lutterworth Area

Part 1, Lutterworth Area, is dedicated to the memory of

**Sir Thomas Cave, Baronet
(1711-1778)**

of Stanford Hall who was the first antiquarian to make a close study of this area.

Sir Thomas Cave, 5th Baronet was born on 27 May 1712. He was the son of Sir Thomas Cave, the 3rd Baronet and Margaret Verney and he was baptised in St Martin in the Fields, Covent Garden, London. He succeeded to the title of 5th Baron Cave in 1734 and was admitted as a barrister to the Inner Temple in 1735. He married Elizabeth Davies in 1736 and became MP for Leicestershire between 1741 and 1747 and between 1762 and 1774.

He was known as an educated man and John Nichols said of him: *"The acquired attainments of Sir Thomas Cave were far from inconsiderable. He possessed a large and well-selected library; and was conversant with the contents of it. Topography, in particular, engrossed a considerable part of the leisure which he could obtain from actual public duties; and, from his local situation, the counties of Northampton and Leicester very naturally excited an equal portion of his attention."* He applied himself *"diligently to collect materials for the History of Leicestershire. He purchased the collections of Mr Peck; and, by his own labours, and the contributions of his friends, has amassed an ample store of MSS, which it is to be lamented he did not live to digest."* The collections were subsequently presented to John Nichols who used them in his monumental work 'The History and Antiquities of the County of Leicester' which is very fully referenced in this current volume.

Sir Thomas died on 7 August 1778 at age 66 and was buried in Stanford on Avon church, Northamptonshire.

(Picture © and courtesy of Nicholas Fothergill, Stanford Hall nr Lutterworth)

Frontispiece: Knaptoft Church and Hall in decay, drawn 1791 by Schnebbelie (Nichols 1810, IV, I, 221)

INTRODUCTION TO THE LUTTERWORTH AREA

The area covered by Part 1 - the Lutterworth Area is the western part of the present Harborough District. Prior to 1973 it was the Lutterworth Rural District, and, apart from the northern end, where several villages are now within the outer suburbs of Leicester (see below), it corresponds with the former Hundred of Guthlaxton. This division of the county may have been named in honour of St Guthlac (673-714), a prominent figure in the Christian conversion of the Kingdom of Mercia. Two of its boundaries follow Roman Roads - the Fosse Way south-west between Leicester and High Cross, and the Watling Street southeast from Highcross to its crossing of the River Swift. The Swift then defines the south-east boundary of the area.

The Hundred of Guthlaxton was originally much larger, embracing all of South-West Leicestershire, but in the reign of Edward III the western half was separated off to create the Hundred of Sparkenhoe, now the Borough of Hinckley and Bosworth.

The northern villages of Guthlaxton Hundred are included in the previous Earthworks volume 'Earthworks of Central Leicestershire' (Aylestone, Knighton, Wigston Magna, Glen Parva, Oadby, Cosby, Blaby, Whetstone, Countesthorpe, Foston, Kilby) (Hartley 1989). These settlements are now in the current administrative areas of Leicester, Blaby District and the Borough of Oadby and Wigston (see plan of Leicestershire and its districts in the Introduction).

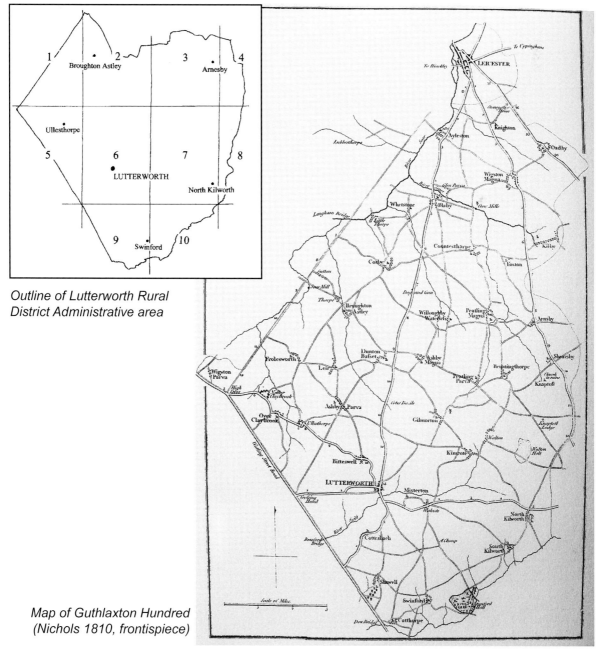

Outline of Lutterworth Rural District Administrative area

Map of Guthlaxton Hundred (Nichols 1810, frontispiece)

3

LUTTERWORTH AREA - THE PARISHES

ARNESBY

Manorial site (fig 1)   *SP617923*

Immediately east of St Peter's church is a pasture field with terraces, ditches and two former fishponds. These are marked on the Second Edition OS 1:2500 maps as "Manor House, site of". The buildings were still standing in the 19th century. Nichols observes *"The old manor-house still remains; and is inhabited by Mr. Adams. The ground about it is moated; and there are vestiges of gardens and fishponds."* (Nichols 1810, 12). Features surveyed in the 1980s include a levelled platform (a) perhaps an entrance court with the site of a gatehouse, and two more levelled platforms (b) and (c) which probably represent the sites of the manor house and outbuildings. These are partly enclosed by a deep ditch (d), which together with the fishponds

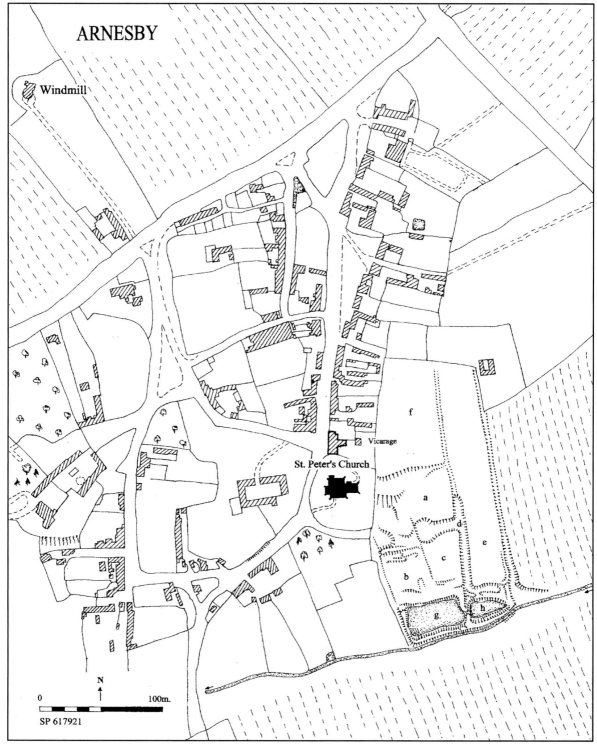

Figure 1: Arnesby manorial site

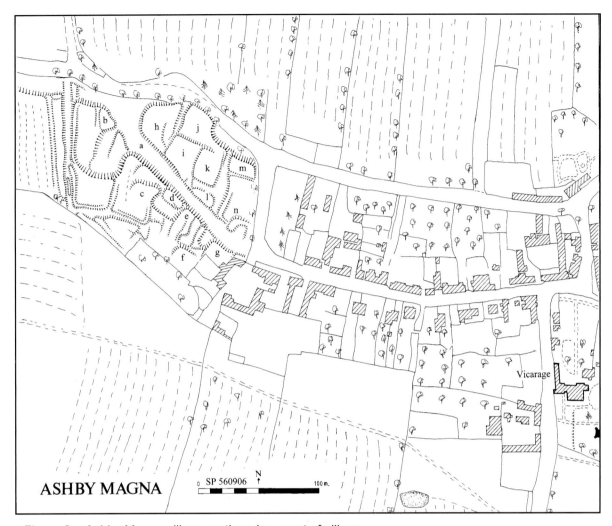

Figure 2a: Ashby Magna village earthworks - west of village

(g) and (h) form a moat-like defensible boundary around three sides of the site. To the east and north of these features are apparently contemporary enclosures, (e) and (f) which may have enclosed a garden and/or an orchard.

The author was shown an engraving said to show the appearance of the buildings on this site in the 18th century, but has not subsequently been able to locate a copy or find where it might have been published.

In 1679 Arnesby still had three open fields, Foston Hill Field, Fleckney Hill Field and Brook Field. M. W. Beresford published a plan of the conjectural layout (Beresford 1949, 90).

ASHBY MAGNA

Village Earthworks (fig 2a)   SP560906
The main street of the village used to continue westwards. Its course is visible in a pasture field as a deep hollow way (a) flanked by platforms (b, c, d, e, f, g, h, i, j, k, l, m, n) indicating the sites of cottages and outbuildings. In three cases (b, c, and n) the platforms are partly surrounded by related embanked enclosures.

Moated Site (fig 2b)   SP565905
To the east of St Mary's church are three or four building platforms (o, p, q, r) and east of them is a small moat. There are the sites of two ponds just upstream from it, with a conduit or supply channel(s) presumably made to bring water from springs in the nearby Conduit Spinney. Partly encircling these features is a broad ditch (t) probably the hollow way of an early route through the village which has been replaced by the present road further north. Some distance down the stream is a large earthwork dam (u), presumably built to retain a fishpond or osier bed in

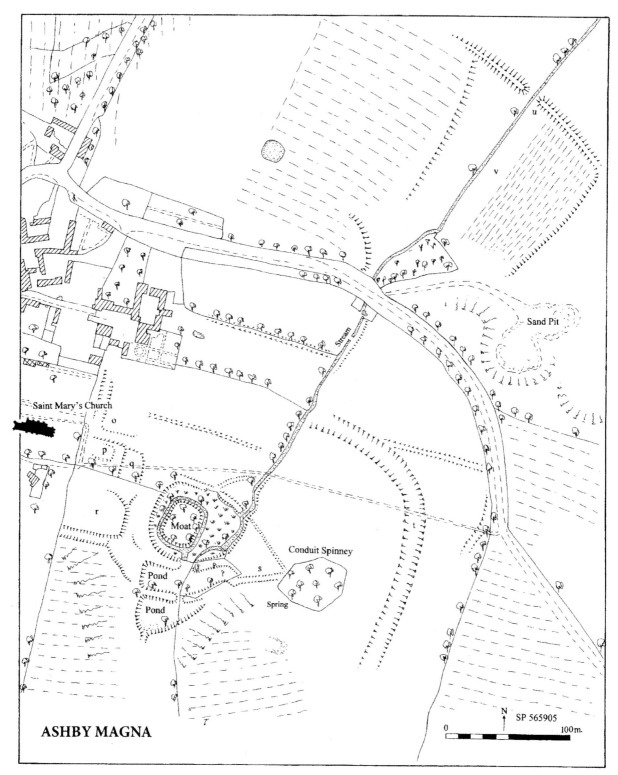

Figure 2b: Ashby Magna moated site - east of village

the area (v). The village fields were enclosed by 1674.

ASHBY PARVA

Village earthworks (fig 3) overleaf   *SP527885*

There are minor earthwork features recorded at various points around the village. Just north-west of the church is a building platform (a), with a small pond, and an old enclosure. To the south-east of this site is another house platform (b) and an enclosure. Further south-east is a length of hollow way, enclosure boundaries, and three small ponds (c). To the north-east of the rectory are three rectangular hollows in a line, presumably remains of an 18th or 19th century

7

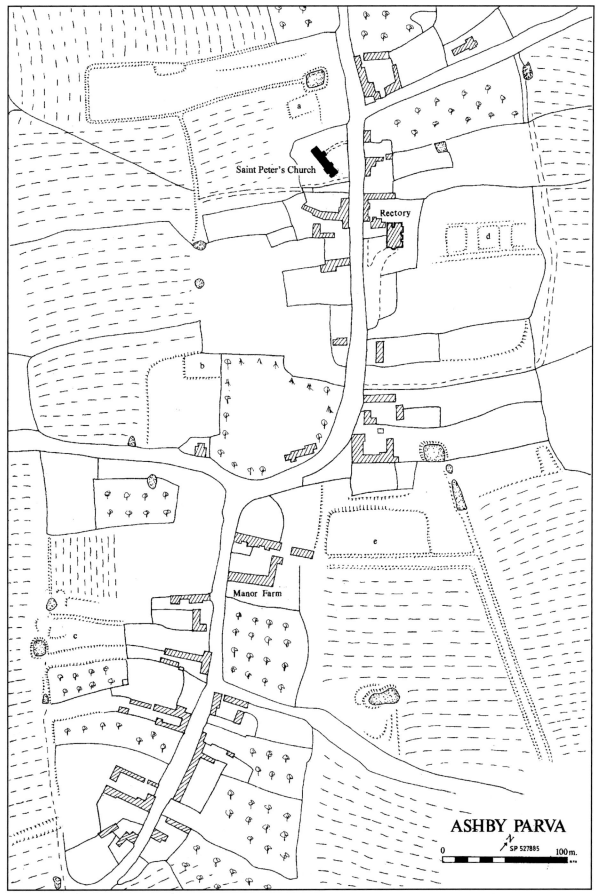

Figure 3: Ashby Parva

garden (d). North of Manor Farm are further enclosures (e) and several small ponds, together with two avenues flanked by ditches, which might suggest that this area was once set out as parkland. Ashby Parva still had open fields in 1638, but they had been enclosed by 1674.

BITTESBY

Deserted Village (fig 4, overleaf)   *SP500860*

At the time of the Domesday survey (1086) "*..it appears, there were five ploughlands; and the land was equal to the employment of four ploughs. One ploughland was in demesne; ten villans, with five bordars, had two ploughs; and there were twenty acres of meadow.*" (Nichols 1810, 117).

In the late 13th century this was, according to Hoskins, "*a flourishing village*" (Hoskins 1944-5, 258). In 1279 there were "*23 villein families each with a virgate of land, and two free tenants with a virgate between them - 25 families in all holding land here*" (op cit, 260 note 18).

The Lay Subsidies of 1327 and 1332 list twelve and nine tax payers respectively, and by 1524 there were just three members of the Salysbury family. A fine of 1572 mentions three messuages, 1000 acres of pasture, but only 40 of arable, suggesting that by this date the lordship was largely enclosed. Hoskins notes that during the early 17th century the process of conversion to pasture seems to have been reversed to some extent, and by 1640 there were 550 acres of arable again (op cit, 258-9). Nichols says: "*The lordship seems to have been converted into sheep-pastures before Burton's time*" (William Burton's book 'Description of Leicestershire' was published in 1622) and goes on to say: "*The whole lordship is almost entirely occupied by one person; and the greatest part of the land has been long since converted into pastures for cattle and sheep*" (Nichols 1810, 117).

There are no buildings on the village site, but the embankment of the Midland Counties Railway was constructed across the middle of it in 1838-40. The village was one of the first to attract the attention of the Medieval Village Research Group, and was Scheduled by the Government in the 1950s, but half the village (the portion west of the railway embankment) had unfortunately been ploughed before the farmer was notified. The earthworks east of the railway line were surveyed on the 3rd September 1985. Near the north end of the surviving earthworks is a hollow way (a) and north of this are three platforms (b, c, d) and a smaller building platform (f). To the south of the hollow way are at least two more building platforms (g, h).

At the south end of the village the original meandering course of the stream can still be seen (i), with two more building platforms (j, k) and the wall footings of a small building (l). The latter may perhaps have been in existence after the desertion of the village, whose earlier houses would have been constructed mainly of mud and thatch. Of the western half of the village we have only the evidence of aerial photographs, which suggest the former existence of three main areas of the village (n, o, r) with hollow ways between them, and at least three building platforms (p, q, s).

BITTESWELL

Mills

In 1361 Simon Pakeman gave to Leicester Abbey various properties in Bitteswell, including a mill. At an even earlier date in 1279 the Abbey are said to have had a windmill "*ad molendinum nostrum*" (Nichols 1810, 40). The Abbey's numerous possessions and tenants here are recorded in their register (Nichols 1810, 40-41).

The parish had been enclosed by 1674. Nichols says this was confirmed by an Act of 1787 (Nichols 1810, 43).

BROUGHTON ASTLEY

The village of Broctone or Broughton derives its second name from the Warwickshire family of Astley who were lords of the manor through the 13th and 14th centuries.

The settlement pattern in this parish does not follow the usual rule in this area of one nucleated village surrounded by its fields. Instead there are three distinct settlements in a line; Broughton Astley, Sutton juxta Broughton (now Sutton in the Elms), and Thorpe or Primethorpe, all in the same civil parish.

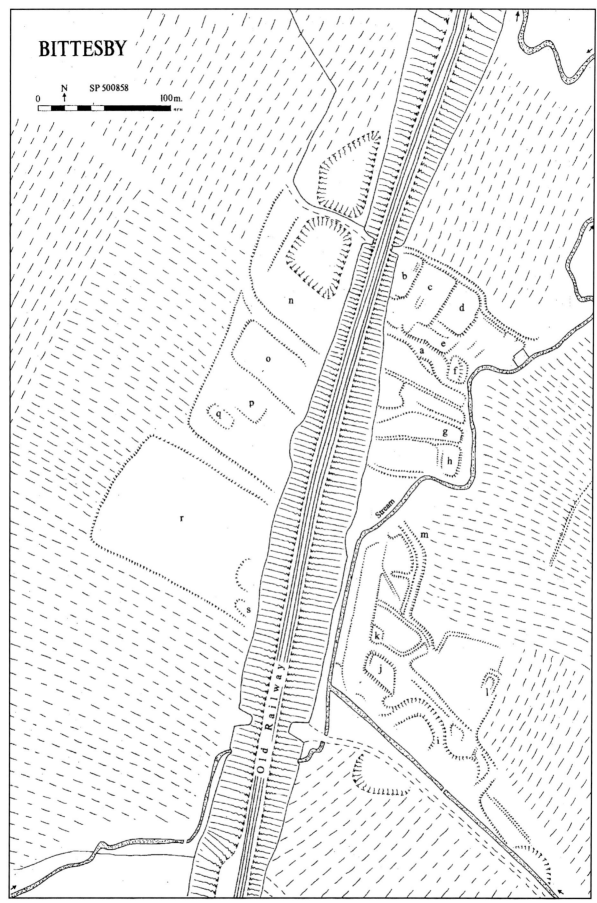

BITTESBY

N SP 500858
0   100m.

o
p
q
n
r
s

b
c
d
e
a
f
g
h
Stream
m
k
j
i
l

Old Railway

Figure 4: Bittesby deserted village

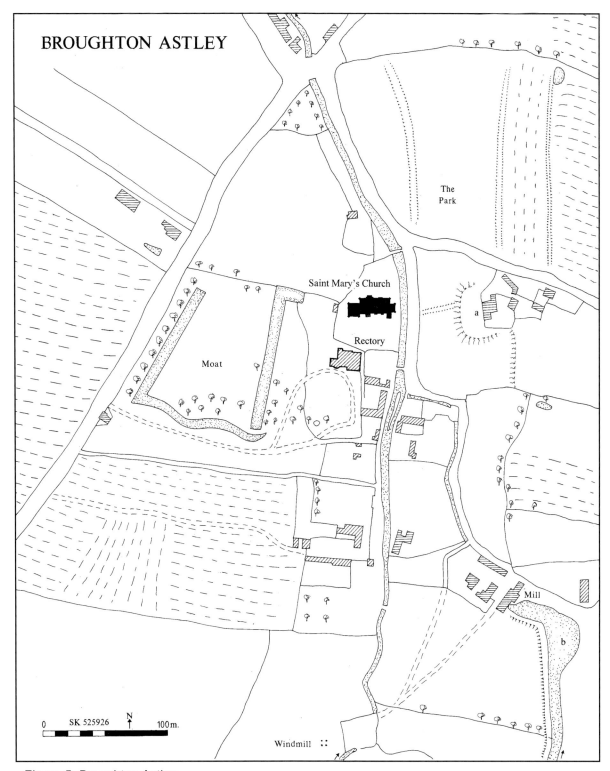

Figure 5: Broughton Astley

Possible Manorial Site (fig 5)   *SP5271 9265*

The White Horse Inn stands on the east side of a raised building platform (a) which may represent the remains of a moated site.

Moat (Garden Feature) (fig 5)   *SP5249 9261*

Just to the west of the Rectory is a large three-sided moat. The First Edition OS 1:2500 map shows the east and west sides straight, while the south side is sinuous. The moat is nearly symmetrical, although there is a narrow causeway in the southeast corner. It seems likely that this moat is a garden feature of late 17th or early 18th century date.

Watermill (fig 5)   SP527 924
The First Edition OS 1:2500 map shows a Corn Mill with a substantial millpond (b) created by a dam. Possibly the site of the mill valued at 2 shillings in Domesday (Nichols 1810, 58).

Windmill (fig 5) bottom of plan   SP526923
'Windmill (Disused)' is marked on the OS 1:2500 map, which shows the four bases which would have supported the cruciform base of a wooden post-mill. This mill is believed to have been previously in use at 'Mount Pleasant' on the south field of the borough of Leicester. It was dismantled and re-erected at Broughton Astley in about 1870. The location is low-lying, by a stream, and it may have been put here more for picturesque effect than as a working mill.

Windmill   SP535936
The First Edition OS maps show the site of another windmill to the north-east of the village.

Primethorpe   SP523931
Primethorpe appears to be a secondary settlement which grew up around a triangular green, between Broughton and Sutton. A ploughland in Thorpe is mentioned in the Domesday survey

Sutton in The Elms Village Earthworks   SP521937
One ploughland in Sutton is mentioned in the Domesday survey. There was also a wood, three furlongs in length by two in width (Nichols 1810, 63). There are slight village earthworks recorded at Sutton in the Elms, showing on aerial photographs near The Grange.

Soar Mill   SP509937
This water mill is a well-known landmark alongside the Fosse Way.

Open Fields
Broughton Astley had three open fields in 1601, Nether, Hungrey, and Oldbradstone.

BRUNTINGTHORPE

Village Earthworks (fig 6)   SP601898
North and west of St Mary's Church are earthworks of a former area of the village, including two hollow ways (a, b), flanked by building platforms (c, d, e, f, g, h, i,) and related enclosures. Near the Manor House is another building platform (j). The block of land around the Manor House is surrounded by a substantial bank (k) and near the centre of the enclosed area is another building platform (l) and a square pond (m) and a possible fish pond (n). Two more ponds (p,r) exist on the east side of the village, with the site of another one (q). Several existing houses in this area have been built within a rectangular gravel pit (o), which must have been abandoned at least a century and a half ago.

Open Fields
In 1606 there were three open fields, Carre, Moor and Olte. By 1625 these were apparently known as Nether, Middle and Upper. Another document of 1713 refers to Carrbrookfield, Outfield and Streetfield. The Enclosure Act was passed in 1776 (Nichols 1810, 66).

CATTHORPE

Apparently also referred to as "Thorpe juxta Lilbourne" after Lilbourne village and castle just to the south in Northamptonshire.

Pond and earthworks (fig 7 overleaf)   SP550780
To the west of Catthorpe Hall is an area of earthwork evidence, including a rectangular platform (a) flanked by a ditch (b) and a bank (c). There is a drained former fish pond (d) and perhaps another one (e) on the slope below Catthorpe Hall.

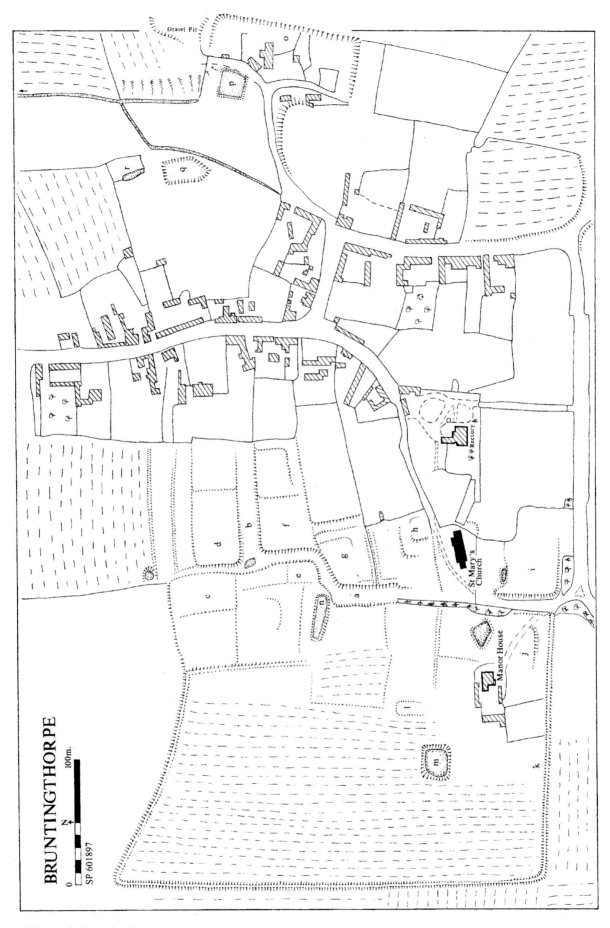

BRUNTINGTHORPE

SP 601897

0   100m.

Gravel Pit

o

p

q

r

d
b
f
c
e
g
n
a
h
i

St Mary's Church

Manor House

Rectory

j

m

k

Figure 6: Bruntingthorpe

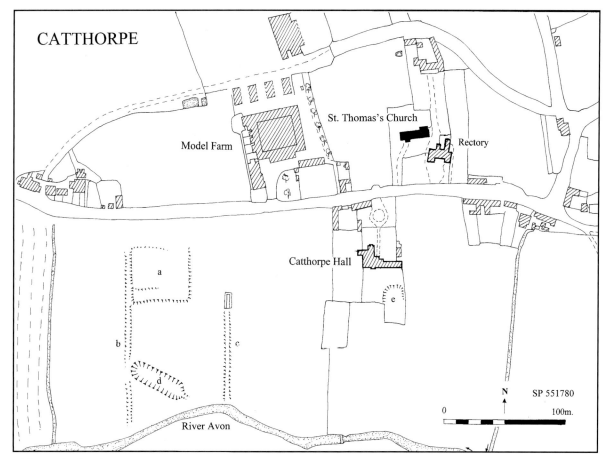

Figure 7: Catthorpe

Mill

In the Domesday survey Maino the Breton is recorded as holding two carucates of land and a mill worth 2 shillings. In 1279 the watermill was held by Roger Malore the Elder. (Farnham 1933, 279). In 1481 Nicholas Cowley died seised of a mill called Luffe's Mill (Nichols 1810, 75). 'Luffemilne' is elsewhere described as part of the possessions of Leicester Abbey, together with the land between the mill pond and the stream course (Nichols 1810, 75).

Dowbridge, (Nichols, 1810, 81, pl XX)

Dowbridge   SP543778

"In the Street Way (Watling Street) ....where Northamptonshire joins the counties of Warwick and Leicester, is Dowbridge, built across the River Avon, consisting of a long stone causey of four arches for an horse, with a stone coping at a height of a foot from the pavement. This causey joins another stone bridge of two arches..." (Nichols 1810, 81).

Lilbourne Castle   SP561774

Immediately over the county boundary in Northamptonshire is the fine motte and bailey site of Lilbourne Castle, still a prominent landmark from the adjacent M1 Motorway.

Open Fields

The open fields of Catthorpe are said to have been enclosed in 1655 (Nichols 1810, 76 and 83-99). Prior to this there were three; Mill Field, Tomley Field, and Street or Biggin Field in addition to the Great Meadow.

CLAYBROOK MAGNA

Also known as Nether Claybrook or Lower Claybrooke.

Village earthworks   SP495889

There was formerly slight evidence of village earthworks at this location.

Mill   SP499891

A mill dam is mentioned in 1638 (Nichols 1810, 110). An earlier reference in an inquisition of 1279 mentions two mills, water and wind, which if correct is an early date for a windmill.

Open Fields

Claybrooke Magna was enclosed by private agreement in 1694.

CLAYBROOKE PARVA

This village, also known as Upper Claybrook, Over Claybrook or Little Claybrook, is described by Nichols as *"a small, neat village upon the turnpike road, containing only ten houses, among which are the parsonage-house, and the mansion-house of Thomas Dicey Esq.: which goes by the name of Claybrook Hall."* (Nichols 1810, 103). The Church of St. Peter, according to Nichols, was "chiefly constructed of such stones as are found at Staunton and Sapcote in this county", with a chancel and tower of free-stone." (Nichols 1810, 107).

Moat (fig 8)   SP495879

In the vicarage garden is a rectangular platform (a) with traces of buildings. It is partly surrounded by two ponds (b, c) forming an incomplete moat. These features together could indicate the site of a former manor house. To the west is a small embanked enclosure (d), and although this contains ridge and furrow it is possible that in late Medieval or post-Medieval times it was used as a garden or orchard. There is a hollow way (e) on the south side, and to the east of the church is another small field (f) which has faint traces of possible earthworks,

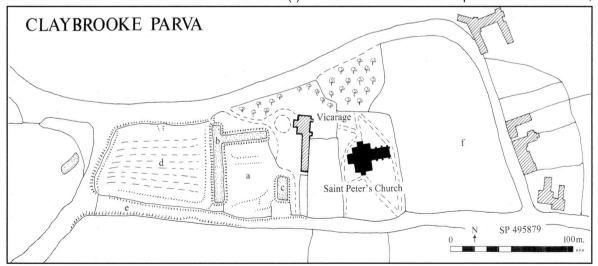

Figure 8: Claybrooke Parva

15

and seems likely once to have had cottages and crofts on it. Across the lane, to the north, is Claybrooke Hall, surrounded by an area of parkland with several ornamental ponds.

Windmill
There is a reference to a windmill here in 1347 (Nichols 1810, 104).

Open Fields
Claybrooke Parva was enclosed by private agreement in 1681. A glebe terrier of 1638 lists many lands and properties in Claybrooke (Magna and Parva) in three open fields; High Cross Field, Middle Field, and Nether Field (Nichols 1810, 110-111). Presumably after enclosure the land made good pasture, for Nichols notes that 50-60 tons of excellent cheese were sold annually to factors from London (Nichols 1810, 129).

Wibtoft Village (fig 9)   SP479876
The village of Wibtoft straddles the Watling Street, and most of it is in Warwickshire. Apparently Ulfric Spot, Earl of Mercia, granted *"the land at Wibtoft"* to one Athelric, about the year 1000. In later years Leicester Abbey's lands here included a mill. (Nichols 1810, 123). Earthwork evidence of former enclosures has been recorded around St Mary's Church on the Warwickshire side and around Alma House on the Leicestershire side.
South of the church is a large building platform (a). To the east of this, beyond a narrow pond, are two old enclosures (c, d). North of the church is another building platform (b) where a croft has gone out of use and been demolished. Beyond it is another platform (f), origin is unknown. North of Alma House is the site of an ornamental pond or sunken garden (g), while to the east are some slight terraces (e), possibly part of a post-medieval garden, or the site of old enclosures.

COTESBACH

Village Earthworks (fig 10 overleaf)   SP535823
On the west side of the village there is hollow way (a) flanked on the west by several old enclosures containing three building platforms (b, c, d). On the east side is another area of old village closes (e) where new houses have been built in recent years. There are more areas of village earthworks, platforms and terraces, at (f) and (g). The village seems to have decreased in size prior to the 18th century, and the loss of a manor house is recorded in the following account:- *"A good farm house, the remains of the old manor or hall-house, outstanding on a knob of ground near the rectory, shews the ancient site of a very large pile of building, which (according to Sir Thomas Cave in 1767) 'in the memory of men now living has been diminished, and the great part of it pulled down; the ruins of which have afforded materials for erecting several new houses in the neighbourhood'."* (Nichols 1810, 148).

Open Fields
In 1606 there were still three open fields, Broadwell Field, Smallwold Field and Swinford Field. They were enclosed during that winter and in 1607 the inhabitants rioted in protest at the way they had been dispossessed.
"In the month of May 1607, a great number of common persons suddenly assembled themselves ...they violently cut and broke down hedges, filled up ditches, and laid open all such inclosures of commons and grounds as they found inclosed, which of antient time had been open, and employed to tillage. These tumultuous persons in Northamptonshire, Warwickshire and Leicestershire, grew very strong, being in some places, of men women and children, a thousand altogether,... and at Cotesbach there assembled, of men, women and children, to the number of full five thousand. These riotous persons bent all their strength to level and lay open inclosures, without exercising any manner of violence upon any man's person, goods, or cattle; and wheresoever they came they were generally relieved by the near inhabitants, who sent them not only many carts laden with victuals, but also a good store of spades and shovels for speedy performance of their present enterprize...."(Nichols 1810, 148).

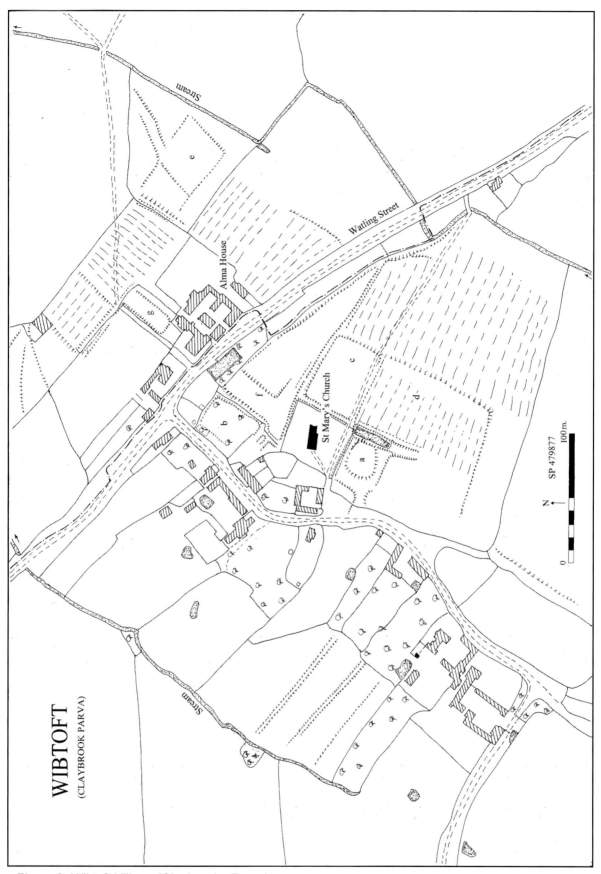

Figure 9: Wibtoft Village (Claybrooke Parva)

17

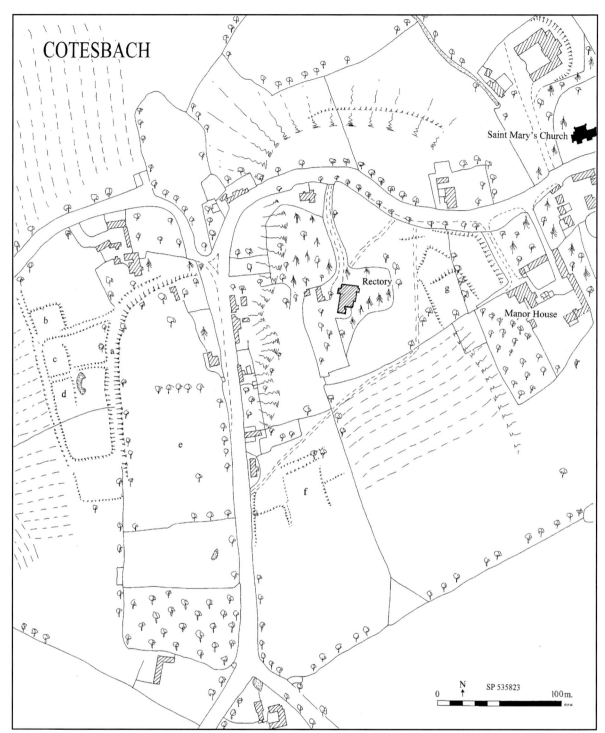

Figure 10: Cotesbach

DUNTON BASSETT

Manorial Site (fig 11)   **SP5475 9053**

North of All Saints Church is the platform of the manor house site (a), with traces of several buildings. It is surrounded by a deep ditch (b), and has outer enclosures (c and d) probably once containing orchards or gardens. There is also a fish pond (e).

To the west are more earthworks, in the centre (g), and the north-west corner (f) of the village. In the parkland south west of the Manor House are additional faint features awaiting interpretation (h), with more features continuing to the west, (not plotted).

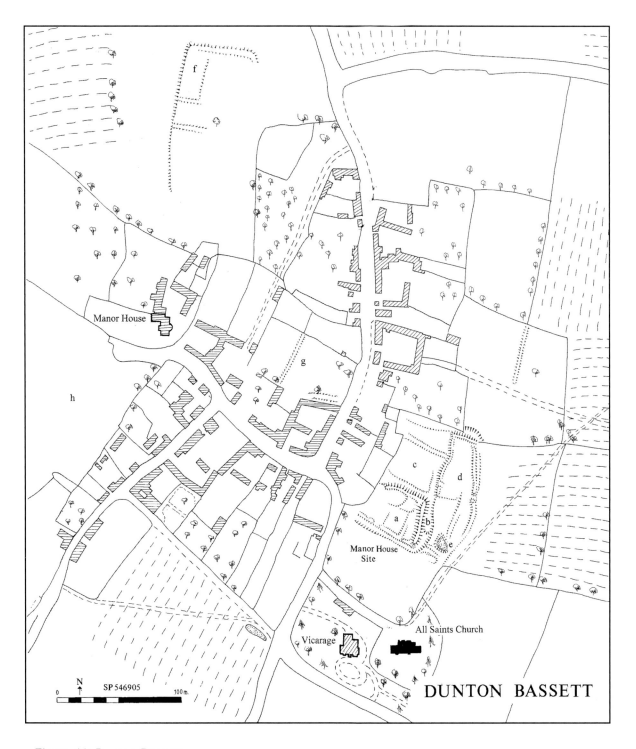

Figure 11: Dunton Bassett

Dunton Water Mill   **SP537895**
In the south-west corner of the parish is the site of a corn mill which had a substantial mill dam
paralleling the stream. In 1296 the Prior of Kenwell held two water mills here.

Open Fields
There were still three open fields in 1674; Olte, Middle and Longslade.

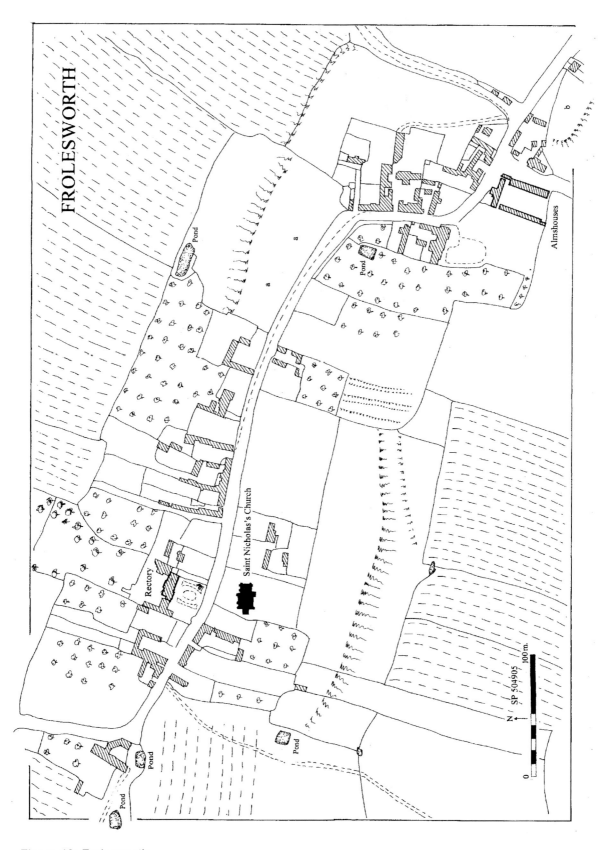

Figure 12: Frolesworth

FROLESWORTH

Village Earthworks (fig 12)   SP504905
The village extends along a ridge, and has the typical rectilinear layout of plots stretching back from the street frontage. There are possible faint earthworks at (a) and interesting 18th century almshouses at the southern corner of the village (Pevsner 1998, 156).

Open Fields
The parish was mainly enclosed in 1674, although evidence of ridge and furrow survived in most of the fields until the 20th century.

GILMORTON

Motte, moats and ponds (fig 13) overleaf   SP569878
Immediately to the west of All Saints Church is an interesting field of earthworks, dominated by a conical mound (a), probably a Norman motte, with an outer enclosure (b) forming a small bailey to the north-west, and both features surrounded by a substantial ditch (c). Knox (2015, 132) suggests the motte has been lowered to accommodate a larger building than the original keep. There are platforms to the south (e, f, g) indicating the sites of at least three buildings. The stream on the west side of the field (d) has had its course diverted to allow the creation of two sets of fishponds (h, i) in the form of ornamental moats. The second set of ponds (i) has been filled with water again in recent years. There is another building platform nearby at (j), possibly part of the adjacent post-medieval farm building.
It would be interesting to have some dating evidence for these various features. The fish ponds could be medieval but it is not impossible that they could have been created or restored in the 18th century to add to the pleasure gardens of the adjacent Rectory.

Open Fields
There were still three open fields in 1674:- Oldmill or Ridgeway, Ursar, and Gawney.

Deserted Village, Cotes-de-Val (fig 14) overleaf   SP553886
In the north-west corner of Gilmorton parish, just north of Cotes-de-Val farm is a roughly rectangular area of earthworks marking the site of the deserted village of Cotes. Nichols describes this as *"a little hamlet called Cotes Devile containing upwards of 300 acres"* (Nichols 1810, 212) and notes that some lands here were held by Thomas de Astley, who died at the battle of Evesham with Simon de Montfort in 1265. He also includes a description of the site of the village :- *"By the many foundations, causeways, &c from time to time frequently discovered by the plough, spade, &c around the present single remaining house (which is in part moated round, and about 40 years ago was wholly so, and the drawbridge remaining), many traces of a considerable village can easily be traced"*...."*Here was formerly a chapel, with a chaplain regularly resident from the mother church; but it has long since been desecrated."* (op cit, 213).
When surveyed in 1980 the earthworks still contained much detail. A hollow way (a) extending east to west, divides the site in two, with another hollow way (b) extending southwards, and others following the perimeter of the site. The north-west quarter of the village is enclosed by a substantial bank (c) and contains several smaller enclosures and at least two building platforms (d, e).
The north-east quarter has remains of one substantial house with a large platform (f), with a hollow in front of it which might be the site of a crew yard for cattle. The south-west quarter also has just one obvious building platform (g), surrounded by more evidence which is hard to interpret. The south-east quarter contains the farmhouse and the moat (k) referred to above, with two more substantial building platforms (h, j) where there are probably the sites of houses and outbuildings, and a smaller house platform (i).
Returning to the south-west quarter, there is pond, now only partially water-filled,) and adjacent to it are two circular features (l, m) which are probably the foundations of two large circular stone dovecotes. On the northern edge of the site is a small mound (n), possibly the site of a windmill.

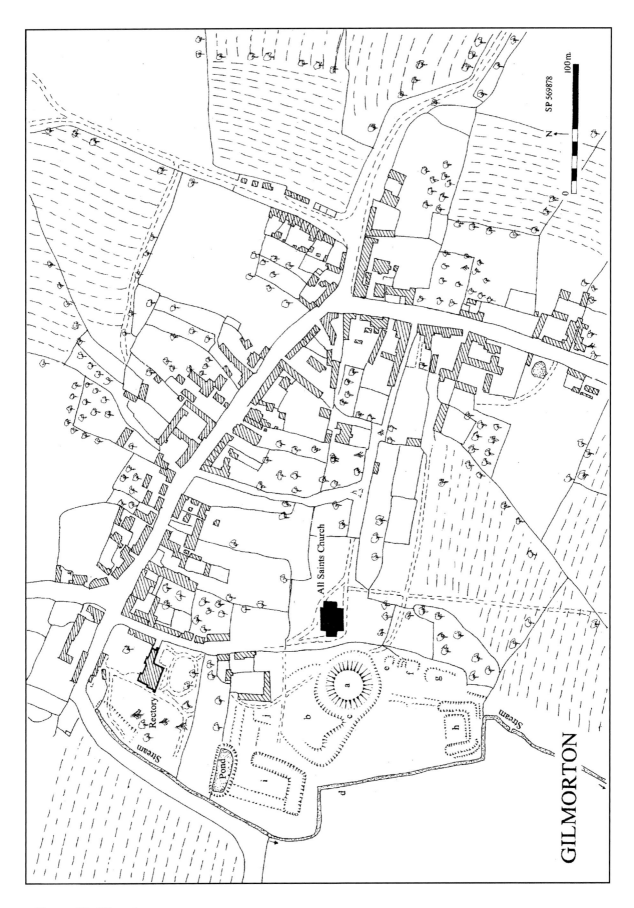

Figure 13: Gilmorton

22

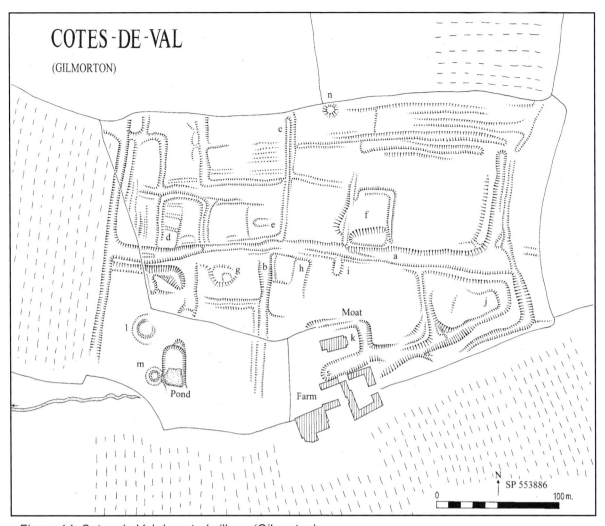

COTES-DE-VAL

(GILMORTON)

Moat

Pond

Farm

N

SP 553886

0   100 m.

Figure 14: Cotes de Val deserted village (Gilmorton)

KIMCOTE & WALTON

Kimcote village earthworks and pond (fig 15) overleaf   SP587865

The area to the north of All Saints Church and Manor Farm seems likely to have been the site of a vanished Manor House. North of the church was a possible building platform (a), which has recently been removed by landscaping, and further to the east is a level terrace (b), perhaps part of a post-medieval garden. Further east again the stream course has clearly been straightened, and is flanked by a long, narrow fish pond (c). There was probably once a second pond (d) indicated by marshy ground on the First Edition Ordnance Survey map. Beyond the stream is a plantation and another possible pond (e).

Just to the east of Manor Farm there are some other slight earthwork features (f) perhaps indicating the site of manorial outbuildings, or earlier cottages cleared to make way for the gardens.

The field across the road, to the south, has two clear building platforms of medieval or post-medieval date (g, h).

Open Fields

In 1606 there were three fields:- Park or South Field, Middle Field and Mill or North Field. South and North Fields still functioned as such in 1679.

Walton village earthworks (fig 16)   SP595871

This village has remained almost entirely within its medieval boundaries, mostly clearly on the west side, where a ditch (a) extends between the village crofts and the ridge and furrow of the former open fields. There are two greens, and a hollow way where an old lane led eastwards from the village (b). There is also evidence of three post-medieval gravel pits (c, d, e).

23

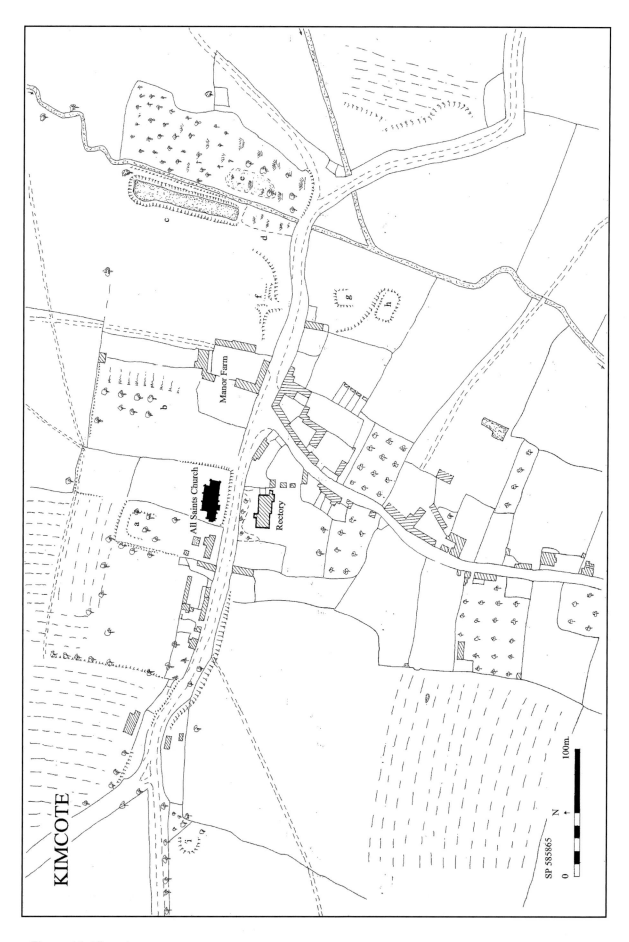

KIMCOTE

All Saints Church

Manor Farm

Rectory

SP 585865

N

0   100m.

Figure 15: Kimcote

24

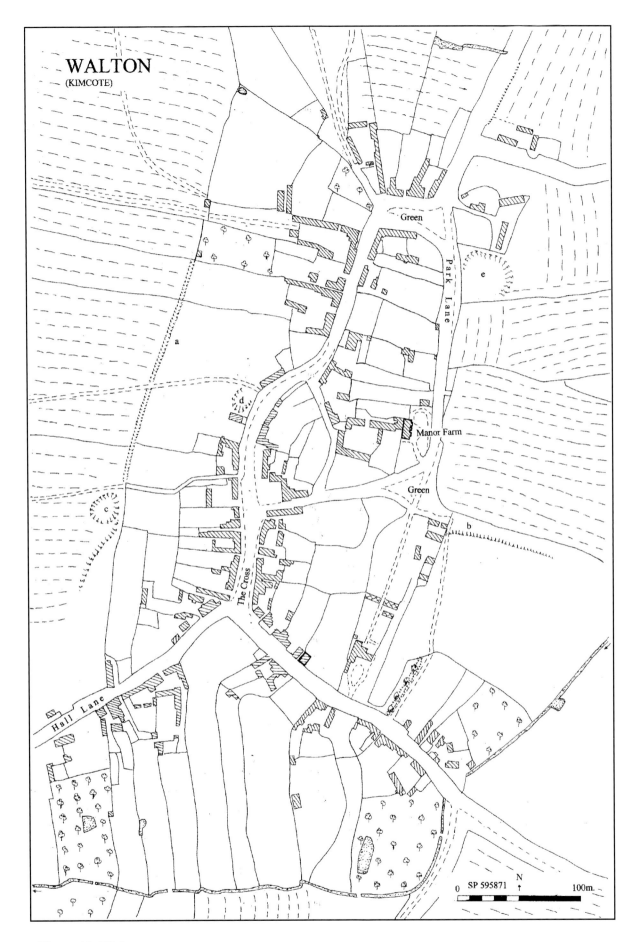

WALTON
(KIMCOTE)

Green

Park Lane

e

a

d

Manor Farm

Green

c

b

The Cross

Hall Lane

0   SP 595871   N   100m.

Figure 16: Walton

25

"Walton, though only a hamlet to Kimcote and Knaptoft, is by far a larger village than Kimcote, containing at this time more than six times the number of inhabitants…. "This hamlet had formerly a separate chapel, which was served thrice a week from the church of Kimcote". Leicester Abbey are said to have held the chapel. *"In Walton stands the base of an old cross."* (Nichols 1810, 215) and the street at the centre of the village is still called 'The Cross'.

Windmill
There is reference to a windmill *"unum molendinum ventriticum"* in 1279 (Nichols 1810, 214).

Walton Holt
This area at the edge of the parish has little evidence of ridge and furrow and was presumably a wood in medieval times.

KNAPTOFT

Deserted village and Hall Gardens (fig 17)   SP626894
The earthworks at Knaptoft have long excited the curiosity of historians, and it was on this site that John Hurst and Maurice Beresford met and decided to form the Deserted Medieval Village Research Group (MSRG). The 60th Anniversary of this founding was marked by a published conference and participants visited Knaptoft and other local sites (Dyer & Jones 2010; Everson 2010, 59-62).

The features visible at the surface represent a typical rectilinear medieval village, overlain by the buildings and gardens of the post-medieval Hall. The village is most clearly seen at the east end of the site, where the main hollow way (a) divides into two ways (b, c). On the north side of (a) are at least two building platforms (d, e). To the south is an apparently later rectangular block of village, containing further building platforms (f, g, h, i, j, k). Further east, (at SP631894) surrounded by the ridge and furrow of the former open fields, is the mound indicating the site of a windmill (l), probably the one recorded in 1301.

The field to the west mainly seems to comprise post-medieval garden features, with a parterre (m) enclosed by an "L" shaped terrace walkway (n). Further down the hillside are what appear to be garden terraces (o, p, q, r). The lowest one (r) has the foundations of a small stone building. The stream course has been altered, with a by-pass channel (s) to pass a rectangular ornamental pond (t) with a central island (or a shallow area) (v). On the north side of the pond is a smaller one (w). The ponds were flooded by means of a dam (u) across the valley bottom. There must have been another pond immediately to the west, retained by another dam (x). North of these features is a linear bank (y) presumably representing the remains of a wall or bank enclosing the north-west corner of the gardens. The ruins of the medieval church still survive, but there is only slight evidence of the 16th century Knaptoft Hall which was the focus of the gardens, and a main reason for the disappearance of the village. In 1301 Knaptoft had 26 tenants, 360 acres of demesne arable, and nine acres of meadow. In the mid 15th century the manor had come by marriage to John Turpin of Whitchester, Northumberland, and by 1524 it was almost entirely depopulated.

Knaptoft Hall was built or enlarged in the 16th century. Nichols notes *"..the old Hall house, which had a circular tower or bastion, of brick and stone, embattled, and was probably built by John Turpin in the reign of Henry VII and enlarged, or at least embellished, by Sir William Turpin, in the reign of either Elizabeth or James…"* (Nichols 1810, 220). The parterres, terraces and ponds noted above were probably created in the latter part of the 16th century. See also Everson 2010 (59-62).

The Turpins joined the ranks of the local gentry and held the manor until 1645. After their departure the Hall was of less importance, and by the late 18th century it had fallen into decay. In Schnebbelie's view of the east front, drawn on September 15 1791, it appears complete, but Pridden's drawing of the north front, done in July of the following year, shows gaping holes in the roof (both engravings in Nichols 1810, 221, Pridden, frontispiece to this section, Schnebbelie overleaf). It was, as Nichols describes *"in a perishing state"* and on a re-visit, in *August 1805 the only remnant was a very small part of the embattled bastion, about two or three yards high..and…a single window of the principal room.."* (Nichols 1810, 220).

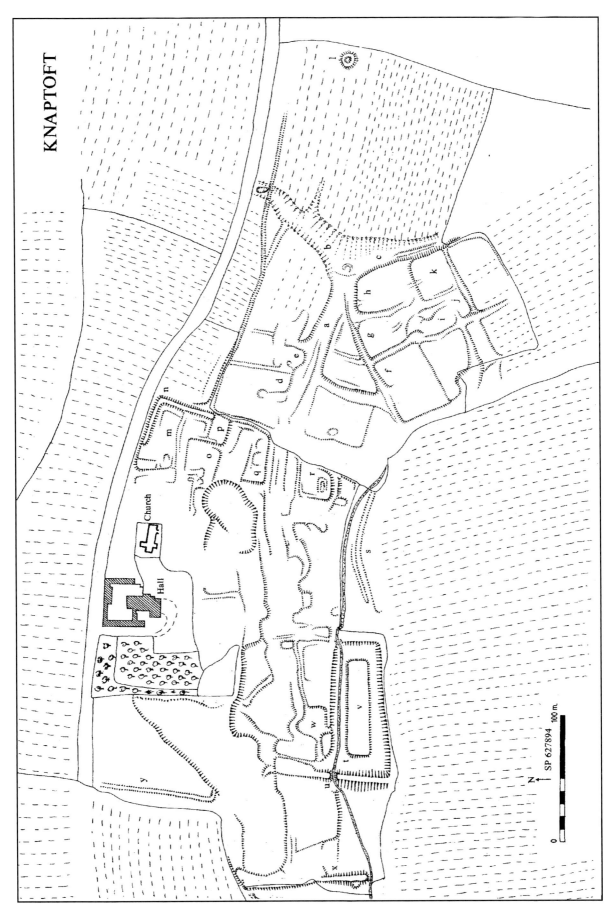

Figure 17: Knaptoft deserted medieval village

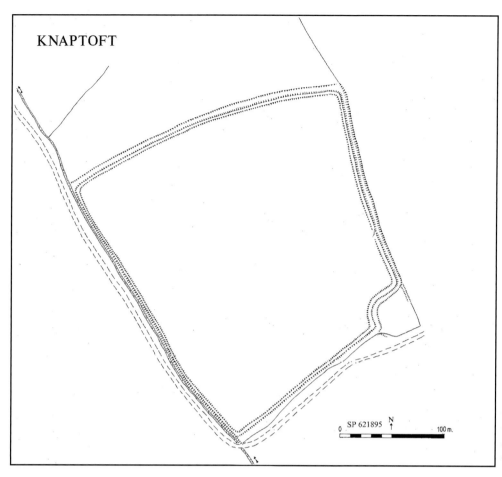

Figure 18: Knaptoft Earthwork enclosure

KNAPTOFT

SP 621895

0   100 m.

N

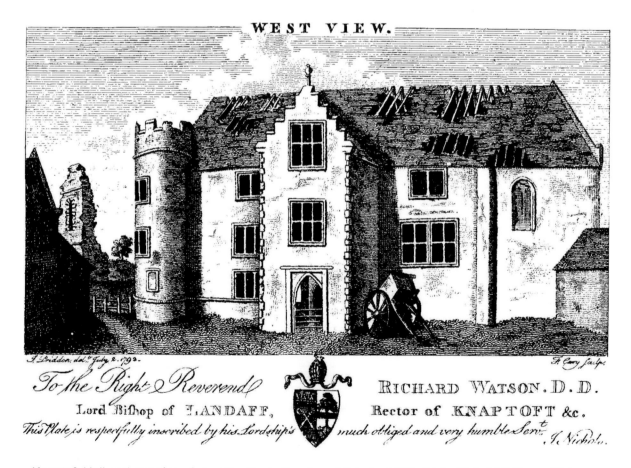

WEST VIEW.

To the Right Reverend   RICHARD WATSON. D.D.
Lord Bishop of LANDAFF,   Rector of KNAPTOFT &c.
This Plate is respectfully inscribed by his Lordship's   much obliged and very humble Serv.t J. Nichols.

Knaptoft Hall and remains of church - illustration from Nichols, 1810, IV, I, Plate XXXII op p221.

Fishponds   *SP623891*

Two fishponds are mentioned in 1301, perhaps those which still exist as fishing lakes about 500m south-west of Knaptoft Church

Earthwork enclosure (fig 18)   *SP 621895*

To the west of the village is a rectangular area enclosed by an earth bank. There are slight ditches outside this bank on the north and east sides, and the stream flows past the west side. The area is called "The Grove" on the Tithe Map and presumably represents a protected area in which trees were grown. It is possible that this may be the area called "Newclose" in 1525 (Nichols 1810, 217)

Open Fields

William Turpin died September 1st 1525, seised of this manor, which is described as containing in total 1300 acres of pasture, 240 acres of meadow, and 40 acres of wood. There were in addition still 600 acres of arable in the Middle Field (Nichols 1810, 217) John Turpin died in 1530 *"seised of the manor and capital messuage of Knaptoft and divers lands....worth £20"*. The lands included The Holm Field, Lady Meadow, Kennell Field, Bradgate Field and Middle Field. Leicester Abbey also held land here called Cottingham Meadow (Nichols1810, 217).

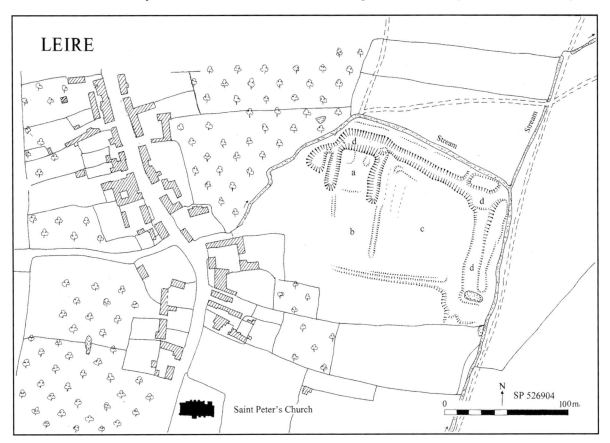

Figure 19: Leire

LEIRE

Moated Site (fig 19)   *SP527902*

North west of St Peter's Church there was a complex of ponds and a moated platform. This site has been largely filled-in, but a survey in the early 1980s recorded a rectangular platform (a), probably the site of a manor house and outbuildings, with an enclosure (b), perhaps a courtyard or garden, to the south. The platform (a) has a moat (d) around three sides, and the moat also extends eastwards as an elongated pond, with an extension southwards. The area (c), enclosed by the elongated ponds probably at one time contained a garden or an orchard. The two streams in the village have had their courses altered to form an additional boundary around the moated site.

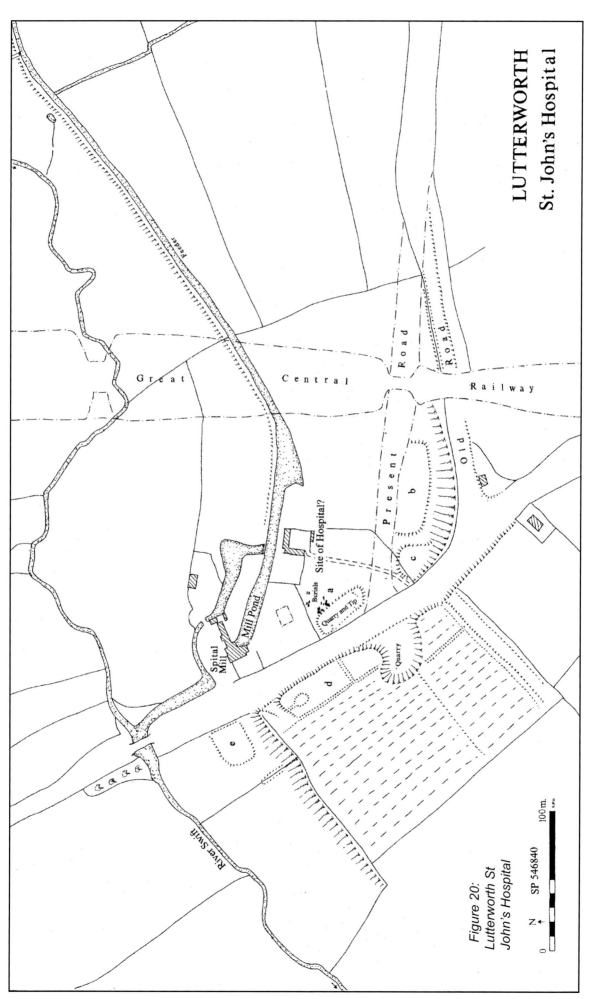

LUTTERWORTH
St. John's Hospital

Great Central Railway

Feeder

Present Road

Old Road

Site of Hospital?

Mill Pond

Spital Mill

Burials

Quarry and Tip

Quarry

River Swift

Figure 20:
Lutterworth St
John's Hospital

N

SP 546840

0   100 m.

30

Stemborough Mill, Leire   SP532910

This water mill site is near the northern boundary of the parish, alongside a track called Stemborough Lane, which leads from Leire to Broughton Astley.

Leire Mill   SP531897

The River Leire is close to its source here, and only a small stream, but some way above Stemborough Mill is Leire Mill, with remains of the mill leet. Dunton Mill, in Dunton Bassett parish, is even further upstream.

Open Fields, Leire

In 1601 there were four open fields:- Over, Lower, Beyond Brook, and Moorhill.

LUTTERWORTH

St John's Hospital (fig 20)   SP546840

The medieval Hospital of St. John lay a short distance south of the town, just across the River Swift. It was founded in 1218, probably by a member of the Verdon family. Under the supervision of a priest it housed six poor men and provided hospitality for poor travellers on one of the main routes between Leicester and London. In its early years it was a wealthy institution, with lands in Gilmorton and elsewhere around the Lutterworth area. The house and chapel were delapidated by 1576, and it had long since ceased to function as a hospital, but continued to provide alms for the poor until after 1676.

Archaeological excavations in 1996 and 2001 revealed 22 graves from a 13th-14th century cemetery (a), nearly all containing adult males. To the west was a post-Medieval gravel quarry and to the south-east were spreads of cobbles, thought to have been used to surface the ground around the Hospital's outbuildings. The excavator considered that the hospital and chapel themselves probably lay further to the south, in the angle between the London and Market Harbough roads (Score 2010, 165-187).

The whole area was largely destroyed by the road realignment of the 1890s and more by recent road widenings and construction of a roundabout. Possible earthwork evidence of the hospital site survived until recently in the form of low platforms (b, c). These would originally have occupied a prominent position at the junction of the two main roads. To the west across the London Road were an old gravel quarry of post-medieval date, ditches and a platform (d) probably indicating a house and grounds, and another possible building platform (e).

Spital Mill (fig 20)   SP546841

In 1577 St. John's Hospital owned two water mills, one of which continued in use as the Spital Mill until the end of the 19th century. The mill dam extended for several hundred yards paralleling the River Swift on its south side. The feeder channel was presumably redundant by 1896 as no attempt was made to retain it when the Great Central Railway embankment was constructed in 1896-9.

Lodge Mill   SP524826

A former watermill on the River Swift with extensive feeder channels.

Windmill   SP550853

This windmill used to stand on the hill north-east of the town.

Windmill   SP539849

A possible mill is marked on the pre-enclosure map at this point, by the road half-way between Lutterworth and Bitteswell

Open Fields

There were three open fields in 1697:- Thunborough, Middle, and Street.

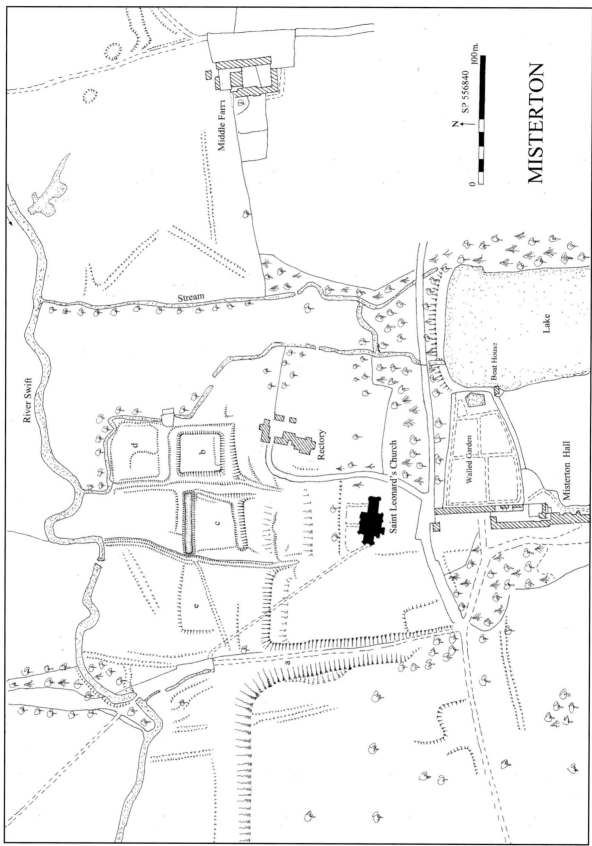

Figure 21: Misterton

MISTERTON

Village and Manorial Earthworks (fig 21)   *SP556840*

The village of Misterton seems to have been almost entirely swept away to create the landscaped park around Misterton Hall, with its large ornamental lake and plantations. St.

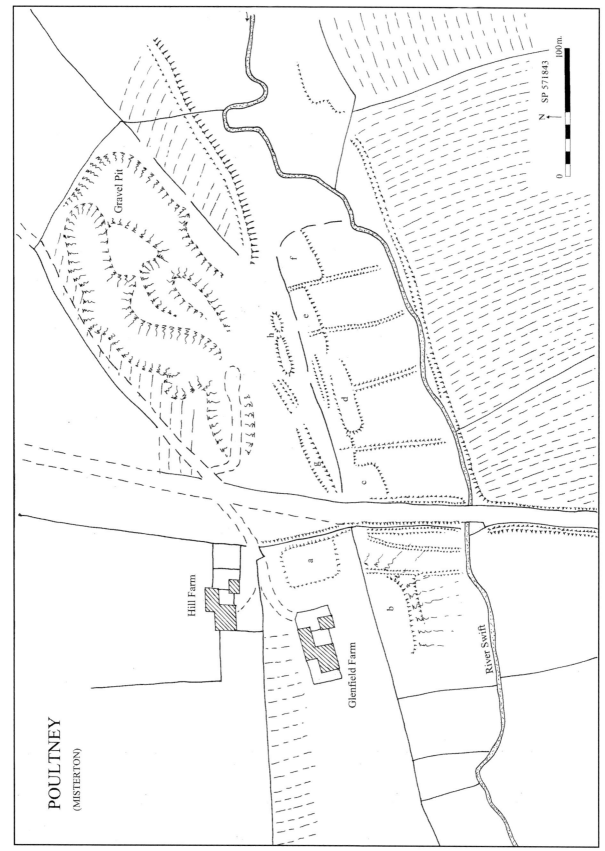

Figure 22: Poultney Deserted Village (Misterton)

Leonard's Church presumably lay near the centre of the village, and to the west is a large hollow way (a) which would have been the major north-south lane through the village. North of the church the land slopes down to the River Swift, and within this area are several features, including a neat rectangular moat (b), an area (c), perhaps once a garden, flanked by narrow ponds, and another enclosed area (d) with the moat to the south, a large ditch to the west, and

33

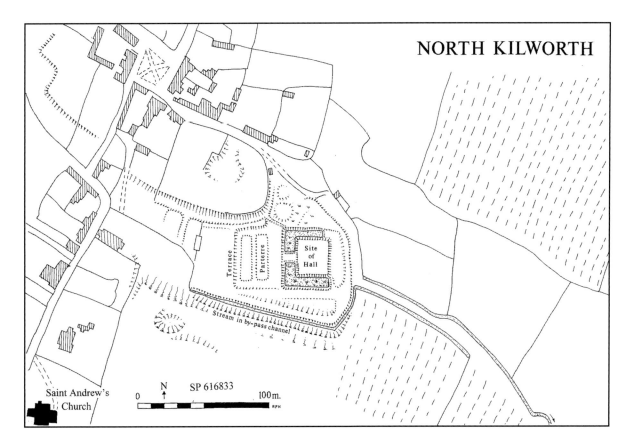

Figure 23: North Kilworth

the altered course of a small stream to the east and north. There is another former enclosure (e) to the west. These features could represent the site of a moated manor house with garden and orchard, which were abandoned when the present Hall was built on the hilltop to the south.

Poultney Deserted Village (fig 22) previous page   *SP571843*

In the eastern part of Misterton parish lay the village of Poultney, the name of which is still preserved in Great Poultney Farm and Middle Poultney Farm. Evidence for the site of the village was elusive for many years, but aerial photographs noticed in 2011 on the 192.com website revealed the characteristic rectilinear plan of a small medieval village just east of Glenfield Farm. Building platforms were indicated (a, b, c, d, e, f) with their plots bounded by enclosure banks and ditches running down to the River Swift. There may have been more features to the north, but this area has been affected by a gravel quarry, with an access track (g) and spoil tips (h). The web photographs were clearly not very recent, as the main field of earthwork remains has since been largely levelled, and very little is now visible.

Sir John Pulteney, who grew up here, became one of England's most wealthy and prominent citizens in the 14th century, and in the 1340s built the superb palace of Penshurst in Kent, much of which still survives.

Walcote Village   *SP567836*

The hamlet of Walcote may have grown in extent to replace Misterton, and it does not seem to have any evidence of village shrinkage.

Open Fields

Misterton and Poultney were enclosed at an early date. In 1625 Walcote had three fields, Middle Field, Buckwell Field and one other.

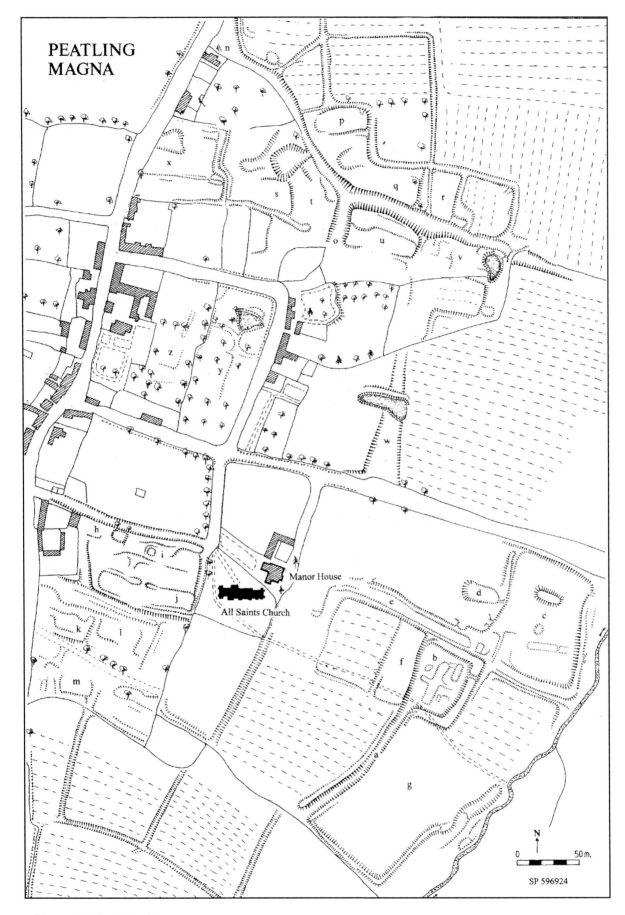

PEATLING
MAGNA

Manor House

All Saints Church

N

0   50 m.

SP 596924

Figure 24: Peatling Magna

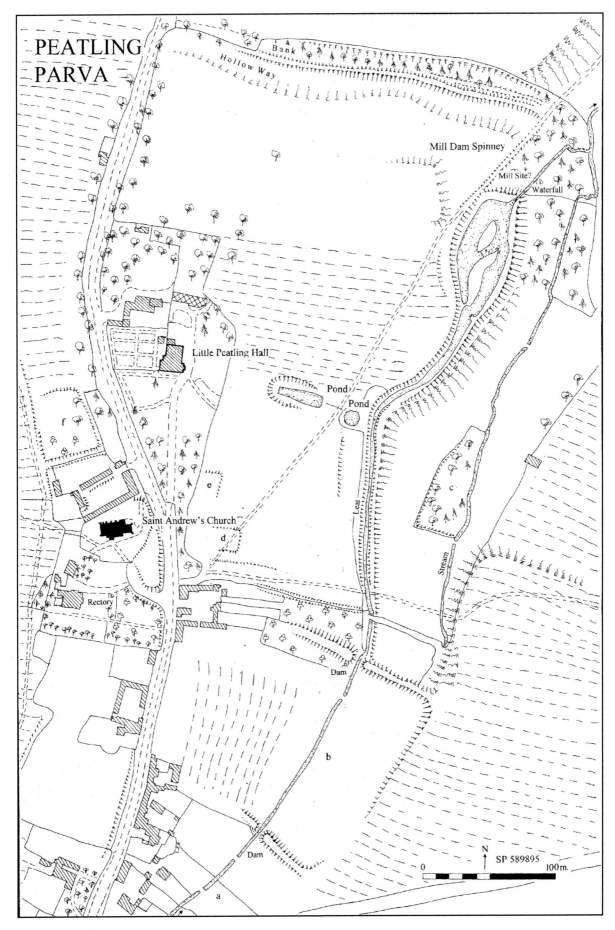

Figure 25: Peatling Parva

NORTH KILWORTH

Nether Hall Moat and Gardens (fig 23) previous page   *SP618833*

The site of Nether Hall is marked by a rectangular moat to the north-east of St Andrew's Church. The moat is water-filled on three sides, but the whole feature is very shallow and presumably intended more for display than defence. Immediately west of the moat is a terrace and a levelled rectangular area, interpreted here as the parterre of a formal garden. There is a by-pass channel, showing how the stream has been diverted to create this low-lying site. Thomas Payne possessed the manor of Nether Hall in 1347, and it was later held by the Belgrave family (Nichols 1810,197-8).

Village earthworks (fig 23) previous page   *SP615834*

There are slight earthworks of two possible building platforms recorded to the west of Green Lane.

Open Fields

Three fields are recorded in 1638:- Mill, Brook, and Holme.

PEATLING MAGNA

Village Earthworks (fig 24) previous page   *SP596924*

Peatling Magna has a remarkable amount of earthwork evidence showing how the village has moved and contracted over the centuries.

To the east of the Manor House (Manor Farm) is an area of old manorial ponds and gardens, with a water supply channel (a), a pond with various islands (b), another pond at a lower level (c), again with islands, and a smaller pond (d) cut into the hillside and presumably fed by springs. There is an embanked enclosure (g), perhaps a plantation or orchard, and an avenue (e) leading from the Manor House into the garden area. Unfortunately the ponds were used as the basis of a new fishing lake in the 1990s, removing a lot of the smaller features.

West of All Saints Church is a field full of evidence of the former village, with at least six probable building platforms (h, i, j, k, l, m). North-west of the present village are two hollow ways (n,o), flanked by yet more building platforms (p, q, r, s, t, u, v) and old enclosures. Another lane led southwards and is clearly visible as a hollow way at (w).

Moving back towards the centre of the village, a post-medieval gravel pit (x) has probably removed evidence of another house site, and in the parkland to the south is more earthwork evidence, with two more building platforms (y, z)

Open Fields

In 1606 there were three open fields, South, East and West. M W Beresford published a conjectural map of the layout (Beresford 1949, 90).

PEATLING PARVA

Formal Gardens (fig 25)   *SP590896*

The area to the east of the village became a landscaped park around Little Peatling Hall in the 18th and 19th centuries. The southern end of this area had two earthen dams retaining ponds at (a) and (b). Further downstream is another basin (c), probably once a pond or an osier bed. A substantial leat follows the contour from dam (b) northwards to a pond with islands in Mill Dam Spinney, probably the site of the medieval watermill, landscaped to make an ornamental pond. A hollow way, presumably the lane to the mill, runs from the present road down to the stream, and is flanked on its north side by a bank.

Between St. Andrew's Church and the mill leat is an area probably landscaped for gardens around the hall, and containing two more ponds, and two building platforms (d, e). There is another platform (f) to the north-west of the church. These platforms probably represent the sites of houses cleared away to create the parkland and give privacy to the Hall.

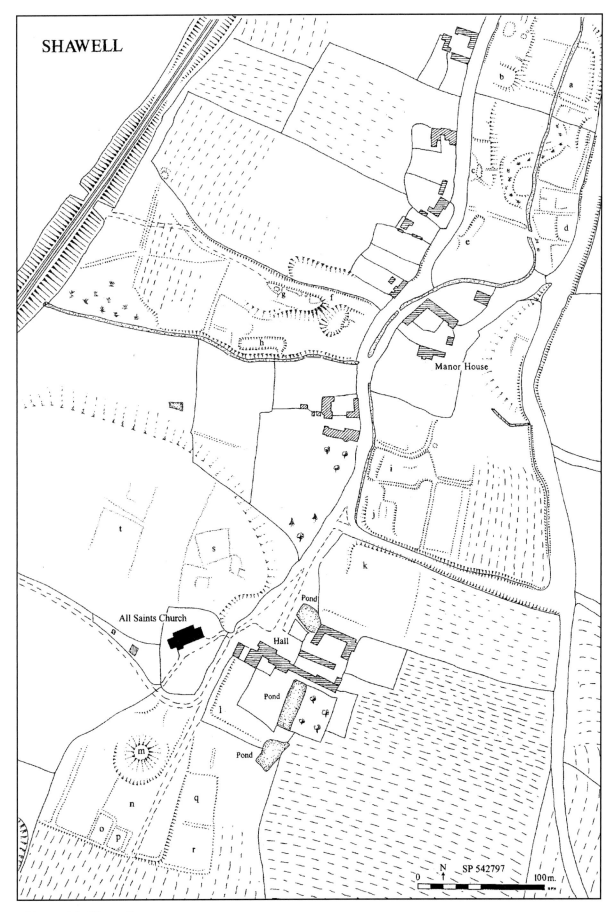

SHAWELL

Manor House

All Saints Church

Hall

Pond

Pond

Pond

N
0   SP 542797   100 m.

Figure 26: Shawell

Open Fields
East Field, South Field and North Field are recorded in 1638. By 1674 they had been enclosed.

SHAWELL

Village Earthworks, Hall Gardens and Castle Mound (fig 26)   SP543800
There are numerous small earthwork features in the village. Beginning at the north end, there is the dam of an old pond (a), and a house platform (b). There are two further platforms showing the sites of former buildings (c, d, e), surrounded by evidence of old enclosures extending back from the street frontages on either side to the stream. A hollow way (f) runs west out of the village, flanked by old quarry pits and also the foundations of at least one building (g). To the south by the stream is a small fishpond (h). South of the Manor House are at least three more building platforms (i, j, k) surrounded by their enclosures and by ridge and furrow.
The Hall has gardens with a pond and an "L" shaped terrace walkway (l) of 16th/17th century style. South of All Saints Church is the best-known earthwork in the village, a conical mound (m) surrounded by a broad ditch. This is thought to be a Norman castle motte. It was formerly surrounded by a series of rectangular enclosures (n, o, p, q, r) which could have functioned as the less defensible outer bailey. These features have been reconstructed from aerial photograph evidence as the field has been ploughed in recent times.
North of the church, in another arable field, James Pickering photographed crop marks of two groups of rectangular enclosures (s, t), perhaps elements of an Iron Age settlement underlying the present village (photographs in Leicestershire Historic Environment Records Centre, Leicestershire County Council).

Open Fields
In 1625 there were still three open fields:- Findall, Bikesdere, and Elm, but they had been enclosed by 1675.

"Holywell Priory"   SP534794 approx.
The site of a small religious house lay just on the Warwickshire side of the Watling Street in Churchover parish. The Victoria County History of Staffordshire identifies it as a chantry chapel belonging to Rocester Abbey in Staffordshire. Founded in the mid-late 13th century, it was abandoned in about 1325 and its function transferred to the mother house. The reason given was that it had become too dangerous for the chantry priest to live in this isolated spot where there were many robbers. (Baugh et al 1970, 247-251, fn 34, 35, 36, 37).

SHEARSBY

Village earthworks (fig 27)   SP623909
Shearsby village is surrounded by earthwork evidence of former buildings and enclosures. St Mary Magdalene's Church stands on a prominent mound (a), the origin of which is not known. To the north are two building platforms (b,c) with enclosures (d) and (e) behind them. At the extreme north end of the village is another building platform (f), with further examples at the south end of the village (g,h), and also the mound where a windmill used to stand (see below). There are old lanes along the south side of the village, surviving as hollow ways, and also on the west side, at (k) where a curving section of hollow way encloses an area of faint village earthworks (i), including two small ponds (j).

Windmill mound (fig 27)   SP623905
A little way south of the village is a circular mound where the windmill used to stand. The former mill tower is marked on the 1904 OS 1:2500 map.

Open Fields
Three open fields are recorded in 1638:- Moor, Brantall, and Rowley. These were later known as Thorpe Hill Field, Branthill Field and Rowlow Field and were enclosed under an Act of 1773.

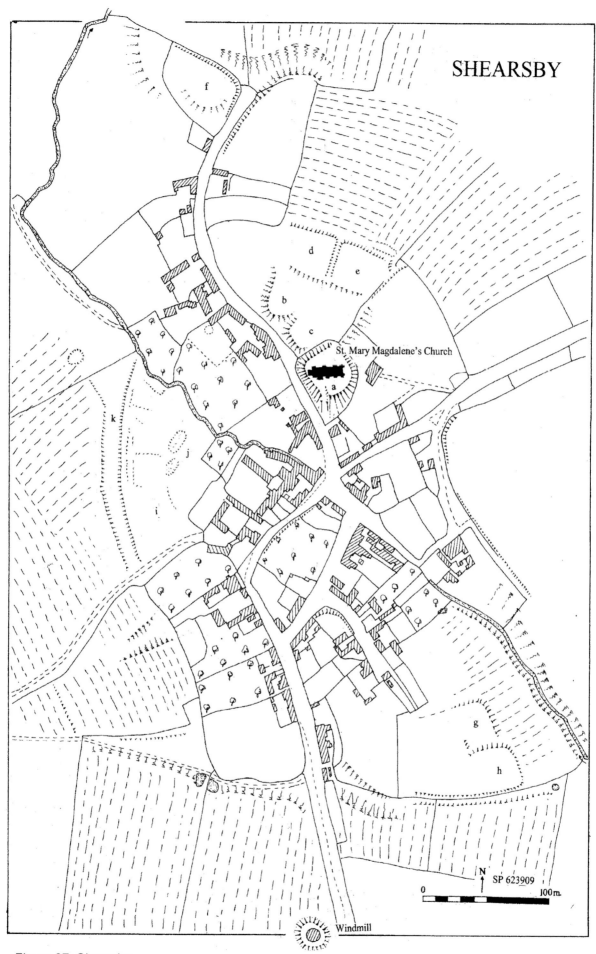

Figure 27: Shearsby

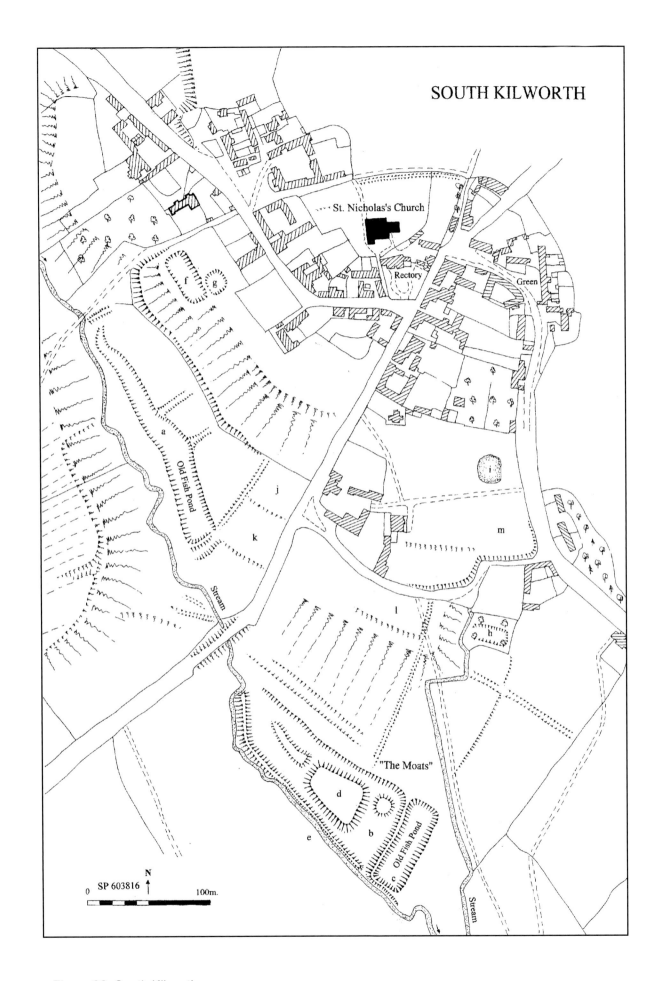

Figure 28: South Kilworth

41

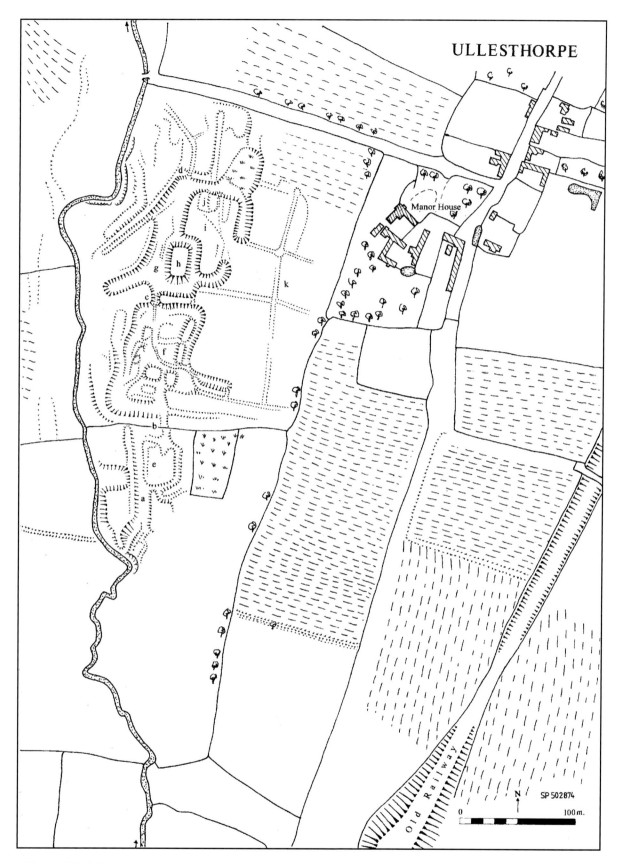

Manor House

Old Railway

SP 502874

N

0   100 m.

Figure 29: Ullesthorpe

SOUTH KILWORTH

Moated site and ponds (fig 28)   **SP603816**

The western edge of the village is defined by a stream, alongside which is earthwork evidence
of old fishponds and moats. North of the main road is a long, narrow pond (a), while to the

south is a moat (b) and another fishpond (c). The moat, as surveyed contains a main island (d) and used to have evidence of two less prominent islands or shallow areas. The stream has been diverted into a by-pass channel (e) which it still follows.

The OS Second Edition 1:2500 map calls this site "The Moats" and has a cross on the island (d) marked "Site of Manor House". A possible clue to the abandonment of the moated site is given in Nichols: " …*in 1633 Thomas Belgrave, esq. settled the manor of South Kilworth, with the water mill there, and also the well-close (where heretofore stood the manor house) on the marriage of his son William….*" (Nichols 1810, 204). The moat has been refilled with water in recent years and the smaller details of the site can no longer be seen.

Up the hillside to the north-west of the old fish pond and moats are more earthwork features, including two fish ponds (f, g) north of the main road, and two more (h, i) to the south. There are three slight terraces or old enclosures (j, k, l) and a larger terrace (m) perhaps an area of former village where the cottages were cleared to make way for a post-medieval mansion which has itself since been demolished. If this supposition is correct, then the various ponds and terraces along the hillside could be interpreted as features in an amenity park around this vanished house.

The main road is the early 19th century Rugby to North Kilworth Turnpike, and there may not have been a route through here previously (Cossons 2003, 67).

Open Fields

There were still three open fields in 1638, named Mutt Field, Wakelow Field and Brook Field. In 1756 the open field of South Kilworth is described as being bounded on the south by the enclosed grounds of Stormere (or Stormsworth, see below under Westrill and Starmore).

SWINFORD

Open Fields

In 1601 East, West, and North Fields are recorded. In 1674 they are recorded as "towards Stanford", "towards Shawell" and "towards Lilbourne" respectively.

ULLESTHORPE

Manorial site (fig 29)   SP501874

West of the present Manor House is a field of earthwork features extending down to the stream, probably representing the site of the medieval manor house with its fishponds and gardens. A supply channel (a) once took water to a series of elaborately-shaped ponds, retained by dams (b, c, d).

The pond created by dam (b) had a shallow central area (e), while the pond (f) created by dam (c) contained nine or ten shallow areas or islands. Water would have flowed into this pond from another, smaller pond probably fed by springs. This could well have been used to rear fish until they were large enough to be released into the other ponds.

Dam (d) retained water in another pond (g) of complicated shape. Within it is a rectangular moated platform (h), probably the site of the medieval manor house, and another platform (i), almost entirely surrounded by a moat. This area (i) might have contained a farm yard with outbuildings, and there is at least one building platform (j).

To the east, up the slope, is an area (k) with no ridge and furrow, which is divided into four by two raised paths. Just to the north are the foundations of three walls. These features appear to be the remains of an area of gardens. The site was surveyed in 1980.

Water Mill

In the Domesday Survey a mill of 16 pence value is mentioned (Nichols 1810, 118)

Windmill   SP506877

The village windmill has recently been restored.

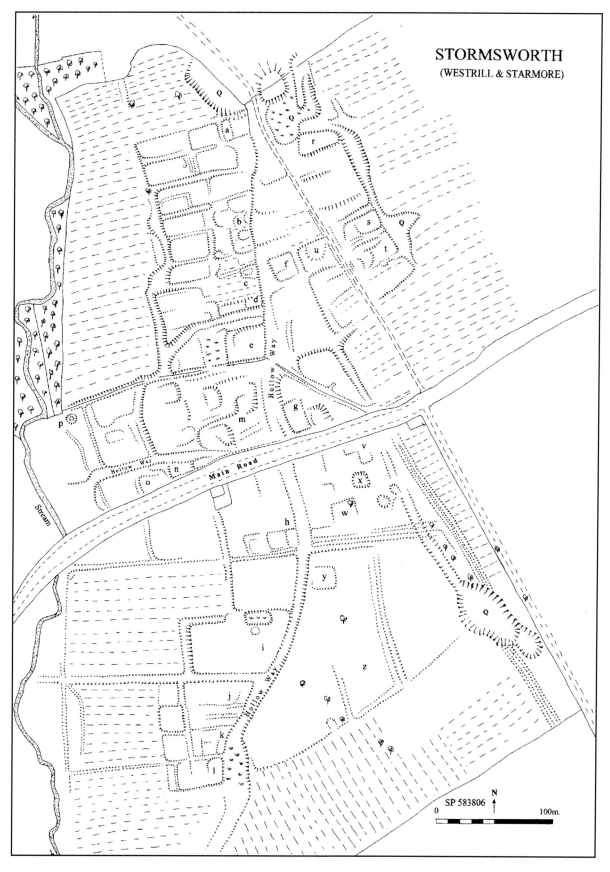

Figure 30: Stormsworth deserted village (Westrill and Starmore)

WESTRILL AND STARMORE

Stormsworth deserted village (fig 30)   *SP582807*

Sir Thomas Cave of Stanford Hall, writing to John Nichols in the late 18th century, recorded that no houses remained, but that in *"particular parts of this lordship may be discovered the lines of old foundations, though the plough has overthrown the vestigia of what buildings heretofore were erected here."* (Nichols 1810, 367).

Hoskins reviewed the documentary evidence in Essays in Leicestershire History (Hoskins 1950, 89-93). The larger manor of *"Stormeorde"* was held in 1086 by the Abbot of Selby, and it had nine ploughlands, occupied by 12 sokemen as their own property. There was also a smaller manor of about 100 acres, with two villains and a cottager. The population was thus about fifteen families, twelve of them freeholders.

Over the next two hundred years the Abbey managed to acquire about two thirds of the land, so that by 1279 there were only nine free tenants and they held only a third of the available land. The two manors were now known as King's Fee (the larger manor) and Mowbray Fee. The Abbot also had the right of fishing on the Avon, and a water mill.

The Mowbray Fee was in 1279 held by the Hospital of St. John of Jerusalem and the land was held by the free tenants of the King's Fee.

The Abbot of Selby held the advowson of the church of Stormsworth, which was built between 1220 and 1279 and appears as a chapelry of Swinford in 1344.

Hoskins concludes that Stormsworth was a flourishing village in the time of Edward I, having some thirty-five households and twice the population that it had in 1086. It continued to be a populous village in the middle of the 15th century, but *"within the next two generations or so the village had disappeared."* (Hoskins 1950, 91). His conclusion is that Selby Abbey gradually acquired land from the freeholders and turned it over to pasture, leaving no livelihood for most of the villagers. In February 1540 all the lands of Selby Abbey in Stanford, Stormsworth, Downton and Husbands Bosworth were bought by Thomas Cave, a member of a Yorkshire family who had long associations with the monastery, but who, as Hoskins remarks "did not disdain to acquire the abbey property when it came on the market." (op cit, 91).

Nichols's correspondent Sir Thomas Cave noted that the north aisle of Swinford church was named *"Stormer aile"* suggesting that it had formerly been used by the villagers of Stormsworth, after the abandonment of their own church (Nichols 1810, 367).

The earthworks of Stormsworth village area are not spectacular. The northern half is Scheduled but the area south of the main road (A427) had not attracted much attention until Mrs Warren of North Kilworth suggested that I take a closer look, and we subsequently made a detailed survey of the whole site.

The village is roughly triangular in shape, flanking a north-south routeway which survives as two lengths of hollow way. Another smaller length of hollow way indicates the old route of the A427 before it was straightened.

The north-west quarter of the village has a very clear rectilinear pattern of crofts, with building platforms at (a, b, c, d, e, m, n, o) and probably elsewhere. The larger and perhaps more prestigious plot extending westwards from (m) has indications of possible outbuildings and crew-yards, and at the bottom of the slope are the foundations of a circular stone building (p), almost certainly a dovecote.

The south-west quarter continues with a clear rectilinear plan, with the sites of buildings probably at (h, i, j, k and l). The enclosure around (i) has a small fishpond. The north-east quarter of the village is less formally organised, but has a back lane flanked by building platforms (r, s, t) and at least three more building platforms (u, f, g).

The south-east quarter is different again, with well-defined building platforms (v, w) and a rectangular hollow (x). There might have been a manor house in this area, with its adjacent closes (z) perhaps once containing gardens and orchards, and including a possible rectangular pond (y). Along the western edge of the village are several quarries (q), dug in post-medieval times probably to provide small stones for road mending purposes.

Stanford Hall and Village (Fig 32)   SP586794

The medieval village of Stanford on Avon lies just inside Northamptonshire. The site of the original manor house is thought to lie just west of Saint Nicholas's Church, in an area later used for a walled garden, with ponds and two prospect mounds inside the wall on the south side. Between 1697 and 1700 Sir Roger Cave built a fine new house on the Leicestershire side of the River Avon, converting part of the fields of Westrill & Starmore into parkland, with magnificent avenues of trees leading north and south, and various plantations. Much evidence of the medieval ridge and furrow was thereby preserved.

During the 18th century the river was dammed to create an attractive lake with two islands, and in addition a smaller serpentine lake was dug to the west of the hall. Within the park there are also two mounds (a), probably created to plant specimen trees on.

The village of Stanford on Avon was much reduced in size, and its focus moved southwards, away from the Hall, leaving well preserved earthworks including numerous building platforms (b, c, d, e, f, g, h, i, j, k, l, m, n, o, p, q, r, s). There are two clear hollow ways (t, u) and a back lane (v). The village earthworks were surveyed for the Royal Commission's *Inventory of Archaeological Monuments in North-west Northamptonshire Vol 3* (RCHME 1981, 176, fig.133), and their plan shows additional village earthworks in the area extending southwards from Saint Nicholas's Church.

Westrill Spinney - Dam and Ponds (fig 31)   SP587803

In Westrill Spinney, north of Stanford Hall, the course of the stream has been modified and a by-pass channel (a) dug into the hillside. In the valley bed a dam (b) was constructed to retain a pond (c), within which are three flat-topped ridges (d, e, f). This seems to be a parkland feature, a plantation, perhaps originally planted with willows as an osier bed, but at present this is just speculation.

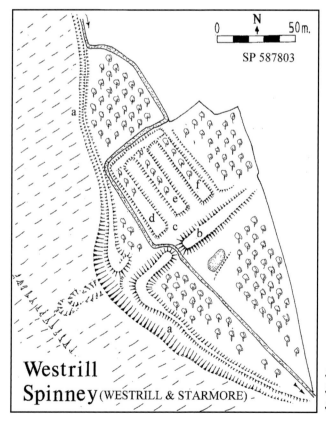

Figure 31: Westrill Spinney, (Westrill and Starmore, Stanford on Soar)

WILLOUGHBY WATERLEYS

Open Fields

There were three open fields, East, Middle and West, in 1601. These had been enclosed by 1674.

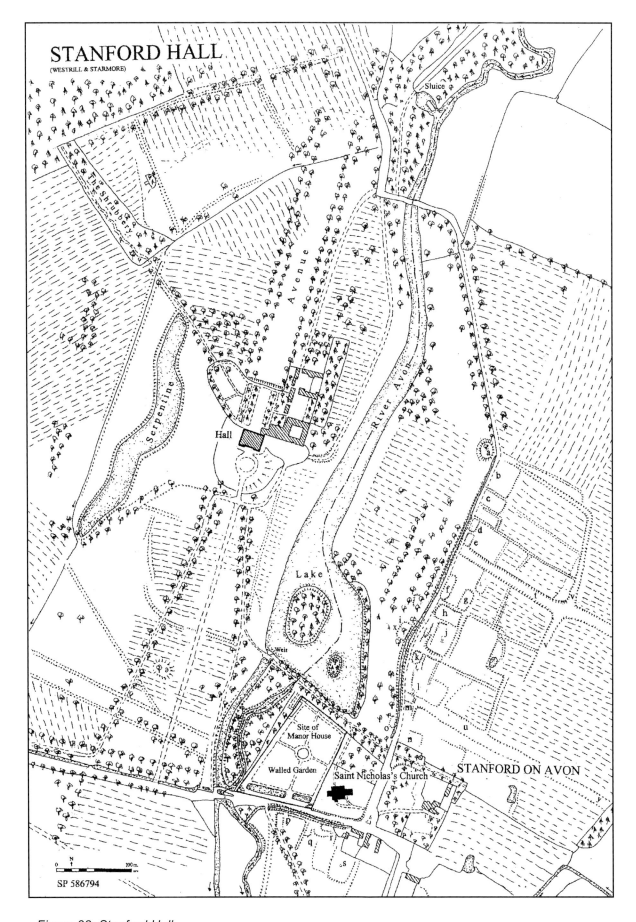

Figure 32: Stanford Hall

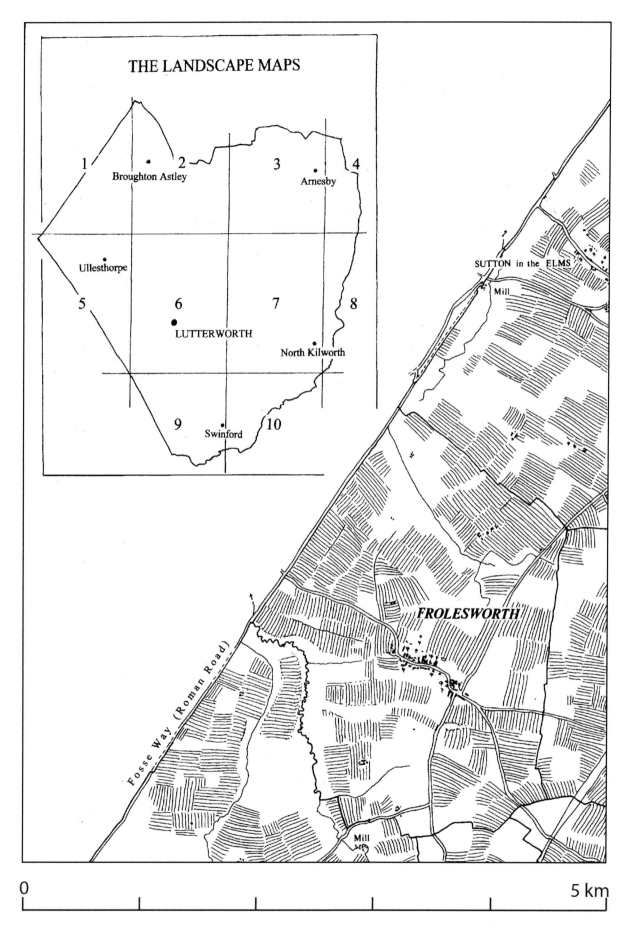

THE LANDSCAPE MAPS

1   2
Broughton Astley

3   4
Arnesby

Ullesthorpe

5   6   7   8

LUTTERWORTH

North Kilworth

9   10
Swinford

SUTTON in the ELMS
Mill

FROLESWORTH

Fosse Way (Roman Road)

Mill

0   5 km

Landscape Map 1

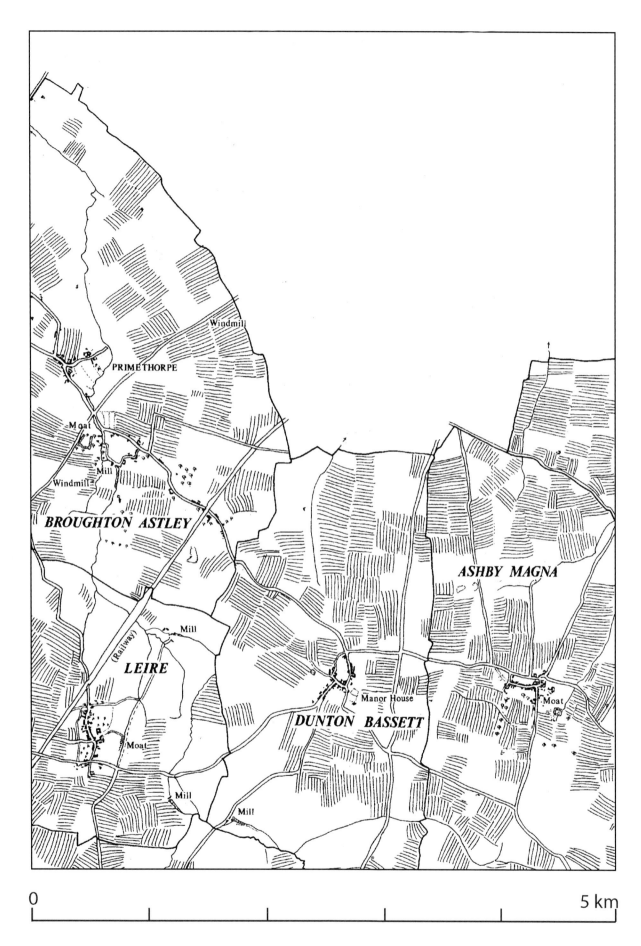

Windmill

PRIMETHORPE

Moat

Mill

Windmill

BROUGHTON ASTLEY

ASHBY MAGNA

(Railway)

Mill

LEIRE

Manor House

Moat

Moat

DUNTON BASSETT

Mill

Mill

0   5 km

Landscape Map 2

49

PEATLING MAGNA

ARNESBY

Manor Farm

Moat

WILLOUGHBY
WATERLEYS

PEATLING PARVA

Hall

BRUNTINGTHORPE

0   5 km

Landscape Map 3

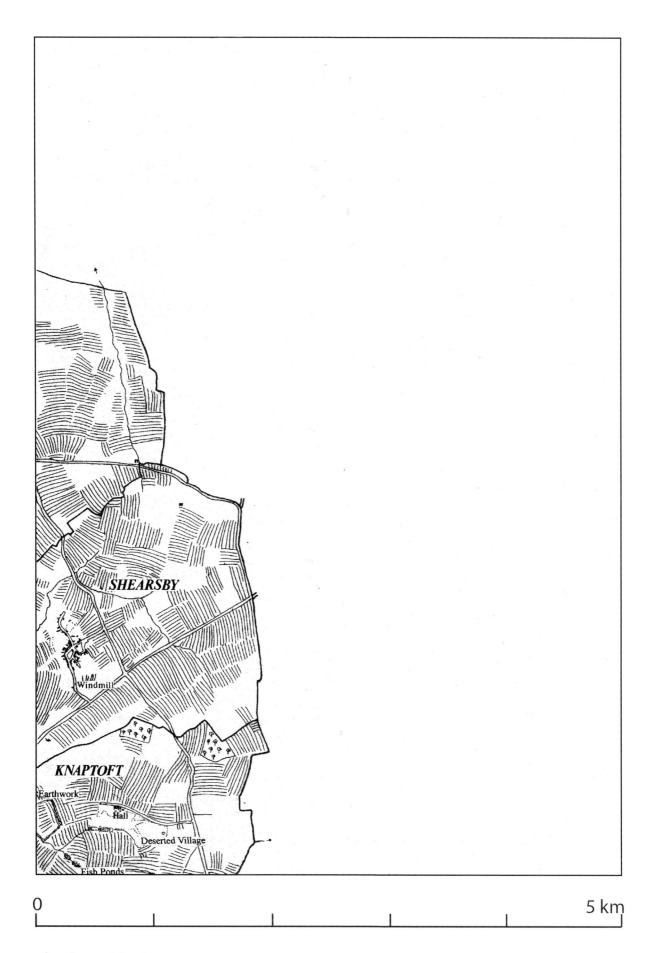

Landscape Map 4

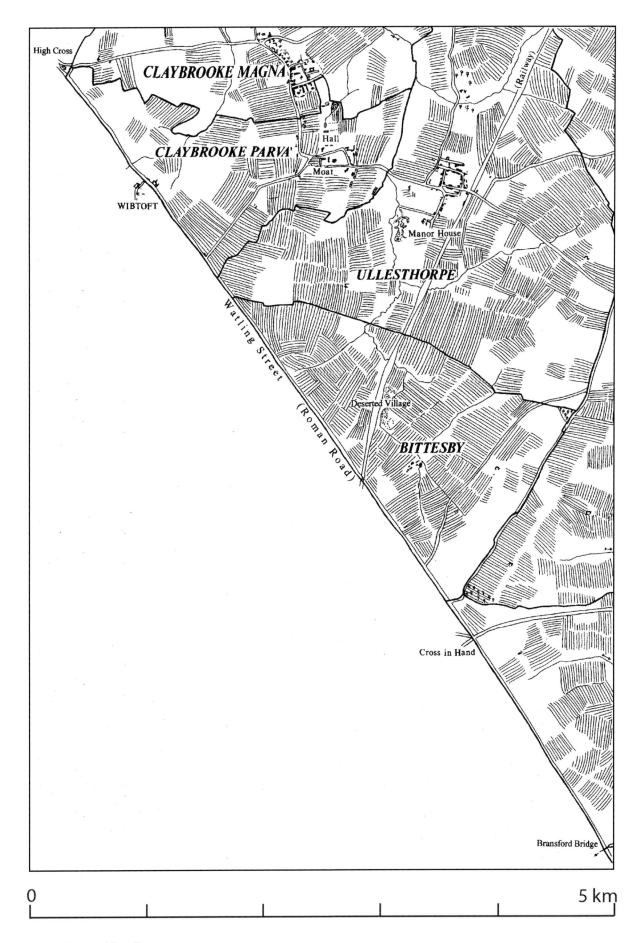

High Cross

CLAYBROOKE MAGNA

CLAYBROOKE PARVA

Hall

Moat

WIBTOFT

Manor House

ULLESTHORPE

(Railway)

Watling Street (Roman Road)

Deserted Village

BITTESBY

Cross in Hand

Bransford Bridge

0   5 km

Landscape Map 5

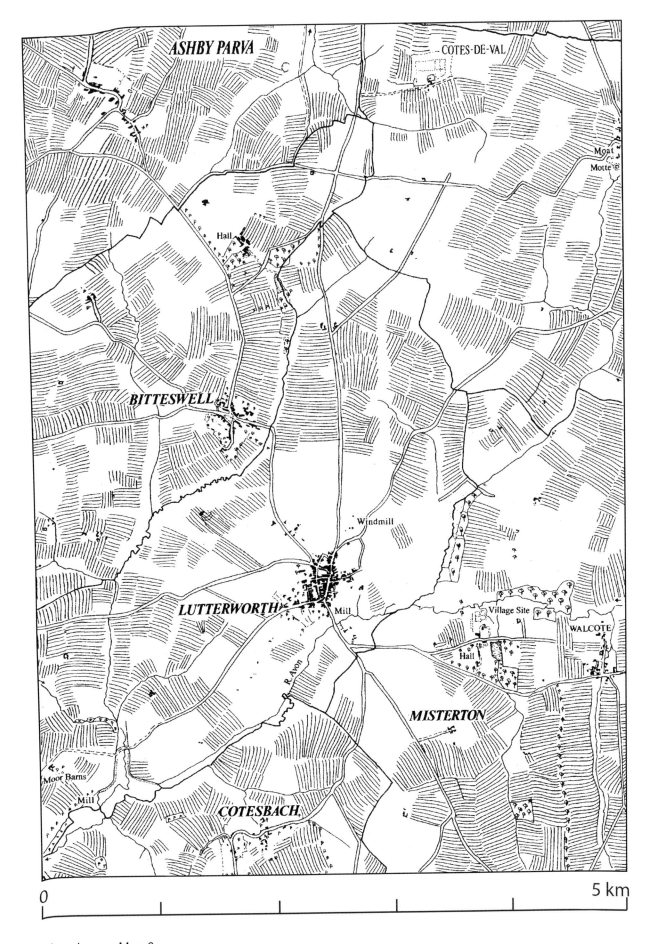

ASHBY PARVA

COTES-DE-VAL

Moat
Motte

Hall

BITTESWELL

Windmill

LUTTERWORTH

Mill

Village Site

WALCOTE

Hall

MISTERTON

R. Avon

Moor Barns

Mill

COTESBACH

0   5 km

Landscape Map 6

53

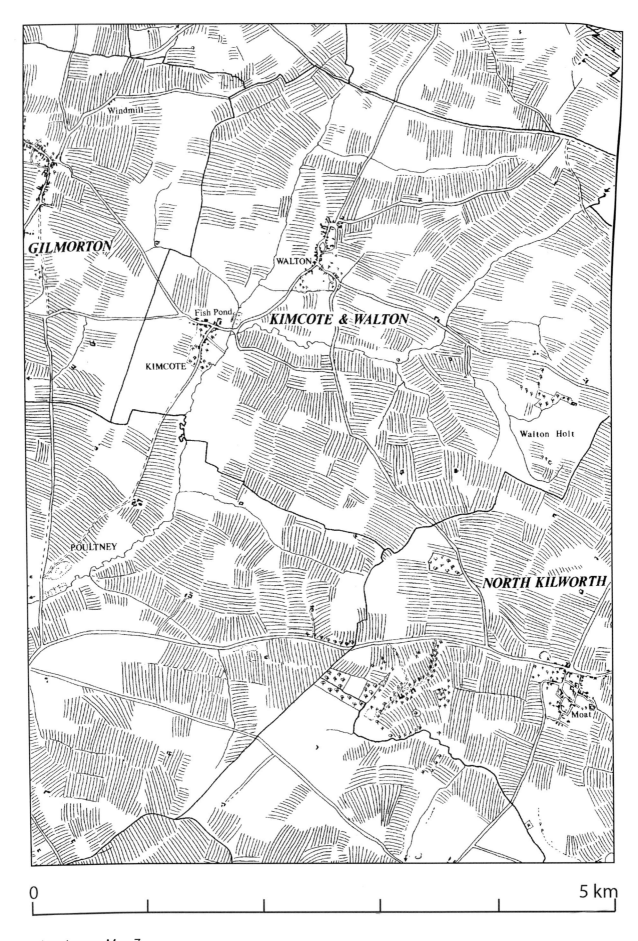

GILMORTON

Windmill

WALTON

Fish Pond

KIMCOTE & WALTON

KIMCOTE

Walton Holt

POULTNEY

NORTH KILWORTH

Moat

0   5 km

Landscape Map 7

54

Knaptoft Lodge

(Railway)

(Canal)

0

5 km

Landscape Map 8

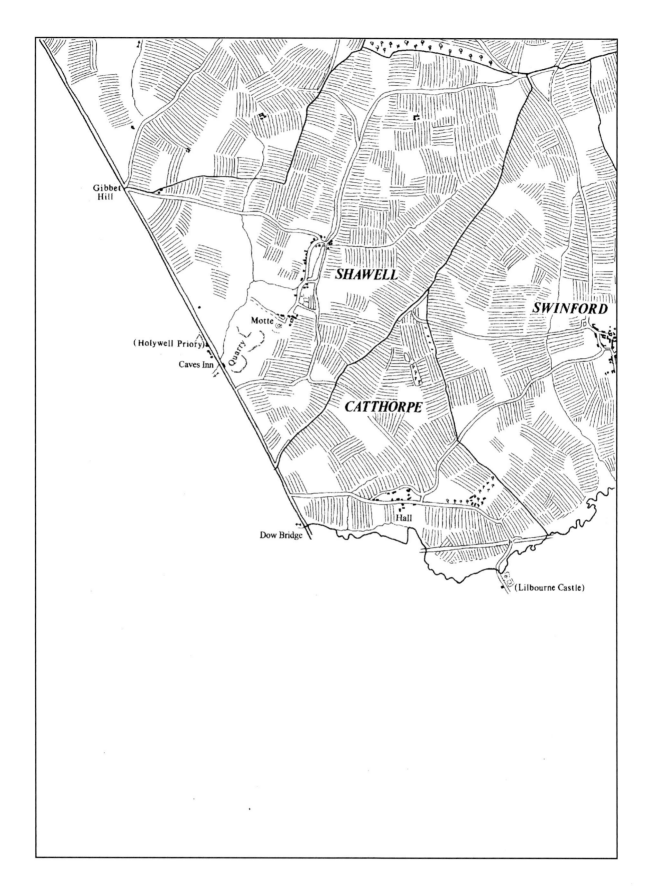

Gibbet
Hill

SHAWELL

SWINFORD

Motte

(Holywell Priory)

Caves Inn

Quarry

CATTHORPE

Hall

Dow Bridge

(Lilbourne Castle)

0   5 km

Landscape Map 9

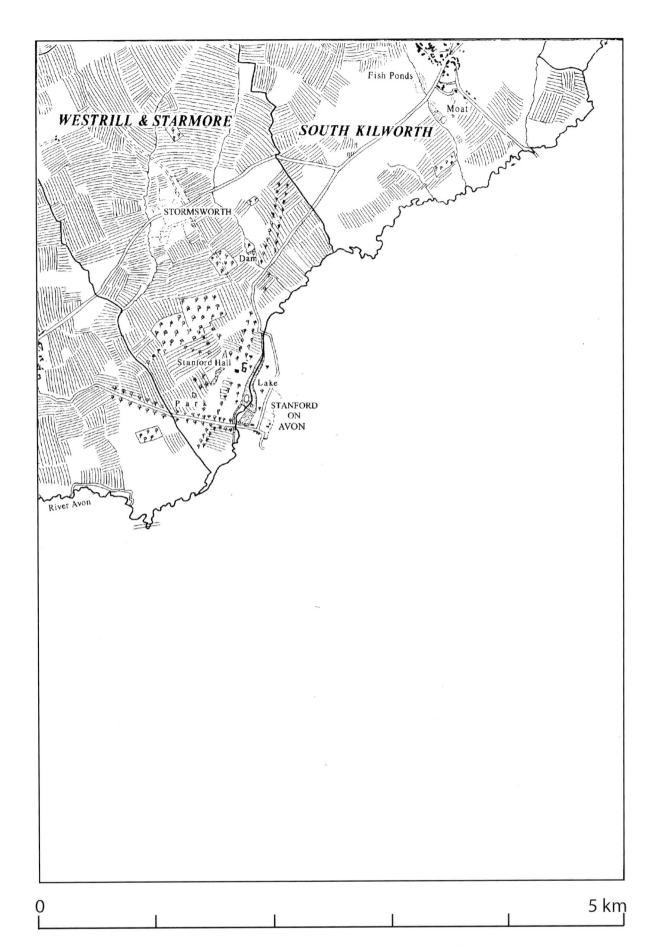

WESTRILL & STARMORE

SOUTH KILWORTH

Fish Ponds

Moat

STORMSWORTH

Dam

Stanford Hall

Lake

Park

STANFORD
ON
AVON

River Avon

0   5 km

Landscape Map 10

The Medieval Earthworks of South & South-East Leicestershire Part 2

Market Harborough Area

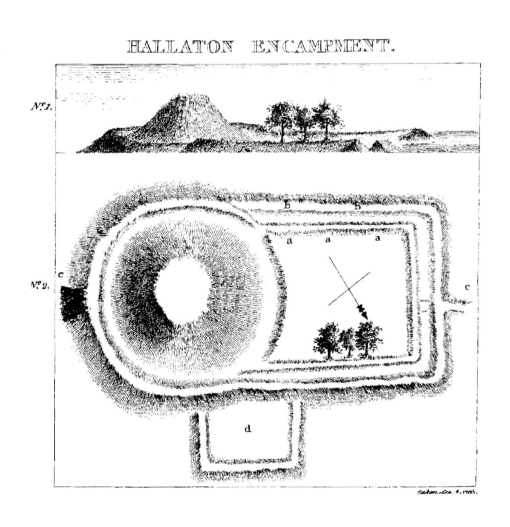

HALLATON ENCAMPMENT.

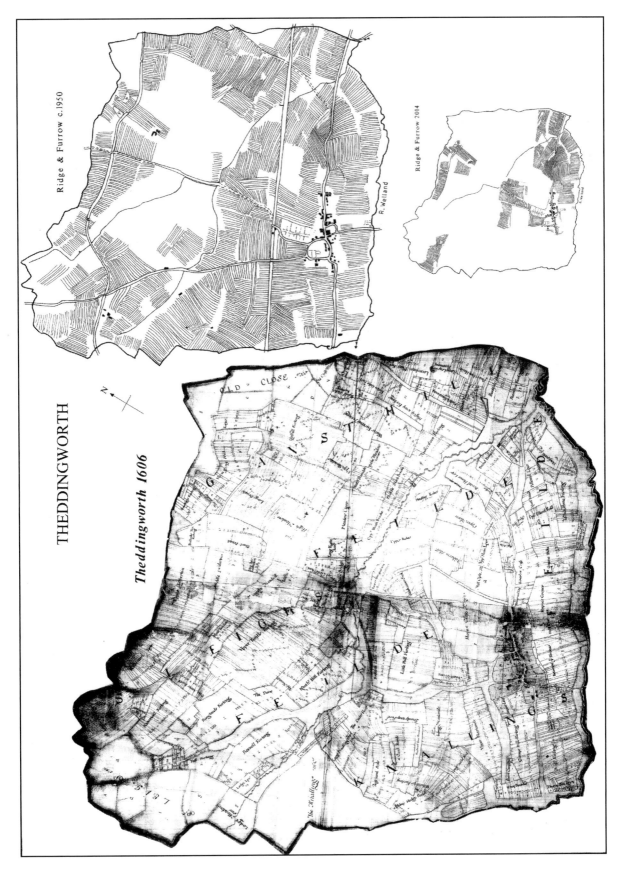

Figure 33: Map of Theddingworth in 1696, showing the layout of the open fields. This is one of the finest surviving open field maps for Leicestershire (copyright: Warwickshire Record Office). The smaller maps show the extent of surviving ridge and furrow in 1950 and in 2014.

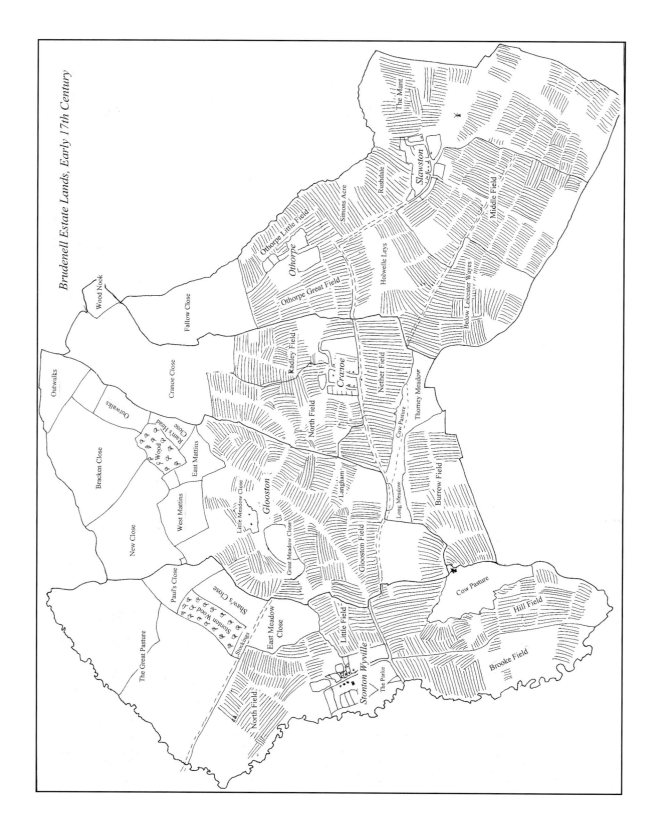

Figure 34: A suggested reconstruction of the landscape of Stonton Wyville, Glooston, Cranoe and Slawston, based on the Brudenell estate maps of the 1630s.

INTRODUCTION TO THE MARKET HARBOROUGH AREA

This volume is a survey of earthwork evidence of Medieval and post-Medieval landscape features in the central part of Harborough District in South Leicestershire. During August 2014 some thirty sites which had not previously been planned were visited, and features sketched from public roads and paths, with details supplemented from air photograph coverage.

The area covered by this report is the central part of the present Harborough District. Prior to 1973 it was the Market Harborough Rural District. A comprehensive survey of the history of this area was published in 1964 as part of the Victoria County History (VCH) series (Lee & McKinley *"A History of the County of Leicester, Vol 5, Gartree Hundred"*) hereafter referenced as VCH for this Part with page numbers to avoid multiple long repetitions.

The parishes are the Civil Parishes defined on the O.S First Series maps in about 1885. These largely follow the Medieval boundaries, and in most cases within this area the same boundaries have been maintained to the present day. The main changes concern Market Harborough, which until the late 19th century was only a very small parish, encompassing the built-up area of the little town. The surrounding fields were still part of Great Bowden parish. Little Bowden, on the south side of the River Welland, was part of Northamptonshire until the 1890s when it was added to Leicestershire.

The area has some parishes with particularly good surviving documents, notably Theddingworth (Frontispiece & fig 33 p 62), Kibworth Harcourt, Little Bowden, and Medbourne, for which we have open field maps. There are also early estate maps of Shangton, Stonton Wyville, Glooston, Cranoe and Slawston (fig 34). A lot of open field information exists elsewhere, for example for Great Bowden, but in the absence of a map much of it is difficult to interpret. Kibworth Harcourt has probably the best range of archival sources, discussed at length in Michael Wood's "The Story of England" (2010), which is a very full but also very readable survey of the history of the history of Kibworth and the surrounding landscape.

Until suppression by Henry VIII in the 1530s, there were monastic houses of varying size and wealth in most parts of England. Within this area the only monastic site with earthwork remains is the small Augustinian house of Bradley Priory in Nevill Holt parish.

Woodland and Deer Parks

Although this area was quite intensively cultivated in the medieval period, there were some areas, mainly on the remoter clay ridges, which were preserved as woodland. This was an important resource for building timber, for firewood, and for seasonal grazing. Woods had to be protected from grazing animals and were usually surrounded by banks and fences. Deer hunting was a an important activity for the highest levels of society, and there are references to a park at Nevill Holt. Such parks had to be enclosed by a pale, usually a ditch with an outer bank topped by a fence, to keep in the deer.

Negative Evidence

Despite the extent and diversity of the recorded earthwork evidence, there are many areas which appear never to have had earthwork features. Around this area these are mainly the low-lying land alongside the River Welland and some of the other streams, which were used as hay meadows in summer and pasture land after the hay crop had been taken. Some parts of the ridges around Stockerston and around Stonton Wood may also have remained pasture land through the medieval period as they were not favourable for ploughing and lay at a distance from the settlements.

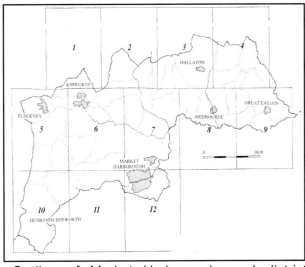

Outline of Market Harborough rural district administrative area. Numbers 1 - 12 refer to the landscape maps at the end of this part.

MARKET HARBOROUGH - THE PARISHES

The parishes of Great and Little Bowden appear consecutively under "Bowden", and the parishes of East, Thorpe, Tur and West Langton appear are listed under "Langton".

BLASTON

Open Fields
The parish was enclosed by the mid-17th century. Prior to this there were three open fields mentioned in 1601 and 1606, South Field, Park Field and Mill Field,

Village Earthworks and Pillow Mounds (fig 35 overleaf)   *SP805955*
St. Giles's Church dates from the mid-19th century, and stands in a field of what seem to be earthworks of a manor-house site. There is an elongated mound (a) perhaps a terrace walkway from a 16th/17th century garden. Near the stream is the site of a fishpond (b), and foundations of two buildings (c, d). The less substantial features (e) may be some sort of garden feature. North of the church the ridge and furrow (f) seems to have been modified to form a series of prominent ridges, which may represent some sort of plantation or orchard. When first surveyed (18th November 1992) (a) and (f) were thought to be artificial rabbit warrens, but they seem too close to the village.

Further east there are village earthworks at (g), and further east again sites of buildings (h, i, j), and more at (k). By the stream south of the village is the site of another fishpond (l), and further east a pair of ponds (m, n). St Michael's Church is a picturesque ruin.

Blaston Hall has very substantial garden earthworks, with a raised terrace (o). It is possible this was once linked to the features surrounding St. Giles's Church.

Hollow Way   *SP814957*
The existing road leading eastwards from Blaston was paralleled on its north side by a hollow way showing its old course. Towards the east end the route divided and there were at least three holloways, two of them to the south of the present road. These features are shown on RAF Aerial Photo Ref: CPE/UK.1925,3165, taken on Jan 16th 1947 (copy ROLLR, Wigston).

BOWDEN: GREAT BOWDEN

Open Fields
The parish was enclosed by 1703. Prior to this there were four fields: Gallow Field, Over Field, Nether Field and South Field.

Village Earthworks (fig 36)   *SP744888*
Great Bowden is an unusual village compared to most in Leicestershire in that it developed around at least four or five open greens, that have been partially infilled in the post-Medieval period. Near the west end of the village is Upper Green, east of the railway is a larger former central green (Green on the plan), both of them very clearly rectangular in outline. The east end of the village does not appear so obviously planned, but contains the largest surviving open space - The Green by the church, linked to the triangular Stock Green. Further north on the edge of the village is Nether Green.

As the village is quite large, with only relatively minor earthworks, the plan included here is a sketch survey at a smaller scale than most of the other plans. based on site visits in 2011 and 2014 and aerial photographs. At the west end of the village is a hollow way (a) with traces of a former building (b) on the north side. A bank and ditch (c) defines the south boundary of this part of the village and at least one bank indicates a former property boundary running down to it. There is another substantial building platform (d) west of Nether Green, and a field with faint earthwork evidence (e) to the north of it.

At the east end of the village is evidence of the boundaries of several former closes (f, g), and to the south, across Dingley Road, is another small field with village earthworks, including two building platforms (h, i). Further south lies Knight's End, another distinct element in the evolution of the village. This area has on its eastern boundary a substantial ditch and bank (j). It is not clear whether these indicate a former fishpond or garden feature, or simply a hollow way and the plough headland of the furlong to the east. South-west of Knight's End are two short lengths of hollow way (k) between furlongs of ridge and furrow.

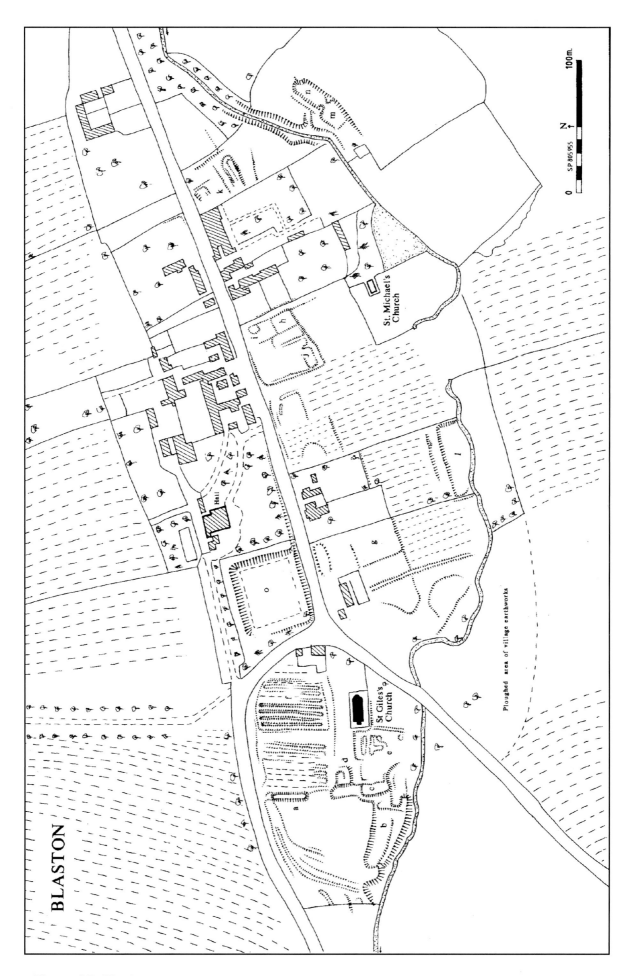

Figure 35: Blaston

Figure 36: Great Bowden

Recent excavations have identified Medieval plots along Sutton Road on the eastern edge of the central Green, with property boundaries (x) and a fish pond (y). (Brown 2010, 95-116).

Windmill Mound   *SP724883*

This hilltop mound marks the site of a former windmill.

Windmill Mound   *SP733884*

A mound on the top of the hill is presumably the site of the windmill. A windmill is mentioned in 1473, and it was blown down in about 1548 (VCH, 41).

Church of St Mary in Arden   *SP741874*

Although not an earthwork site as such, the ancient church of St. Mary in Arden, first mentioned in about 1220, is an interesting survival amongst the 19th and 20th century suburbs of Market Harborough (VCH, 47-8). Prior to enclosure its parish lay scattered in individual properties in Little and Great Bowden, and its origins and status have attracted much speculation from historians. The medieval church was largely destroyed when its steeple was blown down in a gale, possibly the great storm of 1658. It was rebuilt in 1693-4, but subsequently fell into decline and has long been a roofless ruin.

BOWDEN, LITTLE BOWDEN

Until the late 19th century the village of Little Bowden extended alongside the meandering Braybrooke just south of its junction with the River Welland. The layout of the village and its open fields is recorded in detail on a pre-enclosure map. In 1850 the Rugby and Stamford

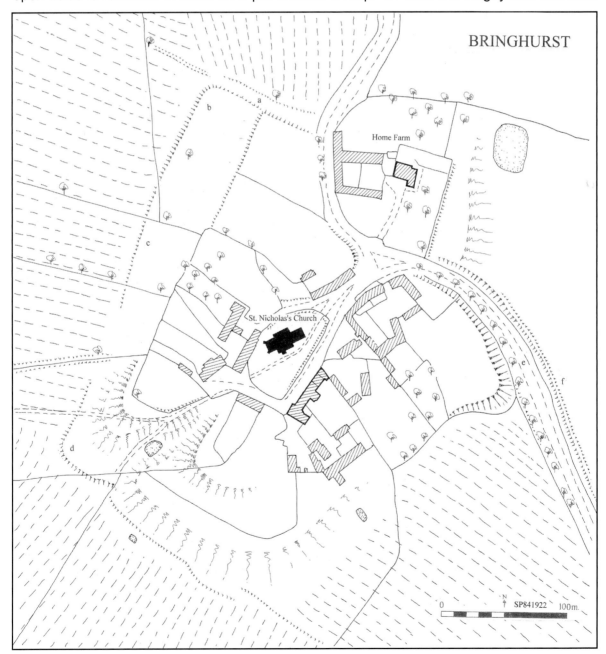

Figure 37: Bringhurst Village Earthworks

Railway cut through the north-west corner of the village, and a few years later the Midland Railway main line to London cut through the eastern flank on an embankment. Although Little Bowden is now surrounded by modern suburban housing there are some slight earthworks alongside the stream course which deserve closer examination. It is now in the civil parish of Market Harborough.

BRINGHURST

Open Fields
There is an Enclosure Act dated 1804. In the 17th century there were references to three fields, at one point called West Field, East Field and South Field, and at another called Bringhurst Field, Drayton Field and Hill Field. A terrier dated 1712 has Bridge Field, West Field and Grove Field. It is possible that Bringhurst shared these fields with neighbouring Drayton (Beresford 1949, 103). They are both unusually small parishes for this area.

Village Earthworks (fig 37)   *SP841922*
Bringhurst occupies the crest of a small hill, with extensive views along the Welland Valley. The church of St. Nicholas sits in the centre of the small cluster of houses. Opposite Home Farm a slight hollow way (a) extends into the fields and marks the northern edge of the village. A boundary bank (b, c, d) indicates the former north-west boundary of the village. The two right-angled corners at (b) and (d) suggest a playing card shape for the maximum extent of the village area, although this is not maintained on the east side. It is tempting to suggest that an Iron Age hillfort might have formed the basis for the Medieval village plan, but only excavation would determine this one way or the other. (Site visited 15th August 2014).

CRANOE

Open Fields (fig 34)
The village had three open fields, South, West and North Fields in the medieval period. By 1637 much land had been enclosed, but Burrough Field (or Nether Field), North Field and Radley Field, are still identified. These were called Burrough Field, Thrally or Thralsby Field and Nether Radley Field in 1679. The village was formally inclosed in 1828, at which date there were five fields - Radley, Burrough, East, Church and Townside (VCH, 82-3).

Village Earthworks (fig 38 overleaf)   *SP761951*
Located on the road (a) from Kibworth to Hallaton, Cranoe village extends up the hillside to St. Michael's Church. Three lanes (b, c and d) have run up the slope and retain evidence in the form of hollow ways. The westerly lane (b) is now a dead-end, flanked by earthwork evidence of terraces with at least two building platforms (e, f). The middle lane (c) remains in use for traffic, and is in places a deep hollow way. The eastern lane (d) only survives as a hollow way in the field, surrounded by other earthwork features. Glooston Rectory stands at the top of the slope and it would appear that the whole area of the village east of the lane (c) was modified in the post-Medieval period to create gardens.

Comparison of the present village layout with that shown on an early 17th century estate map reveals that three substantial houses (g, h, i) were removed, probably in the late 18th or early 19th century, and in fact traces can be identified in the field. To the east of them is evidence of their crofts or closes, that behind (g) being terraced as the slope begins to steepen here. Further up the hillside are platforms indicating the sites of more buildings (j, k, l, m, n to the west of these), from before 1600, and a hollow (o) which may have been an ornamental pond in the Rectory gardens of the 18th century. Building (n) is another one which is marked on the early estate map. Further east on the hillside are two more slight platforms (p, q), possibly the sites of buildings. The Rectory itself was rebuilt during the same period, as the estate map shows the buildings at (r), on the north side of a now-vanished little lane which led east from the hollow way (c) into the open fields.

The village was presumably once laid out more or less as a square in plan. There is however only faint evidence of earthworks in the north-west corner (around s). Returning to the south-east

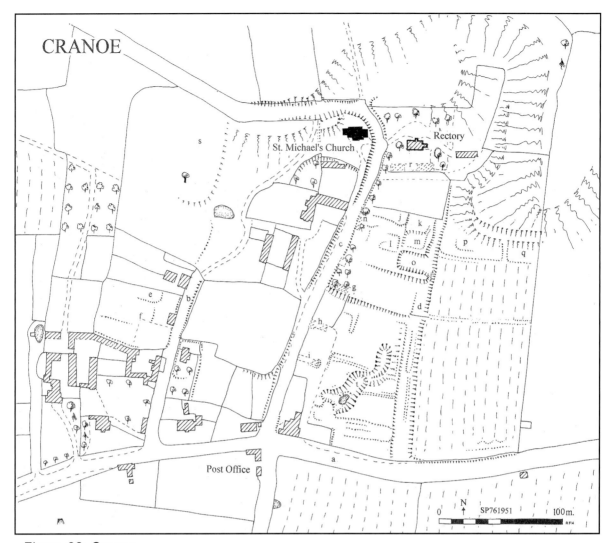

Figure 38: Cranoe

corner, behind the former houses at (h) and (i) there is, in addition to the evidence of old enclosures, a conspicuous hollow (t), probably a 19th century gravel pit. (Site surveyed *c.*2000). J. H. Hill, author of 'The History of the Hundred of Gartree' *c*1875, was Rector here from 1837 to 1886.

DRAYTON
There is an Enclosure Act of 1804 but the history of the open fields is unclear, and it may be that Drayton and Bringhurst shared their fields (see Bringhurst, above). The village of Drayton grew up around a horse-shoe shaped green, of which the present green is the north-west end (VCH, 50).

FLECKNEY

Open Fields
Prior to enclosure in 1769, Fleckney had three open fields, Quisick, Marfield and Hobrook.

Village Earthworks   *SP650935*
Slight earthworks show here on old aerial photographs. In recent years these have been hidden by the growth of vegetation.

Windmill   *SP6393*
The site of a windmill was granted to Leicester Abbey in the 15th century. Later there was a windmill in Mill Field on a hilltop, just west of the village.

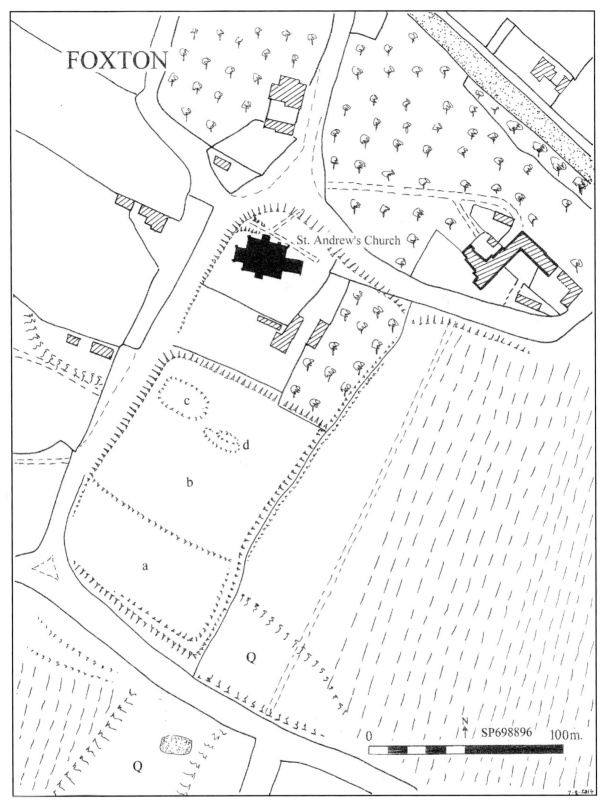

Figure 39: Foxton

FOXTON

Open Fields
In the late 17th century there were three open arable fields. In 1679 Mill Field and Yallo Field are mentioned (VCH, 94).

Village Earthworks (fig 39)   *SP698896*
Foxton is a spacious village with a rectilinear plan, and the houses laid out along six or seven

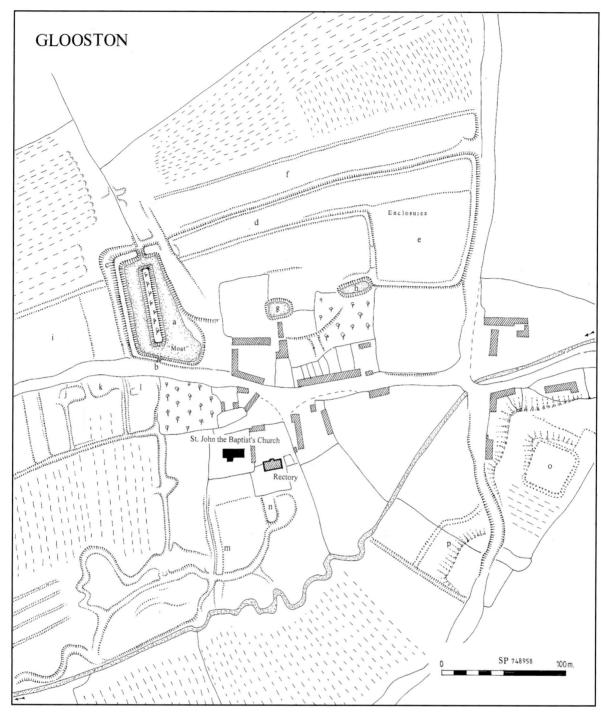

Figure 40: Glooston

parallel lanes. The Grand Union Canal branch to Market Harborough cut through in 1809, leading to some decline of the west end of the village, where there is slight earthwork evidence. St. Andrew's Church stands on a low hill in a southern extension of the village area. South of the church are two substantial old enclosures (a, b) and within (b) are traces of former buildings at (c) and (d). (Site visit 4th August 2014.) In the late 19th century there was a brickworks 150 metres south-west of the church, and clay was quarried from several areas (Q) to the south of the village.

Windmill Mound Foxton   *SP696892*
A mill south of the village was still milling corn in 1885. Permission to build a windmill was granted to Daventry Priory in the late 12th century.

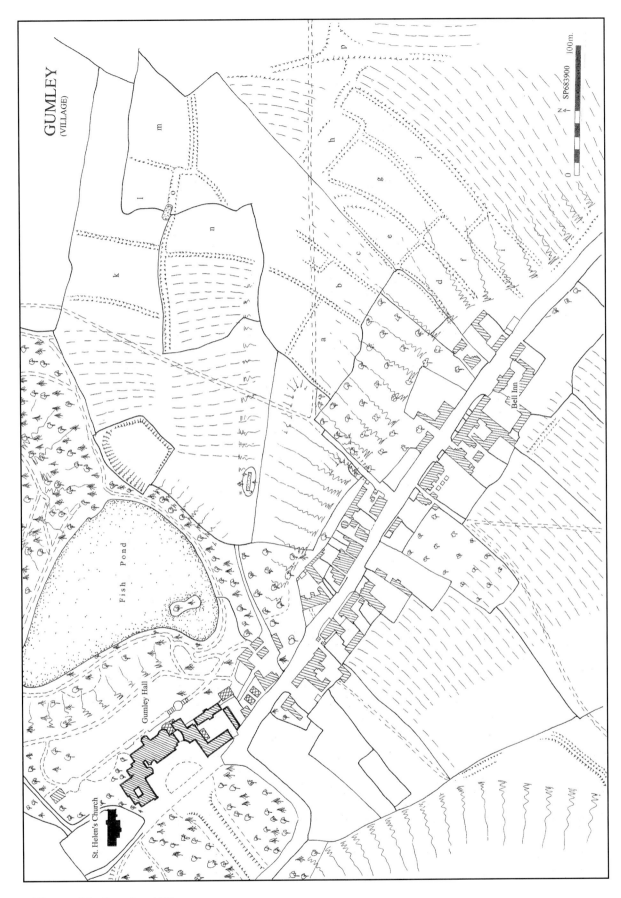

Figure 41: Gumley Village

73

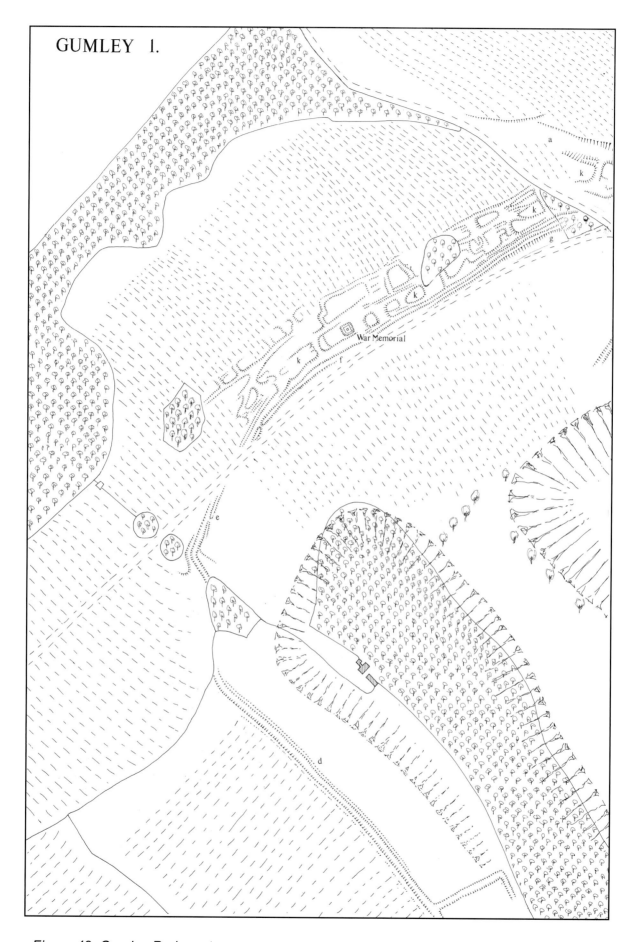

GUMLEY 1.

War Memorial

Figure 42: Gumley Park east

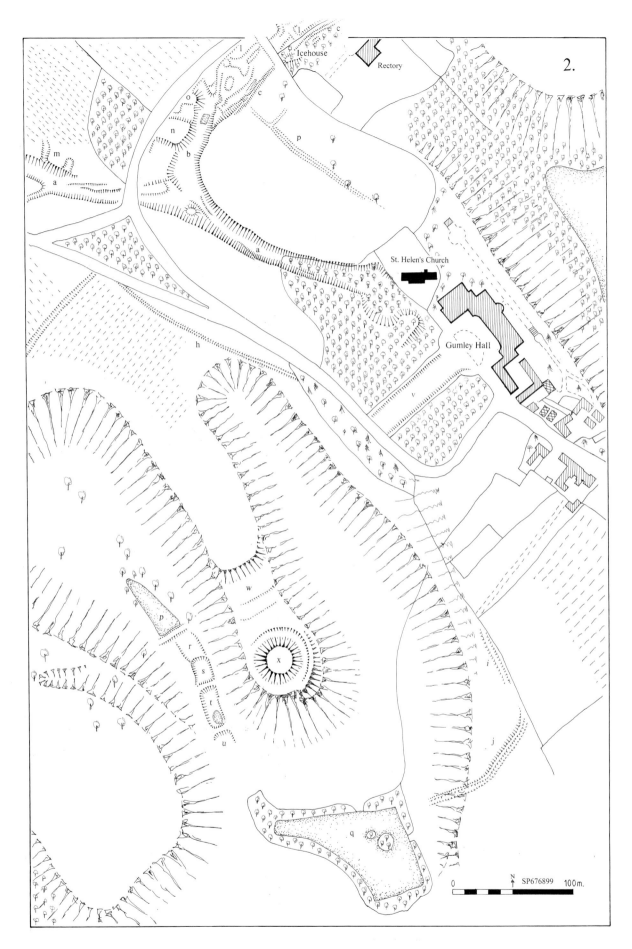

Icehouse

Rectory

2.

St. Helen's Church

Gumley Hall

SP676899   100m.

Figure 43: Gumley Park and Hall west

GLOOSTON

Open Fields (fig 34)
In 1637 the open fields were known as Little Field, Burrough (or Crosborough) Field and Willowsyke Field. By the 1630s about half of the parish was enclosed. Formal enclosure of the remaining three open fields took place in 1828 (VCH, 114).

Manorial Site and Village Earthworks (fig 40)   SP748958
100 metres north-west of the parish church is a moated site (a) with a long, narrow island, a dam (b) to retain the water, and a by-pass channel (c). This is now heavily overgrown, and the surrounding earthworks which once gave it context have been levelled. To the east of the moat there was formerly a long, narrow enclosure (d), extending into a broader enclosed area (e), all surrounded by a bank. A less substantial enclosure (f) flanked (d) on the north side.

Towards the centre of the area defined by the moat and enclosures were two ponds (g, h), and other slight earthworks. There was also another old enclosure (i), west of the moat. These features clearly represent a garden of some sort. As the moated platform is too narrow to have enclosed a manor house, it would seem likely that a large house stood somewhere within the gardens, most probably south of (g), in the area where the present farm buildings stand. However, although the moat, ponds and farm buildings are shown on the estate map of 1637, there is no indication of a house which might match the scale of the gardens.

South of the Rectory are more features; a causeway or dam (m) and a raised terrace, perhaps a garden terrace or the site of a former building (n). To the east, across the stream, are village earthworks, with a ditched rectangular enclosure (o) and a platform (p) alongside the lane. Both of these are probably the sites of vanished houses. (Surveyed 31st October and 1st November 1983).

Windmill Mound   SP752953
This is recorded as being 19m in diameter, 1.3m high, with a cruciform hollow on the top where the base timbers of the mill would have been placed. Nichols mentions a 'tumulus'. (1798, 792). It is shown on the 1637 map and had been mentioned in the 15th century (VCH, 114).

GREAT EASTON

Open Fields
Great Easton has two triangular greens. In 1601 there were still three open fields, North Field, East Field and West Field. Together with Bringhurst Easton was enclosed in 1804 (VCH, 55).

Mill   SP8693
VCH notes "remains of a windmill, north of the road from Great Easton to Caldecott" (VCH, 57).

GUMLEY

Open Fields
There were still three open fields in 1610, Holdgate or Houldgate Field (north-east of the village), Brook Field (south of the village) and Debdale Field or Mill Field to the north-west of the village (VCH, 119). The Inclosure Award is dated 1773 .

Village (fig 41)   SP683900
Gumley village extends down a ridge from St Helen's Church, past the hall, to beyond the Bell Inn. Behind the properties which face the north side of the street there is earthwork evidence of numerous long, narrow closes (a, b, c, d, e, f, g, h, i ,j) extending down the slope to the valley bottom. On the opposite slope are more old enclosures (k, l, m, n), with access from a narrow hollow way (o). At the east end of the site another hollow way (p) extends between the furlongs of the old open fields. These earthworks were first recorded from the air by the late James Pickering, but they are now clearly visible on vertical survey photographs, and easily seen from

the public footpaths across the area. East of Gumley Hall, in the bottom of the narrow valley, is an ornamental fish pond, probably dating from the 18th century, although there do not seem to be records of this.

Park and Hall (figs 42 & 43)   SP679899
The main street of Gumley continues north-westwards past St.Helen's Church as a hollow way (a) leading towards Leicester. Another hollow way (b) branches off and curves around to the east, passing to the north of the Rectory. On the south side are traces of a bank (c), perhaps originally the western boundary of Gumley Wood, which mostly lies further to the east.

To the west of Gumley Hall the ridge which leads towards Laughton has three steep-sided valleys cut into it, with two ridges between them. The steep slopes were unsuitable for cultivation, and much of the area has no evidence of ridge and furrow. To the west of the three valleys is a substantial bank and ditch (d), which turns eastwards at (e) and continues as a fainter feature running along the ridge (f, g). This is visible as far as the road just east of (g). It is possible that it used to continue in the form of the bank (h) which follows the crest of a slope west of the church. Further south is another length of bank (i) and a well-preserved section of bank and ditch (j) descending to cross the valley. These lengths of bank and ditch (d, e, f, g, h, i, j) appear to enclose the area of parkland, and may at some time have enclosed a previously unrecorded deer park.

Along the northern boundary, roughly on the crest of the ridge, is a curious area of earthwork mounds (k-k). There are about thirty in all, mostly rectangular but of different sizes, and it seems likely that they represent rabbit warrens. There are more rectangular mounds or platforms further east (l, m, n, o), the latter two possibly actually the sites of buildings. The field north of St. Helen's Church was formerly divided into at least three parts and the old enclosure banks survive (p). In the central valley in the parkland is a small pond (also p), and earthwork remains of four more (r, s, t, u) downstream. Where the valleys join is a larger pond (q) with two islands. These features probably date from the 18th or 19th centuries.

Gumley Hall was built in 1764 for the antiquary and patron of the arts, Joseph Cradock. The parkland and plantations were apparently laid out in imitation of the Parc de St Cloud in France (VCH, 117). From the west front of the hall an avenue (v) is still obvious, leading between raised terraces. The avenue leads towards the eastern ridge in the parkland, which shows signs of having been cut down in the area of (w). At the end of the ridge is a flat-topped conical mound (x), surrounded by a slight ditch, outside which the natural slopes fall away steeply. This mound, known variously as "Cat Gruff", "Danes' Camp" and "The Mot", is still something of a mystery possibly either constructed as a prospect mound for the 18th century parkland or it might be a Norman motte; the size of the top of the motte is closely comparable with the one at Hallaton. It is also worth noting that Gumley was the site of a royal palace of the Mercian kings, and both Offa and Aethelbald held court here and signed charters in AD 749, 772 and 779. It is

not impossible that The Mot was either a defensive strongpoint or a ceremonial meeting place. Even if the feature we see today is neither of these, it could be that the Normans put a motte here precisely to make the point that they were the new rulers of the land. Gumley Hall (pictured right) was demolished due to delapidation in 1964 although the stable block remains. (Surveyed 1980, additional features noted on field visit, 4th August 2014.)

Gumley Hall

Windmill
A piece of ground *"where a mill lately stood"* lay in Mill Field north-west of the village (VCH 119).

Wood   SP682903
Gumley Wood was one of the few sources of timber remaining in this area in the 18th century (VCH, 117). It has a slight outer bank around parts of the circumference.

HALLATON

Open Fields

In 1601 there were three open fields, Smallwood Field, Barleyhill Field and Fearne Field. A "Mill Field" is mentioned in 1563 and Wood Field and Brook field in 1713. There were four fields prior to enclosure in 1771 - Whetstone, Fearne, Barleyhill and Little fields (VCH, 127).

Castle Hill Motte And Bailey (fig 44.1 and cover illustration Part 2, p59)   SP780967

About 600m west of Hallaton village, above the confluence of two streams, are the well-preserved earthworks of a Norman motte and bailey castle. The conical motte (a) has a summit platform about 20m in diameter and over 7m high. To the north-west lies the sub-circular bailey (b) within a substantial bank and ditch. There are two more enclosures (d, e), possibly used for garden plots, around the eastern side of the motte, taking advantage of space between the defences and the top of the steep, natural banks down to the streams.

Mill Mounds (fig 44.2)   SP787968

North of Hallaton village is an area of spectacular surviving ridge and furrow, within which are two windmill mounds (a, b) . Mound (a) is the smaller of the two, and seems to be the earlier. It lies in a triangular space in the angle between three furlongs of ridge and furrow, and has a hollow in the top. Mound (b) is a somewhat larger conical mound on a site which partly extends onto the ridge and furrow. The plough ridge (c) between the two mounds is a particularly large and fine example. Just to the south of mound (b) is a disused gravel pit.

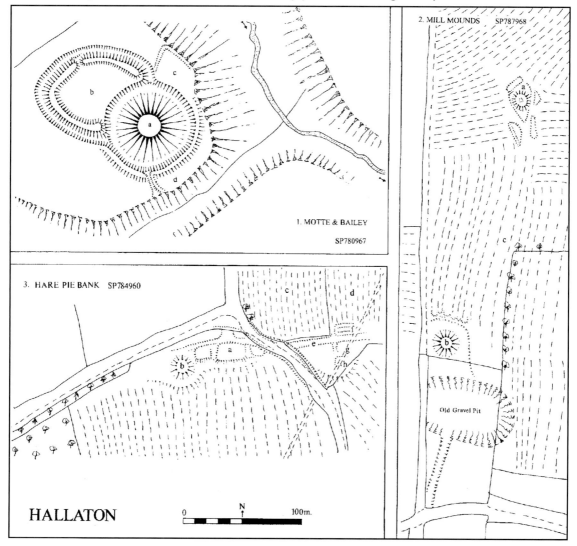

Figures 44.1: Castle Hill Motte and Bailey, 44.2: Mill Mounds,
44.3: Windmill Mound, Hare Pie Bank and site of St Morrell's Chapel

Windmill Mound, Hare Pie Bank and site of St. Morrell's Chapel (fig 44.3)   SP784960

About 500m south of Hallaton village, in the angle of two lanes, are some earthworks on the headland of a well-preserved furlong of ridge and furrow. There are three rectilinear mounds, of which (a) is the middle one and the largest. Just to the west is a windmill mound (b), about 20m in diameter. To the north-east of these features is a field of ridge and furrow, which in the 19th century was divided into two fields called Stowe Close (c) and Saint Morrell's Furlong (d). A hollow way indicates the original southern boundary of these furlongs. There is a rectangular mound (f) in the corner of St. Morrell's Furlong, and two more (g, h) to the south of the hollow way, in a small triangular area. This area is the location for the traditional Easter Monday folk tradition of the Hallaton Hare Pie Scramble and Bottle Kicking. John Tailby reported on this in 1796, noting "*The spot appropriated for the scrambling for the Pies and Ale is....a small oblong bank, 10 yards long and 6 wide; with a small old trench around it and a circular hole in the centre.*" (Nichols 1798, 600).

Recent research by John Morison and Peter Daisley has explored the origins and development of this custom, including the former existence of a small chapel to St. Morrell, which was probably abandoned during the 16th century and is last mentioned in a Glebe Terrier of 1606. (Morison & Daisley, 2000). A resistivity survey in 2011 revealed a buried ditch enclosing an area 30m square, centred on the small mound (h), which is the Hare Pie Bank. Excavation in 2011-2013 showed that the mound or platform (h) had been deliberately created, on top of the foundations of a small building, 5.8m wide and at least 11.5m long, with tiled flooring. This was interpreted as a chapel, and the evidence from pottery and coin finds suggested that it was in use during the 13th - 15th century period (Score & Morison 2014, 55-74).

Cock Abingdon Earthwork   SP774964

In an isolated location 1200m west of Hallaton is a rectangular earthwork enclosure, approximately 90m. x 70m., of unknown date. "*..it is nearly square; the depth of the ditch from the top of the bank about five or six yards; but the depth varies; it having been years past in tillage.*" (Nichols 1798, 601).

Hallaton Wood   SP765976

The wood was important as an area of wood-pasture in the Middle Ages, but ceases to appear in the records towards the end of the 14th century (VCH, 125).

HORNINGHOLD

Open Fields

Horninghold village was extensively rebuilt as a picturesque estate village by the Hardcastle family of Blaston Hall between 1905 and 1911. Prior to the Inclosure Act of 1730 there were three open fields - Moor Field, Hog Field and Little Field. Sir William Turpin was enclosing land here before 1607 and was said to have destroyed a farmhouse. The Enclosure Act was dated 1730, when three fields (Moor Field, Hog Field and Little Field) totalling 916 acres were enclosed. On the eastern boundary of the parish the woods of Muckleborough and Bolt Wood are recorded in the reign of King Henry VI (VCH,154-155).

HUSBANDS BOSWORTH

Open Fields

In the 17th century, Husbands Bosworth had three open fields, North East Field, South Field and West Field (VCH, 33). Somewhat earlier, in about 1500 "t*he Abbot of Leicester had inclosed a common of pasture in Husbands Bosworth called The Dole, adjoining his manor of Pinslade*" (VCH, 32). This would have been in the extreme north-west of the parish, where the Abbey seems to have had other holdings of land here, adjacent to their grange farm which lay just over the boundary in Mowsley parish. Much land in Bosworth was also held by the Abbey of Sulby, which lay just outside the parish, in Northamptonshire. "*In 1764 an Act was passed for inclosing the open and common fields..in the parish of Husbands Bosworth.. computed to consist of about 96 yardlands, and to contain 4000 acres;..*" (Nichols 1798, 464).

Watermill *SP629823*

The supply leat and pond of Husbands Bosworth Mill are well preserved between the River Avon and the Welford branch canal. A mill in Bosworth, very probably on this site, is mentioned in 1086 (VCH, 33)

KIBWORTH BEAUCHAMP

Kibworth Beauchamp and Kibworth Harcourt are two villages sharing a single parish church (St Wilfrid's). Kibworth Beauchamp grew in size during the 19th and early 20th centuries,obscuring any earthwork evidence of earlier changes of plan. The open fields were enclosed in 1779.

KIBWORTH HARCOURT

Open Fields (fig 46)
Merton College in Oxford has owned lands in Kibworth Harcourt for some 750 years and holds a superb archive of documents and maps relating to the village. These have been used by several historians, including Rodney Hilton in 1949, Cicely Howell in 1983, and most recently Michael Wood in "The Story of England" (2010), where Kibworth is used as an exemplar of the history of the villages of England. The map here is redrawn from the 1779 map of the open fields, including the furlong names then in use. This was the map made immediately before the fields were inclosed, when some nine hundred years of farming tradition came to an end. Only a small percentage of the area now retains evidence in the form of ridge and furrow.

Motte (fig 45) *SP680944*
South of the High Street of Kibworth Harcourt (where markets were held until the 18th century) is a low flat-topped mound (a), with the summit area about 25m in diameter, surrounded by a ditch (b). This may have been a Norman motte or defensive strongpoint, although the site is not strategically chosen, being overlooked from the west side. However the context of the site was altered in the late 18th century by the construction of the turnpike road, bypassing the village centre. There are indications of ridge and furrow immediately south of the mound. A relatively recent ditch and fence (c) cut through it to form the southern boundary of the present field.

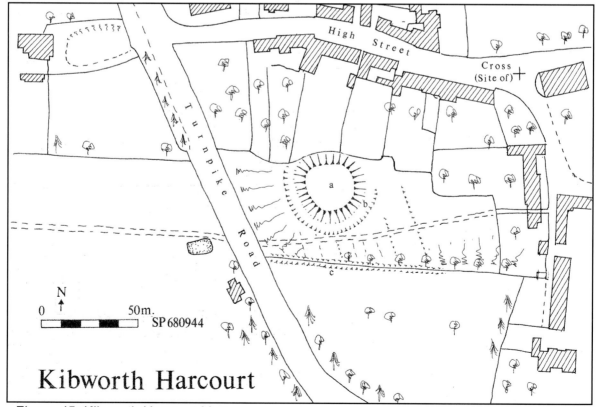

Figure 45: Kibworth Harcourt Motte

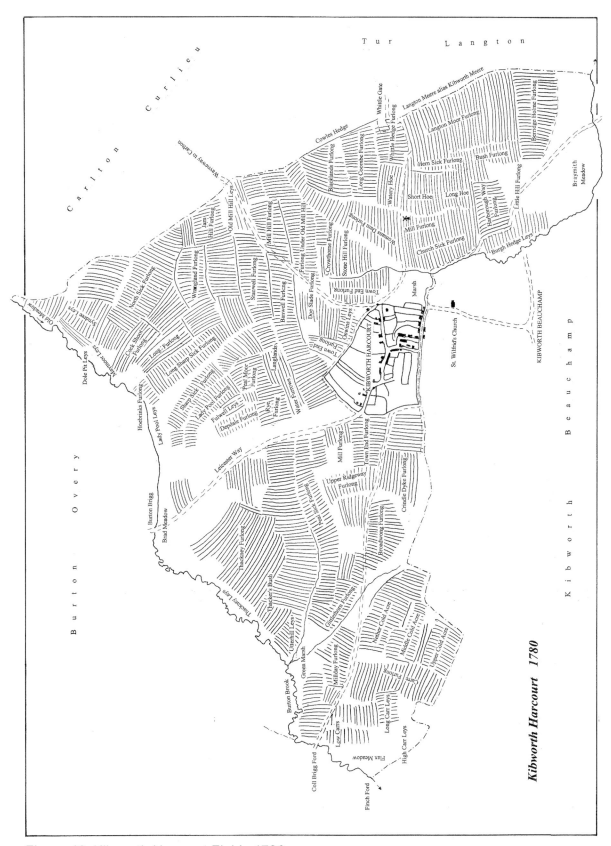

Figure 46: Kibworth Harcourt Fields 1780

Fish Ponds   **SP683946**

Two narrow ponds of unknown date extend along the stream course on the northern boundary of the medieval village.

Windmill Mound   **SP677948**

The mound was excavated by F. B. Aggas in the 1960s, producing millstone fragments and part of a 13th century jar (TLAHS 1967-8, 64).

81

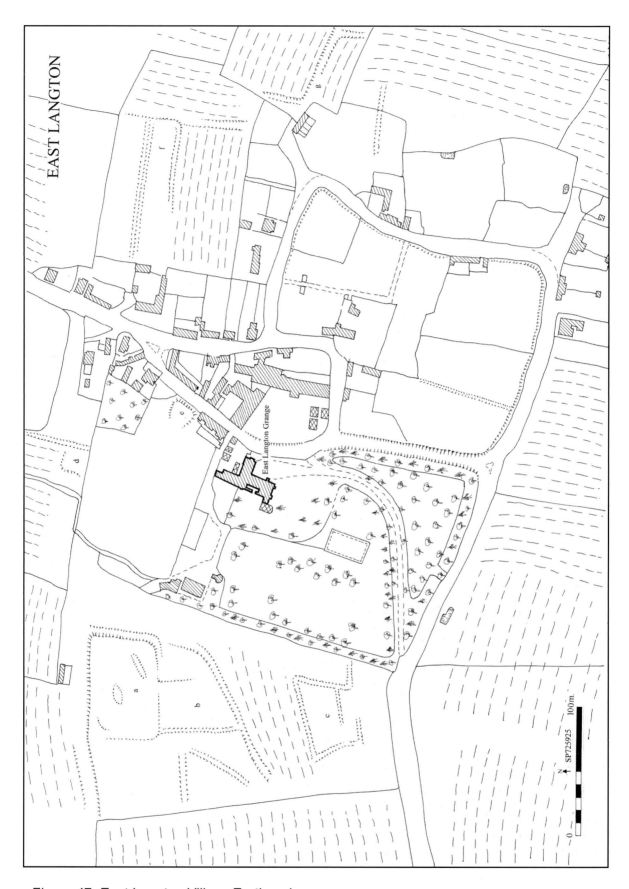

Figure 47: East Langton Village Earthworks

Windmill, Kibworth Harcourt   **SP688944**

This is the only surviving post mill in Leicestershire, dated "1711" on the main post, with the name of the miller, Daniell Hutchinson. It was conveyed by Merton College to a Trust in 1936.

LANGTON, EAST LANGTON

Open Fields
East Langton parish includes the village of Church Langton with its impressive parish church. The exact relationship between these two villages (and West Langton) as regards their open fields is unclear. Church Langton is recorded as having three open fields in 1638, Mill Field, West Field and North Field (Beresford 1949, 108).

Village Earthworks (fig 47)   SP725925
To the west of the village of East Langton is a field with at least three areas of village earthworks (a, b, c). Unfortunately the creation of gardens around East Langton Grange in the 19th century has obscured the relationship between these features and the remainder of the village. North of the Grange are two building platforms (d, e) of unknown date. There are boundaries of an old close in the north-east corner of the village (f), and a length of hollow way (g) further south. Several of the village streets lie in hollow ways. The village and East Langton Grange were extensively rebuilt in the late 19th century by the prominent railway contractor J. W. Logan, and several of the cottages are named after his daughters.

LANGTON, THORPE LANGTON

Open Fields
The open fields of Thorpe Langton were enclosed in 1792 (VCH, 204).

.
Village Earthworks (fig 48 overleaf)   SP740924
Many Leicestershire villages show signs of having been carefully planned at some remote period, but none more so than Thorpe Langton, which when the earthwork evidence is studied can be shown to be a very regular rectangle with the church at its centre. In this case, such is the precision of the original surveyed layout that if lines are drawn between the two corners of the village they cross at the chancel arch of St. Leonard's Church. To allow this to happen the footprint of the village cuts across the line of the road (a) from Kibworth to Welham and Medbourne. Three lanes (b, c, d) extend at right angles from the main road, all set in hollow ways and extending to the southern boundary of the village. Earthworks at the west end of the village include two building platforms (e, f). North of the church are further building platforms (g, h, i, j). There is another large platform west of the church (k), and a an old enclosure boundary (l) to the south. East of the lane (c) is another building platform (m), surrounded with a well-defined enclosure, with another one to the south. The boundary of the village is beautifully defined by the surrounding areas of well-preserved ridge and furrow. (Plan from aerial photos and site visit 4th August 2014.)

Watermill
A watermill is mentioned in 1278, perhaps on the stream which divides Thorpe Langton from Langton Caudle (VCH, 207).

LANGTON, TUR LANGTON

Manorial Site (fig 49 overleaf)   SP708944
This area of earthworks on a south-facing slope near the centre of the village was surveyed early in 1981. Some 200m east of the Manor House is a prominent building platform (a), probably the site of a former manor house, partly surrounded by a dry moat (b). On the east side are foundations of a small building (c), perhaps a gatehouse guarding approach from the lane (d). To the east and south of the moat are old enclosures, including remains of a pond (e), which may once have extended to link up with a drainage channel (f).
Further east, nearer to the present Manor House, is a rectangular enclosure (g) surrounded by banks and narrow hollow ways. At the edges of (g) are the remains of two small buildings (h, i), and just outside the north-west corner of (g) is the rectangular platform (j) for a larger

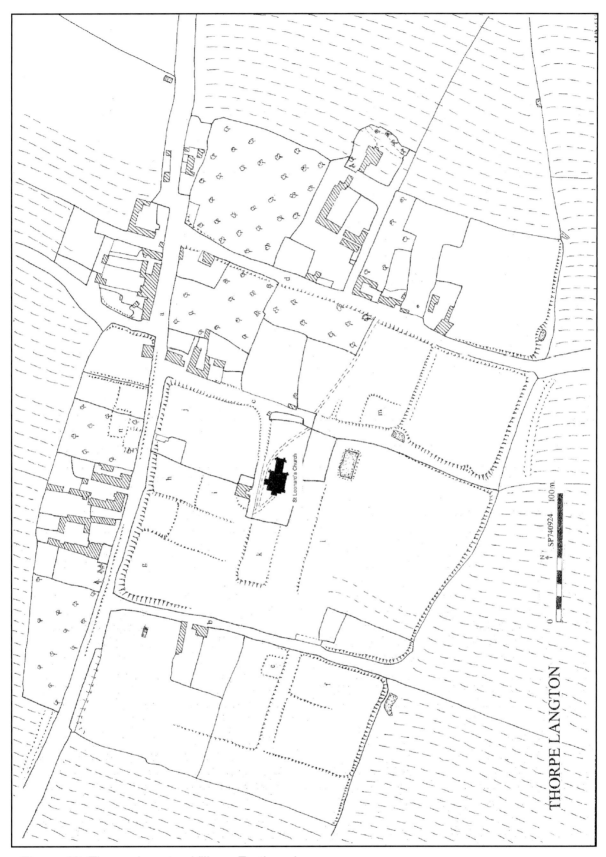

Figure 48: Thorpe Langton Village Earthworks

building. South and west of the Manor House is a terrace (k), a former garden, and on its west side is a drained fishpond (l), which may be the remains of a former moat (see below) with a drainage ditch (m) leading from it down to the stream.

North of the present Manor House is the village's original chapel of St. Nicholas. There was a priest here in 1165, and the chapel was served by Church Langton from 1220 onwards.

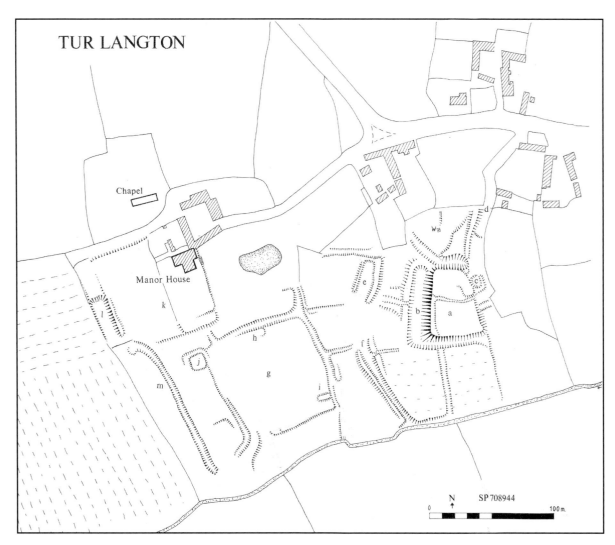

Figure 49: Tur Langton Manorial Site

It fell into disrepair in the early 19th century and was largely demolished in 1866 when the new chapel was opened (VCH, 212). Nichols notes *"near, and a little south of, the chapel is part of a mansion-house standing... It appears...to have been very large and spacious.....the inhabitants say it was wholly encompassed by a moat, of which now some (though trifling) traces remain"* (Nichols 1798, 673). He would seem here to be referring to the pond (I). The Victoria County History considers the present manor house to be the central block of a former "H" plan house, with the original main door on the east frontage (VCH, 209).

It seems probable that the whole area of earthworks here indicates the site of two manor houses and a series of garden features. The gardens may well have developed through from the Medieval period into the 17th century, and it seems likely that the original medieval gardens at the east side of the site were replaced in the 16th century by the more open and formal arrangements further west.

LANGTON, WEST LANGTON

Open Fields
West Langton was enclosed in 1744, prior to which there were three fields, Wheat Field, Bean Field and Fallow Field (VCH, 198).

Village Earthworks and Langton Hall (fig 50 overleaf)   **SP717929**
At West Langton it is possible to see how the creation of a post-Medieval mansion and gardens has led to the removal of an earlier village, but also how clues to this process can survive in the parkland.

85

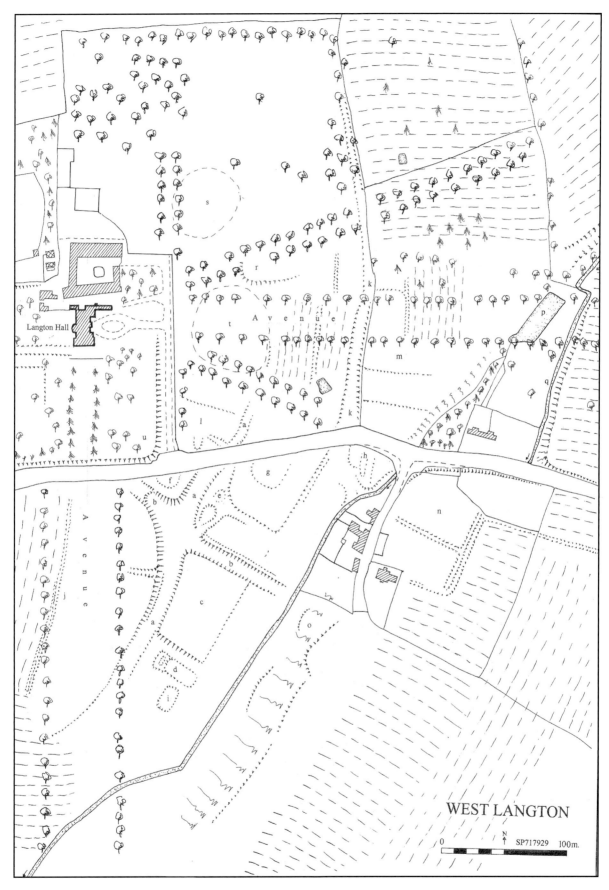

Figure 50: West Langton

The village of West Langton contained five ploughlands in 1086; there were eight acres of meadow and two acres of wood. This little village only makes a brief appearance in Nichols's history, and he notes that Thomas Staveley "*...in 1613 built a handsome stone mansion here*"

(Nichols 1798, 664). This was Langton Hall, and the Hall and its gardens have almost entirely supplanted the village. Close examination of aerial photographs, and a walk along the road (23rd August 2014) revealed a hollow way (a-a-a) extending parallel to the stream, with a branch (b-b) cutting across it from east to west. Between the hollow way (a) and the stream is an old enclosure (c), with foundations of one or two buildings to the south at (d). Further north are more building platforms (e, f, g, h), while to the south of (d) is a rectangular hollow (i), perhaps once a pond.

The western boundary of the village is marked by a bank and ditch (j), partly erased by landscaping for the grand avenue of trees leading south from the Hall. The area is bisected by the Kibworth to Welham road, and to the north of it a hollow way (a) continues for a short distance, with another hollow way (k) to the east extending further north. Returning towards the Hall, there are more slight village earthworks west of the hollow way (a) at (l).

East of hollow way (k) is an old enclosure and terraces near (m), probably also part of the village, and two more old closes across the stream, south of the road (n). There are slight terraces further down the stream (o) which might mark the site of vanished cottages but equally could be natural features cut by the stream, as it has subsequently been straightened in this area. Further upstream is an ornamental pond (p), probably dug in the late 17th or early 18th century to enhance the view along the western avenue from the Hall. The stream course was diverted some distance to the east in an artificial channel (q) cut into the hillside.

Returning towards the Hall, it is clear that considerable landscaping has been done, removing traces of the village and its ridge and furrow. In the avenue leading north-east there is a low platform (r) possibly indicating part of the old village. There are also two areas of disturbed ground (s, t) probably of fairly recent origin. South of the Hall the gardens are on a large rectangular raised terrace (u) which must have buried any traces of the former village in this area.

Windmill Mound   SP722929
Just west of the road junction, south of Church Langton village, is a mill mound approximately 20m in diameter and 2m high.

LAUGHTON

Laughton is a small village, whose size and location seem to have remained remarkably static over the centuries.

Open Fields
Laughton had three open fields in 1601, Coom Field, Nether Field and Mill Field. The parish was enclosed by general agreement in 1663 (VCH, 216).

Watermill
There was a watermill on the Saddington Brook in 1663 (VCH, 217).

Windmill Mound   SP659888
This mill mound is mentioned in the Victoria County History (VCH, 216). There was a windmill in the parish in 1265.

LUBENHAM

Open Fields
Lubenham still had three open fields in 1694, West Field (or Old Mill Field), East Field (or New Mill Field) and Middle Field. Enclosure took place firstly in 1600-1 by agreement and secondly by Act of Parliament in 1766 (VCH, 224).

Village and Thorpe Lubenham Hall (fig 51 and illustration on map page 126)   SP704868
South and east of Lubenham Church there is slight evidence of former enclosures, most obviously (a) near the village school. The River Welland, which marks the county boundary,

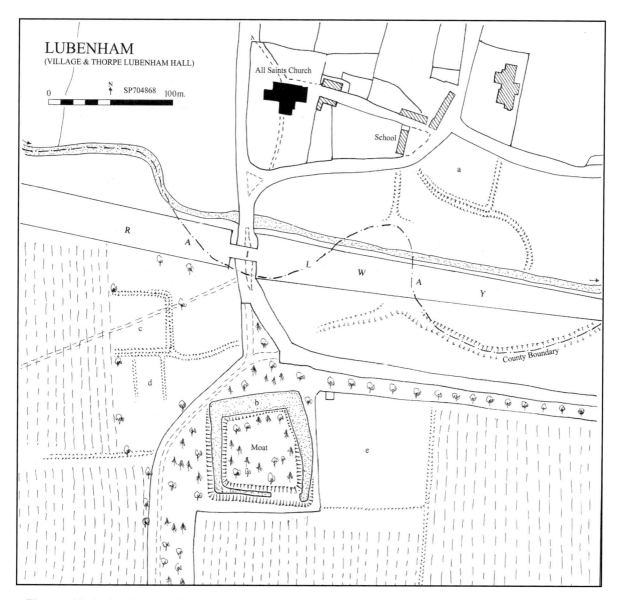

Figure 19: Lubenham, Village and Thorpe Lubenham Hall

used to flow around a series of broad meanders here, but the Rugby to Stamford Railway line, opened in 1850, diverted the river to a straight new course on the north side of the railway embankment. South of the river was the hamlet of Thorpe Lubenham, in Northamptonshire, with a water-filled moat (b), surrounding a rectangular platform. A timber-framed farmhouse was here in 1795 and a view of it was published by Nichols (Nichols 1798, opp page 701), see Page 126 beneath Landscape Map 11. It appears to have been the surviving south-west corner of a 15th/16th century moated manor house with a central courtyard. Enclosures, whether paddocks or gardens, flanked it on the west (c, d) and the east (e). The 1885 Ordnance Survey map shows the moat, but by then the buildings had been entirely cleared away. (Site visit August 4th 2014.)

Old Hall Earthworks (fig 52)   *SP708870*

At the east end of Lubenham village is a field with well preserved ridge and furrow and other earthworks. Just south of the Lutterworth to Market Harborough main road (a former turnpike road) are some old enclosures (a), probably once part of the village. Nichols says that there was formerly a ditch extending further east, but it was filled in to form the course of the turnpike road (Nichols 1798, 700-701). There is a raised bank or old headland (b) extending along the north side of the field. To the south the field has well-preserved ridge and furrow, at some date divided up by a bank and ditch (c), and a parallel ditch further west. The south side of the field extends alongside the River Welland, and there is a subtantial bank (d), probably a terraced walkway. The river now flows in an artificially straight course (e) on the south side of this bank. To the west is the site of the manor house on a platform (f) over 100m square, surrounded by

88

a moat. Nichols in 1798 noted that the south ditch was "very deep within these last fifty years" (p701). The line of the outer bank has been dug away at (g) to drain the moat. Fortunately Nichols includes notes on the site and a sketch (below) of the old Manor House *"drawn some years ago from memory soon after it was taken down"* (Nichols 1798, 699). This appears to be quite an accurate drawing of a building originating in the Medieval period with a central hall, and a porch facing west, a service wing on the south side and an acommodation wing on the north. The building presumably evolved gradually from the 14th or 15th century to the early 17th. It was largely demolished in about 1774 apart from the south wing (VCH, 1964, 220). The 1885 map shows this service wing surviving (f), presumably because it was capable of being adapted for use as an ordinary farmhouse. This map also shows the site of a small fishpond (i) between the moat and the river.

The north and east arms of the moat are still well-preserved today, with traces of a terraced walkway (h) giving views out across the north side of the moat. Farm buildings and a modern house and gardens now occupy the area of the moated platform. The west arm of the moat was largely filled in before the end of the 18th century, and the south arm of the moat has been filled in since 1885.

The terrace walkways would have formed part of the gardens of the manor house, probably extending east to be bounded by the bank and ditch (c). These gardens must have been in existence in the 16th/17th century period, when the manor house was at its peak of importance. (Sketch plot from aerial photos and site visit, August 4th 2014)

Lubenham Manor House (Nichols 1798, op page 701)

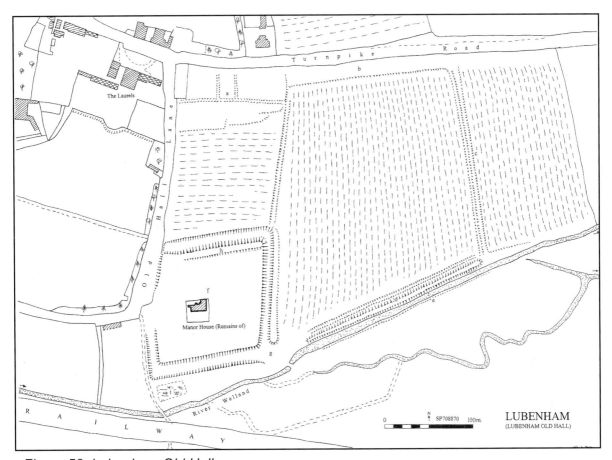

Figure 52: Lubenham Old Hall

MARKET HARBOROUGH

Market Harborough is a classic planned medieval market settlement, created in the late 12th century on a spot which had previously been part of the open fields of Great Bowden. Until the 1890s the parish was tiny, just enclosing the built-up area, and despite its impressive appearance, the church of St. Dionysius was a chapel to the mother church of St. Mary in Arden in Great Bowden.

"Kings Head Close" (figs 53 & 54)   **SP 734875**

Nichols published a plan (figure 53; Nichols 1798, op page 478) of this embanked rectangular enclosure which formerly existed behind Kings Head Yard to the east of Church Street. It seems to have extended about 150m north-south and 70m east-west. The ancient parish boundary of the town used to follow the north and east sides of this enclosure, suggesting that it dated back at least to Medieval times. The area was developed in the 19th century and again in the 20th, and no evidence of the close seems to survive. Details from Nichols' plan are here drawn up (figure 54) on the basis of the 1885 OS map. The corners of the close were at a, b, c and d, with a substantial bank extending from a to b, and partly surviving between a and d. One building (indicated by the dashed line at 'e') existed inside the close, on the lane linking it to the King's Head Inn (f). Nichols states that at the time of his survey the ditch enclosing the site had gone, but enough of the banks remained to show the form of the enclosure. His text tells us, amongst other information, that the surviving "*rampart*" was "*at this time elevated no higher above the field than a low terras-walk..*" He also notes that in the north-west angle was a large walnut tree (Nichols 1798, 486). The King's Head Inn (f), half of which is still an inn (2014), is said by Nichols to have been "*an antient manor-house*", which seems very likely (*op cit*). These clues suggest that the close might possibly have been an enclosed garden for the manor house. The King's Head is certainly in an historic part of the town centre, opposite the ancient "Three Swans" Inn (g) and now next to the Town Hall and Court House of 1788 (h).

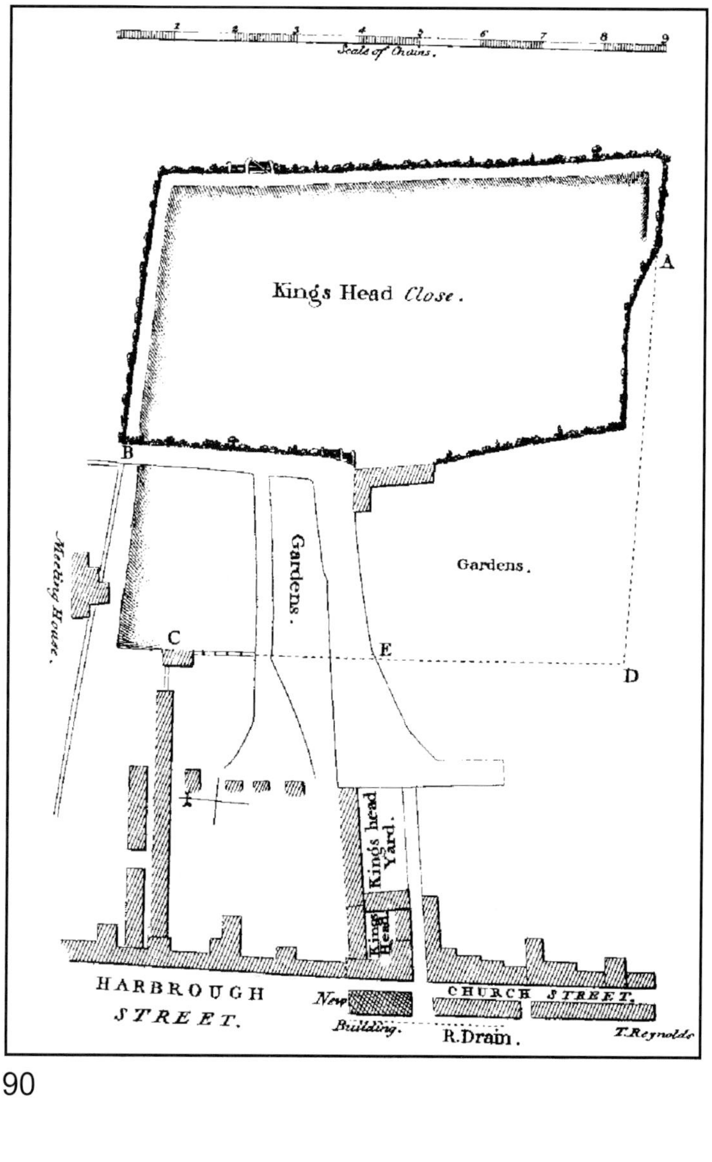

MEDBOURNE

Medbourne lies close to the site of a Roman small town, and inherited its role as a market centre, receiving the grant of a market and fair in 1266 (VCH, 233).

Open Fields

There were three open fields - Bridge Field, Dale Field and Marsdale Field (VCH, 235). The high ground on either side of the road to Nevill Holt appears to have been enclosed when Nevill Holt was imparked in the 15th century. This was the last Leicestershire open field system to be enclosed, with the Act being passed in 1842 (map in Leicester, Leicestershire and Rutland Record Office).

Figure 53: Kings Head, Market Harborough (Nichols 1798, 479)

KING'S HEAD CLOSE

(MARKET HARBOROUGH)

Figure 54: Market Harborough Kings Head Close

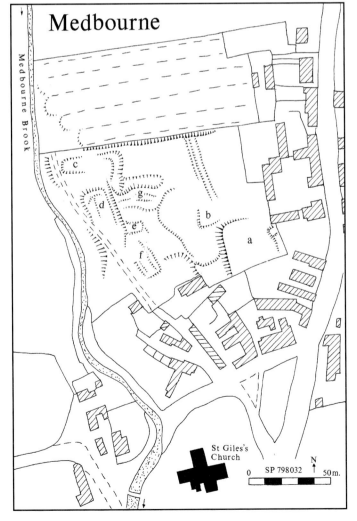

Village Earthworks (fig 55)
SP7980932

North of St. Giles's Church, in a field sloping down to Medbourne Brook, a small field shows earthwork evidence of part of the village which has been abandoned at some time in the past. As surveyed (25th September 1981) there was a levelled terrace (a) and at least half a dozen building platforms (b, c, d, e, f, g). The sites (d) and (e) have evidence for the foundations of stone walls.

Windmill, Medbourne

A windmill is mentioned in 1571. A smock mill was standing in the mid-18th century, and was demolished in 1902, the tump still being visible in 1960 by the Slawston Road (VCH, 235).

Figure 55: Medbourne Village Earthworks

91

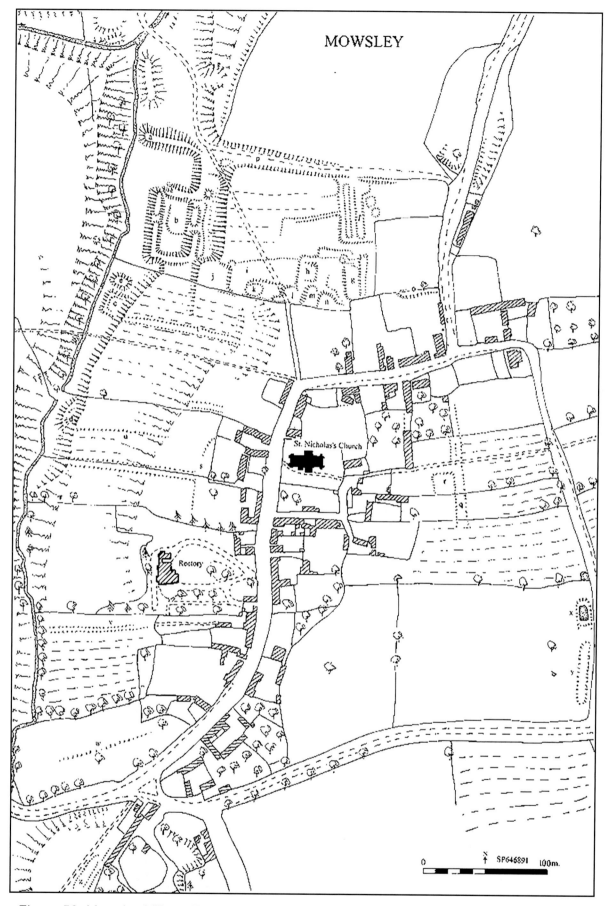

Figure 56: Mowsley Village Earthworks and Fishponds

MOWSLEY

Open Fields

Mowsley had three open fields in 1628, Millhill (or Mill) Field, Beesick Field and Swarborough Field. These were enclosed in 1788 (VCH, 253). The mother church was at the now deserted village of Knaptoft.

Village Earthworks and Fish Ponds (fig 56)   SP646891

The most conspicuous earthworks in Mowsley village are those of the fishponds north west of the parish church. A substantial dam (a) would have created a pool stretching some 300m south up the valley. Alongside this was a rectangular pond (b) partly cut into the hillside. Further upstream were smaller side ponds (c) and (d), also perched in the hill slope, and a small island (e) perhaps for water fowl. Returning to the side pond (b), just to the north-west of it are the foundations of a small circular building, perhaps a store house. (Surveyed 27 Jan 1982)

To the east is a raised terrace or platform (f) with two elongated hollows and two smaller hollows to the east. These may also have been ponds, but of a more ornamental kind, perhaps part of a garden. Just to the south is a complex of building foundations, with building platforms (g) and (h), shallow terraces (i) and (j), and more small building platforms or heaps of demolition rubble (k, l, m, n). There is another substantial bank (o). The whole area of these earthworks, including the ponds, would seem most likely to represent a 15th or 16th century garden. There should logically be a mansion house somewhere on the site but at present it is not possible to identify this. Being built with more valuable materials, when it was no longer used it may well have been dismantled more systematically than the smaller buildings, and the components taken away for use elsewhere.

The fishpond field is referred to as "Brabazon Close" in some accounts, implying that it was once owned by the Brabazon family who held land here. On the north side of the close is a substantial hollow way (p) with a lane leading out of the village towards Saddington. East of the parish church are traces of an old hollow way (q) and a building platform (r). West of the church are more faint earthworks (s) and a series of old enclosure boundaries leading down to the stream, including (t, u, v, w). Small areas of quarrying can be seen to the east (x, y).

At the south end of the village there is a possible building platform (z). This is likely to be of post-medieval origin, as 50 metres to the west is a deep gravel pit, probably dug in the 18th century. After it ceased production cottages were built in and around it, probably in the early 19th century. (Site visit, 4th Aug 2014)

Pinslade Grange Moated Site (fig 57 overleaf)   SP634871

This is an isolated moated site on a small spur of land in the angle between two streams. Unlike many moated sites, it is in an elevated position with extensive views towards the east. The moat (a) is mostly cut into the hilltop, but has a retaining bank where the land slopes down on the east side, and still retains some water in this area. The platform (b) is some 30m square. Outside the moat, on the north side, is a hollow (c), probably the remains of a small fishpond. The two steep-sided valleys (d) and (e) enclose the site on its western and southern sides, and below the point where they meet the ground has been dug out to create a fishpond (f). On the west side of the site a fairly straight section of bank, with an outer ditch, connects the two valleys to form the remaining boundary of the site. The moated site is believed have enclosed the main building of the Pinslade Grange farm of Leicester Abbey. The Abbey held lands here in the years before 1254.

The Northampton to Leicester road passes the site on its west side, and the moat is clearly visible. The road became a turnpike under an Act of 1765 and the growing use of the road by stage coaches probably explains why the moat was noticed as a feature of antiquarian interest at least as early as 1787. (Site plotted from aerial photographs and viewed from the road, August 4th 2014).

Windmill Mound, Mowsley

The VCH notes a mound in Mill Field, possibly the site of the windmill held by Robert de Mowsley before 1338 (p253).

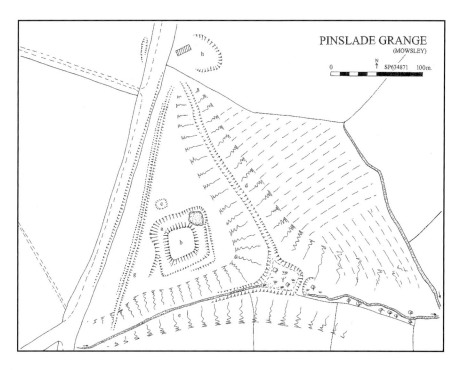

PINSLADE GRANGE
(MOWSLEY)

N SP634871 100m.

Figure 57: Mowsley, Pinslade Grange

NEVILL HOLT

The VCH states that *"the township of Holt was created in the 12th and 13th centuries from assarts made in the woods east of Medbourne"*. The parish was enclosed in the late 15th or early 16th century (VCH, 246).

Hall Gardens and Village Earthworks (fig 58)   *SP 816936*

Nevill Holt Hall is one of the most picturesque sights in Leicestershire, with the medieval great hall linked on the east to St. Mary's Church and on the west extending through a range of buildings of 16th to 19th century date. It occupies a superb site with extensive views to west, south and east over the Welland Valley. The survey was done on July 5th 1983, with an additional visit to confirm details on August 23rd 2014.

Hidden behind the hall are a few cottages of the original village, along the old main street (a-a) which can be seen continuing as a hollow way further south. Successive owners of the Hall wanted privacy, and diverted passing traffic along a tree-lined drive to the west. A straight cut-through (b) gives access to the village and service buildings. On its south side a high wall forms the northern boundary of the formal gardens, while to the north, in what became parkland, are earthworks of a vanished part of the village, with building foundations at (c) and (d) and platforms (e) and (f). South-east of the hall are more buildng platforms (g, h). Due south of the hall are the foundations of a substantial building (i), with a building platform to the south. These might be the remains of 15th or 16th century outbuildings, demolished before the mid-17th century, as they are not shown on a plan of that date. They lie alongside another abandoned hollow way (j) which would once have given access to the hall and village. Between the two hollow ways (a) and (j) is a rectangular area (k). This may be the southern part of the old village, mostly levelled off by later landscaping of the grounds.

There was certainly a formal garden north-west of the hall, as it is marked on the mid-17th century (redrawn here) plan and several features survive. The orchard (l) was flanked on the east by a low raised walkway (m) and on the north by a higher terrace walkway (o), called "The Stand" in the 17th century. It still provides extensive views over the gardens to the south and out into the parkland to the north. To the east the walled kitchen garden and yards still exist. Returning to the former orchard, the 17th century plan shows another terrace walkway, *"The Mount"* which would have been at (n) but has been entirely removed, probably in the late 18th or early 19th century. Part of the spoil may have been used to create a prospect mound in line with the great avenue leading westwards towards Medbourne. Going back north to the park, the fish pond (q) seems likely to be a post-medieval amenity in the parkland, as do two other small ponds which survive as earthworks at (r) and (s), surrounded by small enclosures.

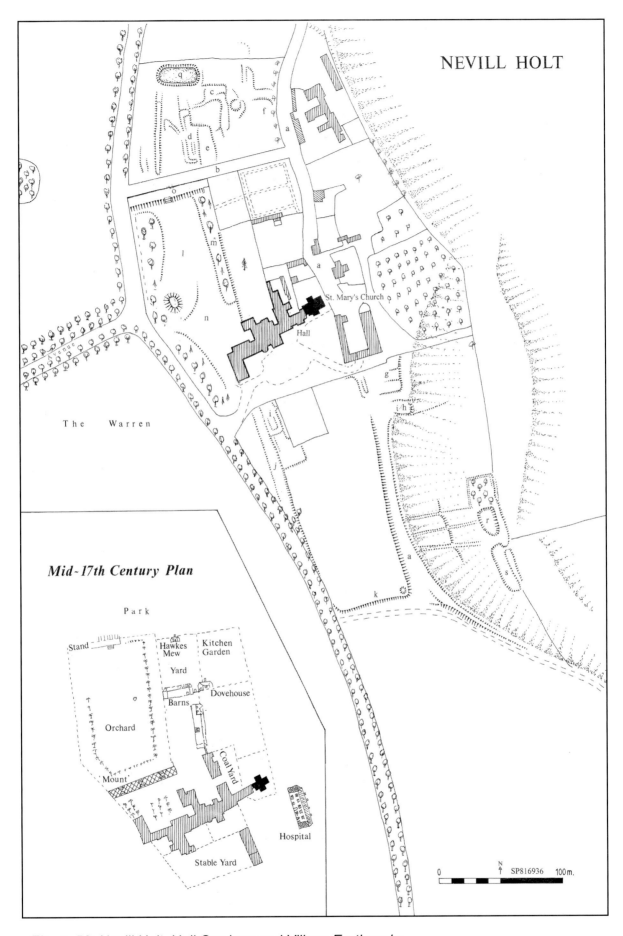

NEVILL HOLT

q

c

f

a

d

e

b

o

m

l

n

St. Mary's Church

a

Hall

g

h

i

j

The Warren

Avenue

r

a

s

k

Mid-17th Century Plan

Park

Stand

Hawkes Mew

Kitchen Garden

Yard

Dovehouse

Barns

Orchard

Coal Yard

Mount

Hospital

Stable Yard

0   SP816936   100 m.

Figure 58: Nevill Holt, Hall Gardens and Village Earthworks

Park   *SP8293*

Field names in this area include First and Second Great Park, and Little Park. In 1448 Thomas Palmer was licenced to impark 300 acres (Cantor 1970-1, 23). The area had been disparked by 1641.

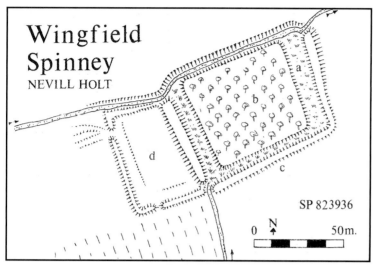

Figure 59: Nevill Holt, Wingfield Spinney Earthwork

Wingfield Spinney Earthwork (fig 59)   *SP823936*

This small earthwork comprises a moat (a), enclosing a level platform (b), approximately 50m square. It is sited at the junction of two streams, which now flow through the moat. To the west is an area (d) enclosed by a bank, which continues (c) to enclose two side of the moat. Much of the site was heavily overgrown when visited (18th May 1984) and its origin and purpose remain unknown.

Prestgrave Deserted Village (fig 60)   *SP828932*

Nichols notes the former existence of Prestgrave *"..a depopulated hamlet, situated in the South-East extremity of Holt lordship, adjoining on the angle of both Easton and Drayton-field, was originally a part of the Soke of Easton, and possibly may have been the site of a grange belonging to the abbey of Peterborough". "There still remain evident traces of streets or lanes, and foundations of houses, many of which were discovered by the plough when the close was in tillage." (Nichols 1798, 523)*

The site was relocated in the early 1980s through fieldwork and documentary study by Miss Edna Linford. It lies 1.5km east of Nevill Holt, in a valley bottom, alongside a stream which has been diverted in recent times. The field survey published here was done on the 18th of May 1984. On the south side of the stream was a hollow way (a), and evidence of the village lies on either side of the point where this track would have crossed the stream. In pasture on the west side of the old stream course were at least five house platforms (b, c ,d, e, f), and across on the east side were three larger platforms (g, h, i). The field to the south has been levelled by ploughing, but a scatter of medieval pottery sherds has been identified around (j).

Further north there is another possible hollow way (k), and to the north-west a bank (l) and an "L" shaped excavation. This feature also seems to have been noted by Nichols, who remarks that *"...the East and North sides of the foss or moat still continue visible".* Nichols continues *"..There are nearly 200 acres of this depopulated village in what is called at this time Holt Lordship, very rich land, the present owner Cosmas Nevill esq. And it is supposed that nearly the same quantity of land, antiently belonging to Prestgrave, has been added to Easton and Drayton fields..."* (op cit).

Bradley Priory (figs 61 & 62)   *SP823953*

Bradley Priory was a small Augustinian house established in the early 13th century (certainly before 1234) in the pastures and woods at the northern extremity of Nevill Holt parish. The founder was Robert Burnaby (Liddle & O'Brien 1995, 14). Hardly any trace is now visible, but the Ordnance Survey plan and a site visit (5th November 1981) have recorded some details (figure 62). The site lies alongside a small stream (a-a) and was presumably accessed via the lane to the present Priory Farm, extending as the hollow way (b) with a fragment of a ridge and furrow field to the north. On the south side of the hollow way part of an old enclosure (c) survived, with perhaps another to the west. Across the stream was an area enclosed by a ditch and bank (d-d). This was probably part of the Priory's precinct boundary. It may originally have been a

PRESTGRAVE
(NEVILL HOLT)

Old Course of Stream

Hollow Way

(Now in Culvert)

0   N   SP 828932   100 m.

Medieval pottery scatter

Figure 60: Nevill Holt, Prestgrave

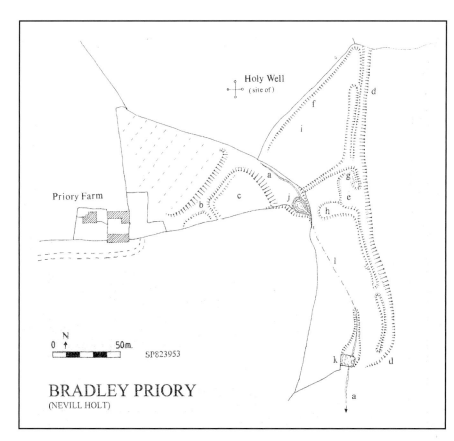

Figure 61: Bradley Priory, Nevill Holt

water-filled ditch, and it is widened out to form a pond at (e). To the north a bank (f) is probably another length of the precinct boundary, but not so well-preserved. Between the ditch (d) and pond (e) were the foundations of a small building (g), perhaps a store house. To the west was a platform (h) on which another building presumably once stood. Further north at (i) the Ordnance Survey recorded "*possible building-steads, uneven ground, nettles etc*".

In the valley bottom was a small pond (j), with another downstream at (k). Between these features the stream ran in a culvert (l), probably originally constructed for the Priory to take the water under their buildings so it could be used for sanitary purposes. This might suggest that the conventual buildings were in this area, and the Ordnance Survey record a ploughed area with "*building debris*" about 50m west of (l). They also noted the site of a Holy Well to the north of the Priory site.

The illustration below is a view of Priory Farm, drawn by John Tailby and published by John Nichols (1798, opp page 509). The building was demolished *c.*1820.

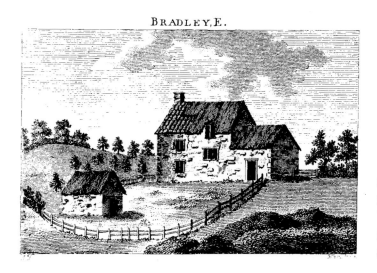

Bradley Priory Farm by John Tailby from Nichols, 1798, opp p. 509

SADDINGTON

Open Fields
Saddington had three open fields in 1601: Linborough or Limborough Field, Breach or Mill Field and Pesell or Peasehill Field. They were enclosed in 1770 (VCH, 284).

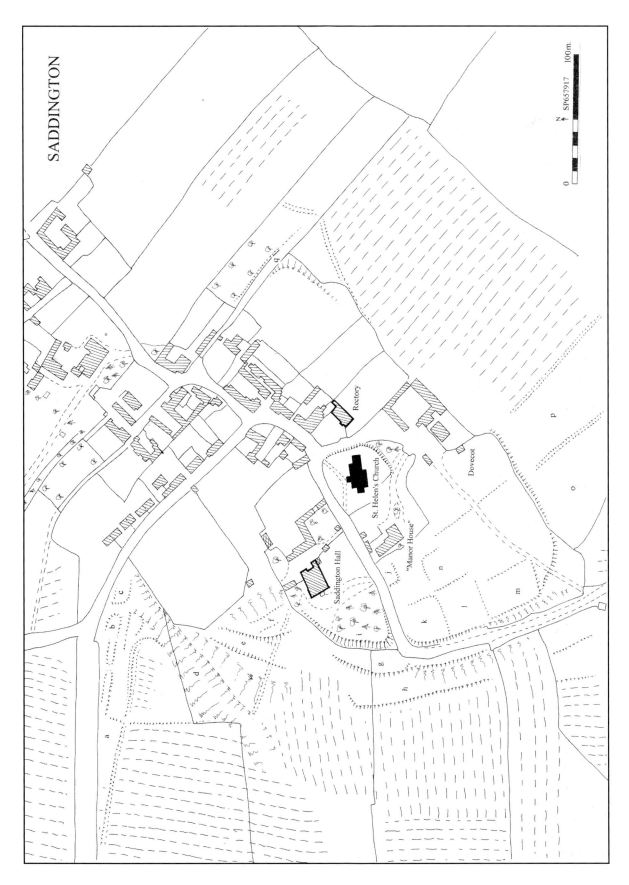

Figure 62: Saddington Village Earthworks

Village Earthworks (fig 62)
SP 657917

Study of aerial photographs, followed by a field visit on 15th August 2014, revealed a fair amount of earthwork evidence. The village is still surrounded on its west side by well-preserved ridge and furrow. North of the village a large plough-headland (a) ends in two mounds (b, c) of unknown purpose. Between these features and the village is a small, steep-sided valley (d) and a possible hollow way (e). The path along this hollow way continues along a slight terrace (g) to join the present road. Below it to the west is another large plough-headland (h).

There are slight earthworks of a possible building platform (f) north of Saddington Hall, and the west end of the hall gardens is on a terrace (i) which may have been the site of earlier buildings. Across the road, next to Manor House, is a building platform (j), with three more (k, l, m) extending southwards along the lane and possibly another (n) behind them. This field is sub-rectangular, with a dovecot on the east side, and presumably represents the manorial site which would probably have included outbuildings, gardens and an orchard. To the south across the stream are two old enclosures (o, p).

The graveyard of St. Helen's Church is raised some 4m above the surrounding ground to the south, where a hollow way descends to the farmyard. The Rectory lay just to the east and further east still is another hollow way (q) with a lane leading south-east out of the village.

SHANGTON

Open Fields

The parish was enclosed by 1679. Prior to this in 1625 the names of two open fields, Beck Field and Middle Field, are recorded (VCH, 295).

Village Earthworks (fig 63)   SP714961

Shangton village is "L" shaped in plan. The north end extends along a west-east lane. At its west end there is evidence that an area has been abandoned to pasture, leaving building platforms (a, b, c, d) alongside the lane, and old enclosures (e) behind them to the north. South of the lane is an old enclosure (f) and foundations of a small building (g). To the east of these is an area of ridge and furrow, which was divided up into a series of closes (h) at some point and later converted back into one large field.

A lane branches off the first one, leading south past the Hall. A 17th century map in the Northamptonshire Record Office shows this as a considerable building which has since gradually reduced in importance. There is evidence of former extensive gardens, including a large terrace (i) south of the Hall and a possible avenue (j) down to the stream. The map also shows the pond, further north, with its waters extending much further up the valley than they do now. Across the road from the Hall is the Rectory, with a garden terrace on its south side, probably of 19th century date.

South of the parish church is a more puzzling area of earthworks. There is a hollow way (k) showing the old course of the lane south out of the village towards Market Harborough. The modern road runs on a diverted, probably 19th century, course a little to the east. West of the hollow way (k) is an area of earthwork remains, including building platforms (l, m, n, o and possibly others). Further west, in a field now levelled by ploughing, the area of earthworks used to extend into (p) and there are at least two old enclosures (q) further west.

Possibly after the buildings in this area had been demolished, a dam (r-r) was built across the stream, perhaps a partner to the one north of the Hall. It would have created a narrow lake extending to the west up the stream valley. (Site surveyed 22nd October 1981 - south of the church, and 1st December 1999 - remainder of village).

Shangton Grange (fig 64 overleaf)   SP722973

Just over 1Km north-east of Shangton is a place sometimes in the past known as Hardwick and now called Shangton Grange Farm, with the farmhouse at (a) on the plan. This was a grange farm of Leicester Abbey, and the moat (b) which would have defended the Abbey's farm buildings still exists on three sides of the present farmyard. The platform (c) would have measured some 80m by 60m. In 1885, and on a 17th century map, the moated platform is shown at least partly in use as an orchard. A levelled platform to the east (d) may have been made with spoil from the moat and used as a level platform for outbuildings. It appears to overlie earlier features which probably constitute the remains of the village of Hardwick. Within a rectangular plot there are several enclosure boundaries and the foundations of at least two stone buildings (e, f) and probably a third (g). It is not at present possible to say whether these

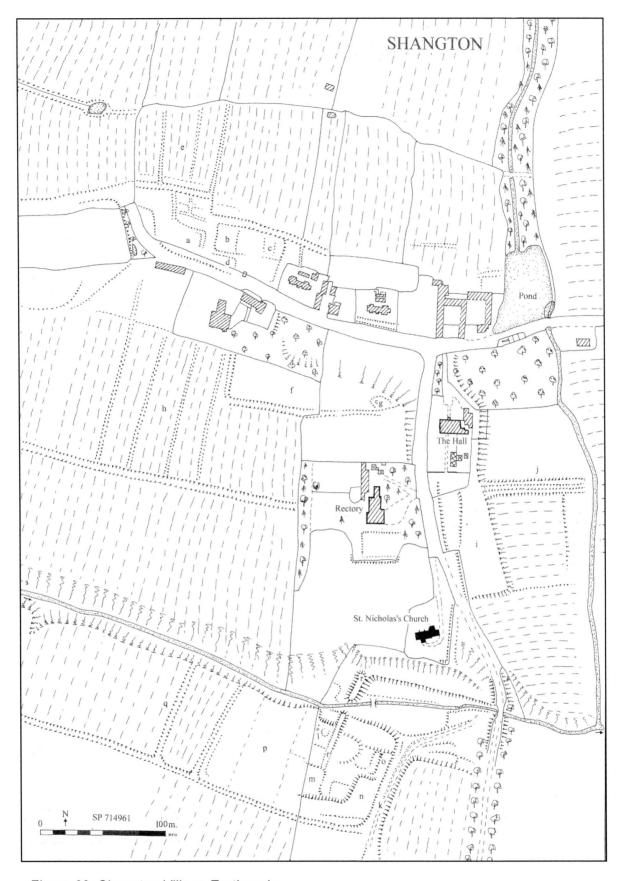

Figure 63: Shangton Village Earthworks

buildings went out of use when the grange farm was built, or continued in use as dwellings or storehouses alongside the monastic farm. To the south is a pond (h), possibly a fish pond associated with the grange farm, although it could be a flooded gravel pit. There is another post-medieval quarry east of the village at (i), probably a gravel pit. (Survey 6th October 1981)

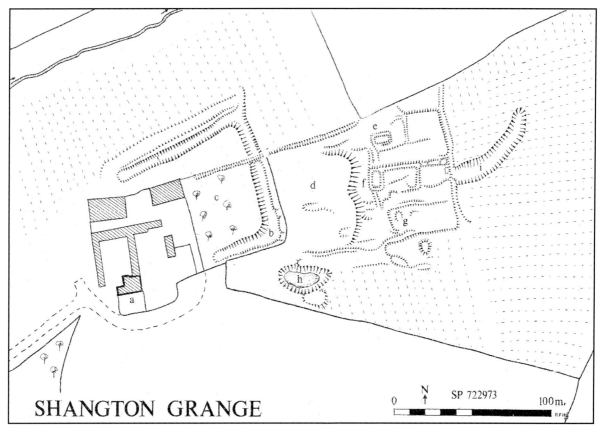

Figure 64: Shangton Grange

Victoria County History notes that Hardwick Manor was apparently given over to pasture at an early date and probably all enclosed by 1464 (VCH, 295).

Earthwork on Gartree Road (fig 65)   SP724967
Alongside the Gartree Roman Road in Shangton parish are slight remains of a site which has long intrigued antiquarians. The road descends into a hollow to cross a small watercourse (a-a). On the south side of the road are remains of what seems originally to have been a rectangular enclosure with a western ditch (b) a southern bank (c), and an estimated line of the east side in the field across the stream (d), as noted by the Ordnance Survey. They also recorded a quarry pit (g) and another one north of the road at (h). R. A. Rutland, the then Keeper of Antiquities at Leicester Museums, visited in 1973 when the site was threatened with disturbance and recorded an additional bank parallel to the Gartree Road with corners at (e) and (f) indicating former west and south sides. The present author visited in 2000, finding the site considerably overgrown, but with two ponds, one in the quarry pit (g) and another in a nearby hollow at (i). There also appeared to be a low platform at (j). The origin of the site remains obscure and only likely to be ascertained by excavation.

The Gartree Bush   SP716972
The meeting place for the Hundred Court of Gartree was in Shangton parish, at a place called the Gartree Bush. Nichols published an interesting description and plan of the site (provided by John Tailby) with its history as far as it could then be determined (Nichols 1798, 791-792, plan opp p.865), see plan within John Tailby dedication, page 60, Part 2 this volume. At that time the site was marked by *"four venerable wide-spreading decayed elm-trees"* and the stump of another, alongside the line of the Roman road from Leicester to Medbourne. Elderly local inhabitants reported to Mr Tailby that there had formerly been *"a white thorn-bush, (long since decayed), under or round which the court business was transacted"*. Tailby reported *"the impanneling of the jury, paying the chief rents, &c, used to be performed on this spot, and they afterwards adjourned to Tur-Langton to dine."* (*op cit*). "The Court Bush" is marked on a map of 1637 by James Spencer (Northamptonshire Record Office, map 580).

102

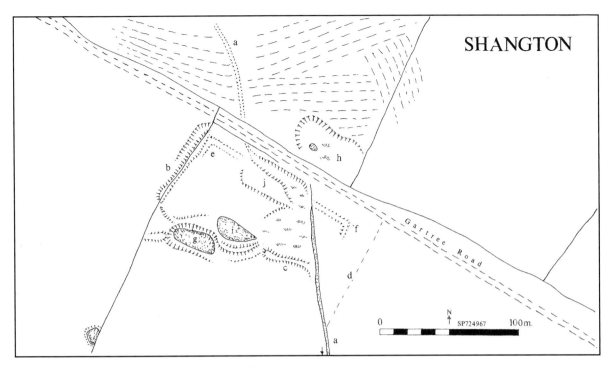

Figure 65: Shangton, Earthwork on Gartree Road

Fishponds   SP714971, SP716964

The sites of two fish ponds were noted by J. R. Branson in 1976 (Leicestershire Heritage and Environment Record). The first is in "*Conduit Spinney*", suggesting that this pond was supplying water via a conduit to Shangton Hall. The second pond is also likely to have formed part of the post-medieval amenities of the Hall.

Windmill Mound   SP718962

J. R. Branson noted remains of a mill mound in 1976. There was a windmill in Shangton in the 13th century (VCH, 295).

SLAWSTON
Open Fields

Three open fields are known to have existed in Slawston. In medieval times they were simply known as East Field, Middle Field and West Field. By 1476 one had become Berehylfield (VCH, 299), and by the time of the Brudenell estate survey in the 1630s they were called Hollywell, Middle and Burroughill Fields (VCH, 300). They were formally enclosed in 1793.

Village Earthworks (fig 66 overleaf)   SP780944

There is some evidence of shrinkage of the village at its east end, with evidence of three old enclosures, (a) north of All Saints Church, three more further west (b), and another with a possible building platform (c). On the northern edge of the village is a hollow way (d), with a branch into the fields. Further west are more old closes, bounded by a ditch (e) and bank (f). Nearby is a section of back lane, and a hollow way (g) shows where it used to continue westwards. Another old enclosure existed to the north, its former northern boundary indicated by a ditch (h).

South of the church were two more old enclosures (i, j). A raised track (k) crosses this area. It was presumably built to improve access to the church. (Site visit, 4th August 2014).

John Tailby, who provided a great deal of local archaeological information for Nichols's History of Leicestershire, was a resident of Slawston, although he was not complimentary about it "..*The town is long, narrow and, in general, dirty;*", but he admitted that the church "*as you approach towards it through the town, has a pretty appearance.*" (Nichols 1798, 797).

103

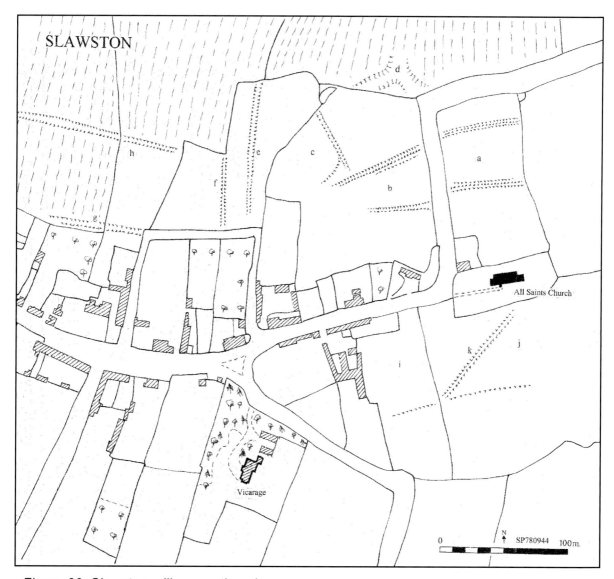

Figure 66: Slawston, village earthworks

Windmill Mound   *SP782942*

Windmill Mound   *SP 787933*

A mound about 9m in diameter and 1m high. A windmill is mentioned in 1637, and there was a derelict mill on top of Mill Hill until 1928 (VCH, 300).

Othorpe Village (fig 67 & fig 34)   *SP770955*

The present Othorpe House stands on the site of a small village in the northern part of Slawston. On the Brudenell estate map dating from the 1630s it is shown surrounded by its two open fields, Othorpe Great Field to the west, and Othorpe Little Field to the east. The authors of the Victoria County History considered that Othorpe was "*probably depopulated in the late 14th or in the 15th century*" but this seems to conflict with the evidence of the map. They note further that Othorpe "*became an important sheep pasture under the Brudenells*" (pp299, 300). The estate map shows a large close, Fallow Close, occupying most of the area north of the village and this was presumably the main area of sheep pasture. Most of the site east of Othorpe House has been levelled in recent times, but old aerial photographs allow us to reconstruct its appearance. The lane (a-a-a) leading north from Slawston to the former area of wood and pasture passes straight through the site, with a branch to the east (b). There were several old enclosures (c, d, e, f, g, h, i, j, k), and it seems likely that there were once buildings in (c, d, e, h, k). Area (d) is within another old enclosure extending northwards up the hill to join two more (l, m). Within (m) are a building platform (n) and an old pond (o).

104

OTHORPE
(Slawston)

SP 770955

0 ... N ... 100m.

Figure 67: Othorpe Village

SMEETON WESTERBY

Open Fields

There were two open fields in 1690, Riggs Field and Nether Field. The fields were enclosed in 1779 as part of the Kibworth Act of that date (VCH, 185).

Village Earthworks (Smeeton) (fig 68.1)   SP678927

From the crossroads at the centre of the village Blacksmith's Lane (a) extends as a hollow way (b). The field to the south contains several building platforms (c, d, e, f) and a hollow (g), perhaps an old pond. There is another building platform further south (h) next to Christ Church, which was built on this site in the 19th century.

Returning to the crossroads, a lane continues west in a hollow way (i). In a paddock to the north of this are four more building platforms (j, k, l, m), while to the south is a well-preserved furlong of ridge and furrow. The main north-south lane through the village continues a little further southwards as a hollow way (n).

Returning to Christ Church, there are old gravel pits (o) and (p) to either side of it. The quarry (p) was still in use in the late 19th century. (Site visit, 15th August 2014).

Village Earthworks (Westerby) (fig 68.2)   SP676926

This plan overlaps slightly the plan of Smeeton, and the point marked "X" is common to both plans. The hamlet of Westerby extends along a west-east street on a low hilltop with extensive views. There are remains of several old closes north of the street, at (q, r, s, t), and a small terrace (u) to the south, which may be part of a 19th century garden. Near the west end of the hamlet is an old quarry pit (v), and the topography of the east end of the village has been dramatically altered by a large and deep gravel quarry (w). This quarry (of which (o) and (p) to the north in Smeeton fig 68.1 are extensions) had gone out of use before the Ordnance Survey map was made in 1885 and has subsequently become a picturesque area of allotment gardens. The gravel pits were presumably in use in the late 18th and early 19th century period for road surfacing. (Site visit 15th August 2014).

Windmill

A windmill stood half a mile west of the village in 1885. It is said subsequently to have been blown down "*with the miller inside it*" (VCH, 185).

STOCKERSTON

Open Fields

Stockerston had three open fields, South Field, Bridge Field and Sweethedge Field. John Burton (see below) was enclosing land between 1580 and 1607, and the whole lordship was probably enclosed before 1674. We are told that it made rich grazing land (VCH, 306).

Garden, Hall and Village Earthworks (fig 69 overleaf)   SP836975

Extending west up the hillside behind Manor Farm is an area of massive building foundations and garden terraces, surveyed on the 11th November 1982. The main area of foundations is around (a) which presumably was the site of the mansion. To the west is a well-preserved levelled parterre (b), flanked on three sides by raised terrace walkways. To the south is a smaller terrace (c). To the east down the slope are more terraces (d, e), probably the site of another parterre, then terraces at (f), (g) and (h). This would have been a costly and magnificent garden of late 16th or 17th century date. To the east across the road are more earthwork remains, with a building platform (i), and another one (j) which is partly surrounded by an "L" shaped pond (k). A drainage chanel (l) probably once conveyed water away from the whole area of gardens, supplying en route a fishpond (m). This area was presumably also laid out as gardens, but it is not possible to say whether it was created at the same time as the main area of terraced gardens, or represents the site of an earlier manor house.

To the north, along a small stream valley, are remains of two more ponds (n) and (o) surrounded by raised banks, probably also part of the amenities of the mansion gardens and park. Just east of Manor Farm, across the lane, is a raised area (p) of sub-rectangular plan, probably the former site of at least two buildings. This seems likely to be remains of the village, an area which was cleared away when the inhabitants were rehoused further to the south. Perhaps created at the time of this southwards move of the village is an area of small fields (q), of which the boundary banks survive. The hedges had been cleared away and the area made into one large field again by the time of the 1885 map survey.

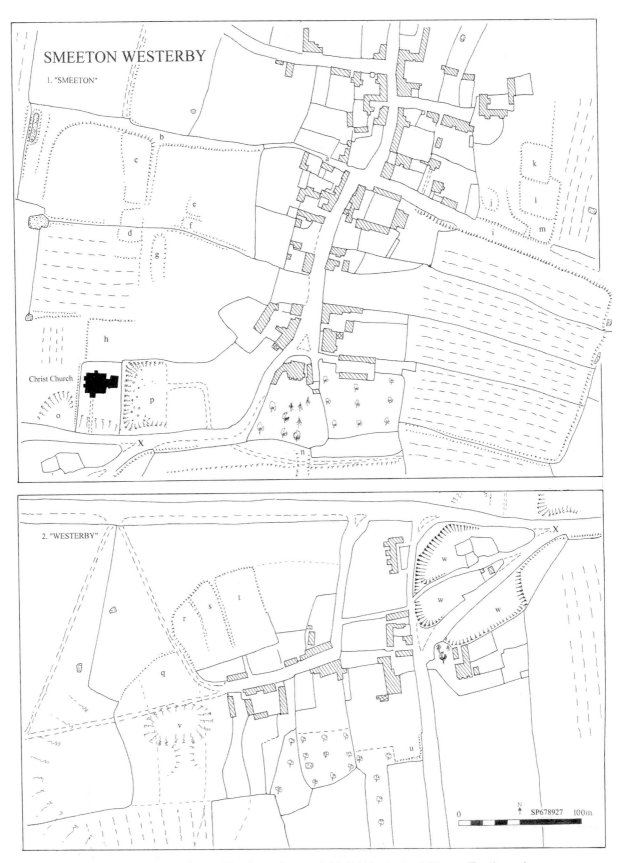

Figures: 68.1 Smeeton Village Earthworks and 68.2 Westerby Village Earthworks

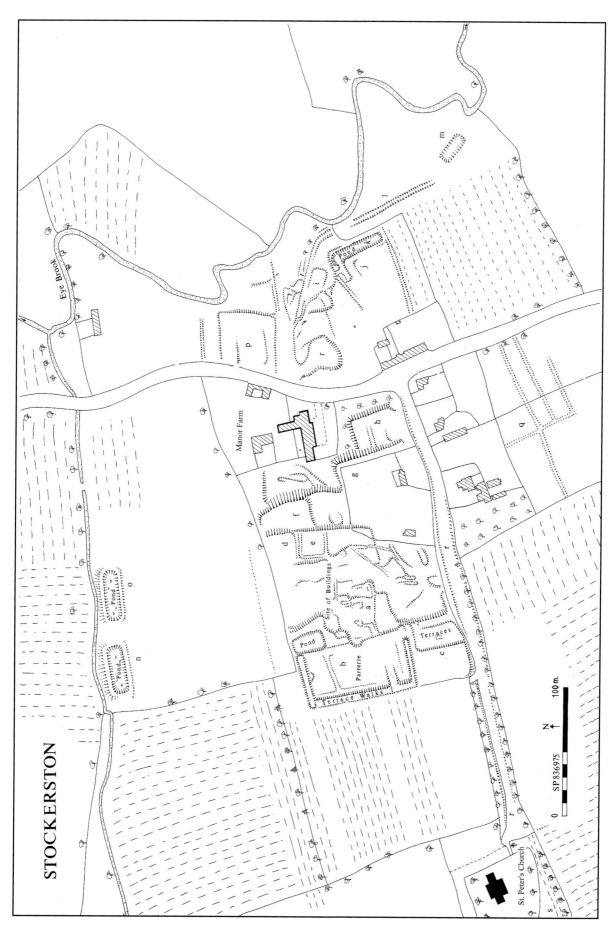

Figure 69: Stockerston, Garden, Hall and Village Earthworks

The family most likely to have built this house and gardens are the Burtons. In 1580 the manor of Stockerston was sold to John Burton of Braunston (Rutland) whose son Thomas was created a Baronet in 1622, and whose grandson Sir Thomas sold it to Sir Charles Duncombe in about 1685 (VCH, 304).

The mansion and gardens were probably abandoned before the end of the 17th century, and a new Stockerston Hall was later built just to the west of St. Peter's Church. This is described by the VCH as a building of c1800, standing on the site of an earlier building, with a window opening of 17th century date in the cellars (VCH, 303). The lane which gives access to the church and hall is clearly ancient and runs along a deep hollow way (r).

Watermill

A watermill at Stockerston is mentioned in 1086 but not after 1685 (VCH, 306). This probably lay on the Eye Brook east or south of the village.

Holyoaks Village (fig 70)   SP843957

In the southern extremity of Stockerston parish the farm called Holyoaks Lodge is thought to stand on the site of a vanished hamlet, but there does not appear to be any surviving earthwork evidence. In December 1496, Sir Robert Brudenell is said to have turned the area over to cattle pasture, destroying seven messuages, and evicting thirty people. *"They have departed thence and are either idle or have perished."* (Hoskins 1944-5, 254). This was about half of the township, and Brudenell continued purchasing and leasing more land until about 1507 (VCH, 306).

A survey of 1606 recorded *"Upper and Nether Holliocks"* with two closes of meadow and a small wood. In 1652 *"Upper Holliock"* had a two-storey tenement and *"Nether Holliock"* also had a house in it (VCH, 306). By 1796 there was just one house, the lodge building, and John Tailby drew it in that year to provide an illustration for Nichols' History (below, Nichols 1798, plate LXXXV, 509).

Watermill

A mill is mentioned at Holyoaks in 1086 and 1303, presumably a water mill. The site is probably now below the waters of the Eyebrook Reservoir.

HOLYOKE.E.   Vol.II.Part II.Pl.LXXXV.p.509

Holyoaks Manor House (Nichols 1798, 509)

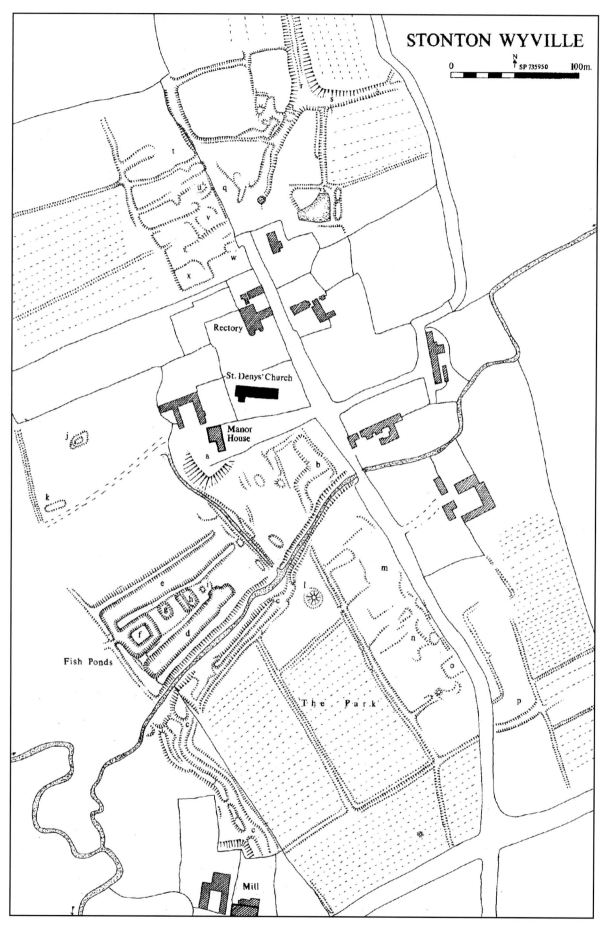

STONTON WYVILLE

0   SP 735950   100m.

Rectory

St. Denys' Church

Manor
House

Fish Ponds

The Park

Mill

Figure 70: Stonton Wyville, Village Earthworks, Manorial Site, Fishponds, Watermill, Park

STONTON WYVILLE

The Wyvilles were tenants of the manor from 1086 until at least 1494, after which it was first leased and then purchased by the Brudenells who started to build up an estate in the area. In the 17th-19th centuries it was sometimes called Stonton Brudenell.

Open Fields (Fig 34 p 62)
In 1601 there were three open fields, Mill Field, Brook Field and Hardwick Field. The 1635-7 Brudenell estate map shows Brook Field and Hill Field south of the village, and North Field just north of the village, and Little Field east of the village. The northern part of the parish was taken up by The Great Pasture and Stonton Wood. A few years earlier, in 1631, Lord Brudenell was offering the tenants inducements to agree to enclosure of the open fields, and the village seems to have been completely enclosed by the end of the 17th century (VCH, 310).

Village Earthworks, Manorial Site, Fishponds, Water Mill, Park (fig 70)   SP735950
Only a handful of houses near the church now remain at Stonton Wyville, but plentiful earthwork evidence remains to show how the village formerly extended both to the north and the south. It was partly replaced by the gardens and park of the Manor House, which have themselves been returned to pasture land in the post-Medieval period.

The Manor House is a building of medieval origin, standing on a substantial platform (a). Its position may suggest that it represents only one wing of a formerly larger house. The manor is recognised as the oldest of the Brudenell estates and the family is well represented by monuments in the church. To the south of the house are remains of a fishpond (b), together with other earthworks, presumably the site of a garden. There have clearly been substantial alterations to the watercourse to allow water to be diverted; on the south side of the existing stream is an embanked channel (c-c-c) which fed water to the water mill further south. To the west are the earthworks of a remarkable complex of fishponds, with the main ponds (d) and (e) flanking a raised platform.

At the west end of this feature is a small moat surrounding a rectangular platform (f), while further east are two small ponds or tanks (g, h) and the foundations of a small building (i). The moat may have formed a protected area for water fowl, and the small building may have been a storehouse for equipment such as nets or baskets. Fish caught in the larger ponds may have been put in the small tanks so as to be accessible when needed for the table.

North of the fishpond complex, in an area which was probably also part of the gardens, the stream seems to have been diverted into a channel with two right-angled bends to add to the supply for the ponds. There are also foundations of two small buildings (j) and (k).

South of the mill channel is a field named "*The Park*" on the estate map of 1637. There is a very low, conical mound (l), perhaps a tree mound or a prospect mound to give views over the park. Clearly this area had at an earlier date formed part of the village, with the sites of houses at (m, n, o) and probably elsewhere along the street frontage. Behind these to the west are the banks and ditches of several old enclosures (gone by the time of the 1637 map), and underlying the whole field is the Medieval ridge and furrow. There are probably sites of more houses and old enclosures around (p) on the east side of the street.

At the north end of the village the main street continues as a hollow way (q) into the field, and a branch leads off north-east to another junction with hollow ways (r) and (s) continuing north and east respectively.

West of this junction is another old enclosure and building platform, and there are two old enclosures and a pond south of hollow way (s). (Site was surveyed 1-5 October 1981).

Windmill Mound   SP745942
A low mound 16m in diameter on the top of Langton Caudle hill. A windmill is shown here on the map of 1635-7.

THEDDINGWORTH
Open Fields (Frontispiece Part 2 and fig 33 p 62)
A remarkably detailed (and very large) map of Theddingworth village and its open fields was surveyed and drawn in 1696 by Robert Hewett for the Hon. Richard Newdigate of Arbury in Warwickshire, the then owner, and is now preserved in the archives of the Warwickshire County Record Office (CR136/c1876), reproduced in colour opposite page 60 in this volume and the ridge and furrow on page 61. There were three open fields, Gausthill Field, Sleighs Field and Knallings Field. All three fields are referred to by other names as well during the 17th century (Beresford 1949, 113). The detail of the map is remarkable, with full details of the holders of the strips and closes.

The parish was enclosed by an agreement made in 1713 between the freeholders and the lord of the manor (who sold the property a year later)(VCH, 316). Figure 33 displays how much of the open field system survived as ridge and furrow in 1950 and also in 2014, showing that here, as elsewhere, there has been a considerable loss of evidence in recent years.

Village Earthworks (fig 71)   SP665856
The lane running north from the village takes a curving course towards the west on its way, but an earlier and more direct route can be seen in the form of a hollow way (a) running straight down the field. This is flanked by earthworks of old house sites and closes, with numerous building platforms including (b, c, d, e, f, g, h, i, j, k). Between these in several places the old property boundaries can be seen extending at right angles from the hollow way. To the east of (k) the site of another building can be seen (l), near a small hollow way which probably formed the start of path along the back of the properties. The present lane may have originated by people using (or being required to use) a similar path on the west side of this part of the village. (Plan based on aerial photos, survey work in the 1970s by T. Pearce, K. Gowland and others, and site visit 4th August 2014). The whole area of these earthworks had been turned over to pasture land by 1696, when the Newdigate estate map was made.

To the south of the area described above is another area of earthworks (surveyed 28th March 1988). A hollow way (m) seems to have provided access to the centre of this area, and around it are several old closes containing building platforms (n, o, p, q, r, s, t). To the east, north of All Saints Church, is another field with with some old enclosure boundaries.

The 1696 map shows houses in several locations where they no longer exist, including at (t) and (u) in the earthworks already described, and also along the main road frontage at (v, w), (x) and (y). Three more houses are shown along the road frontage at the west end of the plots containing sites (p, r, s), and a larger "L" shaped farmhouse or manor house at (z). a hundred metres north-west of this point, a circular feature (aa) appears on old aerial photographs. This no longer exists, but seems likely to have been the foundations of a circular stone dovecote of medieval type. It is not shown on the 1696 map.

Windmill Mound   SP666858

Watermill   SP6685
The VCH notes "indications of the medieval mill site on the river and remains of fishponds nearby". There is no obvious evidence now of earthwork features. There were two mills in 1086 (VCH, 313, 317)

Hothorpe (Northants)   SP668851
The hamlet of Hothorpe belonged with Theddingworth but lay over the Welland in Northamptonshire. It was largely depopulated by the mid-16th century, and the first Hothorpe Hall was built on the site c1600. John Cook of Hothorpe Hall demolished the last few cottages at Hothorpe in about 1830 and built new houses in Theddingworth for his tenants (VCH, 313).

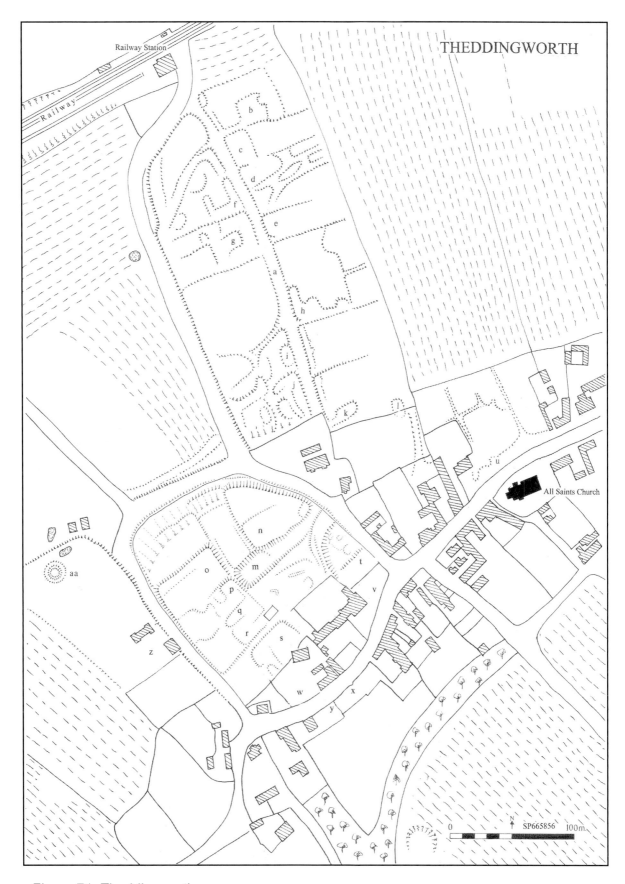

Figure 71: Theddingworth

WELHAM

Open Fields

Welham had open fields in 1601 but was then enclosed by agreement, probably by 1606 (VCH, 333)

Village and Hall Earthworks (fig 72)   SP765924

Much of the present layout of Welham village can be attributed to one man, Francis Edwards (d.1728-9). Nichols records how Edwards *"built the town in its present state..... It formerly stood on the south side of the canal"* (Nichols 1798, 865). Edwards was a visionary who was somewhat ahead of his time. He believed that by providing a bridge across the Welland here he could establish a new routeway between Leicester and London to replace the one through Market Harborough. Surprisingly even at this date the river crossing was heavily used by carts bringing coal from north-west Leicestershire to villages in Northamptonshire (VCH, 333).

It seems likely that Welham was already much decayed as a village, for there is plenty of earthwork evidence all around the existing houses. South of the Manor House is a large building platform (a), probably the site of the medieval manor house, surrounded by a moat (b), with a drainage channel (c). The whole site lies within a large embanked enclosure (d). North of the moat are earthworks of an outer court with a building platform (e), perhaps the site of a barn or other farm building. Towards the church was another enclosed yard or garden (f). The enclosure (d) around the moated site probably also contained gardens or orchards, and in the corner to the west are remains of a small pond (g). The northern boundary of (d) is not a continuous bank, for at (h) there is a section of broad ditch, probably once a pond, also occupying part of the moat. This may be part of a more modern garden scheme relating to the present Manor House. Between enclosure (d) and the river is a broad ditch (i), which appears to be an attempt to straighten the river course in this area, or possibly a leat to supply a watermill.

On the north-west side of the village is an irregular hollow way (j), possibly widened by quarrying for gravel and flanked on its south side by more building platforms, for example (k). To the east across the lane is more evidence of the medieval village, with old enclosures (l, m) and sites of former buildings (n, o, p). Possibly these buildings represent another manorial site, for immediately to the east is another enclosure which could have been a garden or orchard. There is a substantial boundary bank and ditch (q), a feature (r) which might be ponds or building foundations, and two more sites of buildings (s, t). Faint and narrow ridge and furrow underlies the area.

Francis Edwards began to build a mansion for himself opposite the junction where the road over his new bridge joined the village street. The Victoria County History suggests that this was originally intended to be a large inn for travellers, based on the Red Lion in Northampton (VCH, 332). The new house and village were all to conform to a rectilinear geometrical layout, most clearly seen in the surviving garden walls (u) and the straight frontage of the properties further east. Nichols notes *"To the new house, gardens were laid out and planted in a very magnificent style; the walls of which are now standing; and the lands, together with what the house stood upon, are converted into pasture.."* (Nichols 1798, 865). There is no sign of the hall, unless the pond (w) indicates the flooded cellars. On the south side of the street was a fashionable "canal" or long, narrow pond, possibly once continuing at (v) towards the church yard.

Between the *"canal"* and the river is a terraced area (x), probably more of Edwards' gardens, and some more slight earthworks (y) which could be garden features or surviving evidence of the old village. (Site surveyed 18th and 23rd May 1985, with the help of S. Barker).

Watermill A mill is mentioned in 1086 and 1220 (VCH, 334). Its remains may lie amongst theearthworks along the river, specifically at (i) and (y), noted above.

WELHAM

Site of Hall

Garden Walls

Gate
Gate

St. Andrew's Church

Vicarage

Manor House

Canal

R. Welland

Bridge

0   N ↑   SP 765924   100m.
RFH

Figure 72: Welham, Village and Hall Earthworks

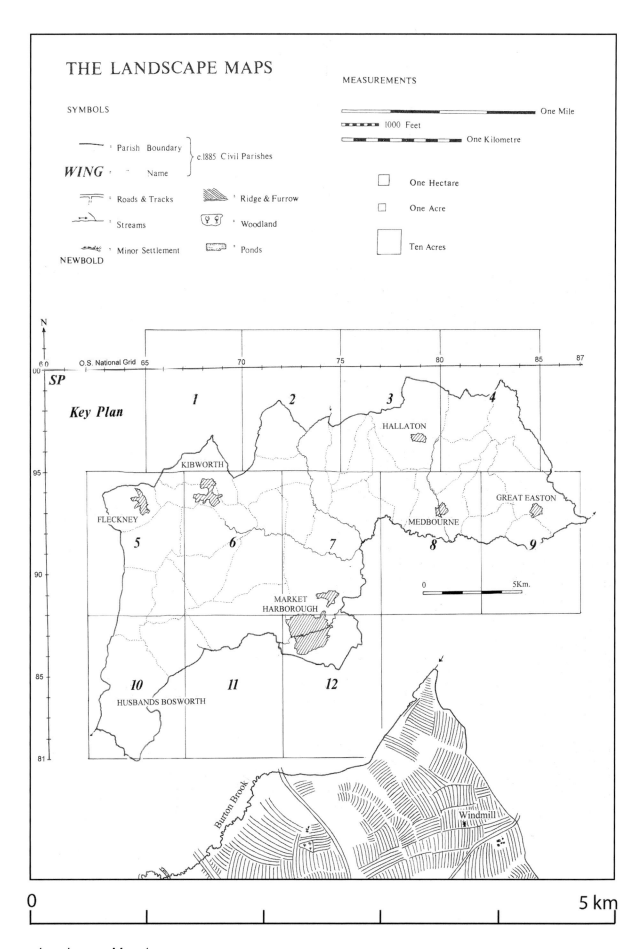

THE LANDSCAPE MAPS

SYMBOLS

MEASUREMENTS

——— : Parish Boundary ⎤
⎟ c.1885 Civil Parishes
WING : Name ⎦

——— : Roads & Tracks

——► : Streams

——— : Minor Settlement
NEWBOLD

▨ : Ridge & Furrow

🌳 : Woodland

▱ : Ponds

◻ One Hectare

▫ One Acre

◻ Ten Acres

One Mile

1000 Feet

One Kilometre

Key Plan

N

O.S. National Grid

SP

1   *2*   *3*   *4*

HALLATON

KIBWORTH

FLECKNEY   *5*   *6*   *7*

MEDBOURNE

GREAT EASTON

8   *9*

MARKET
HARBOROUGH

10   *11*   *12*

HUSBANDS BOSWORTH

Burton Brook

Windmill

0   5 km

Landscape Map 1

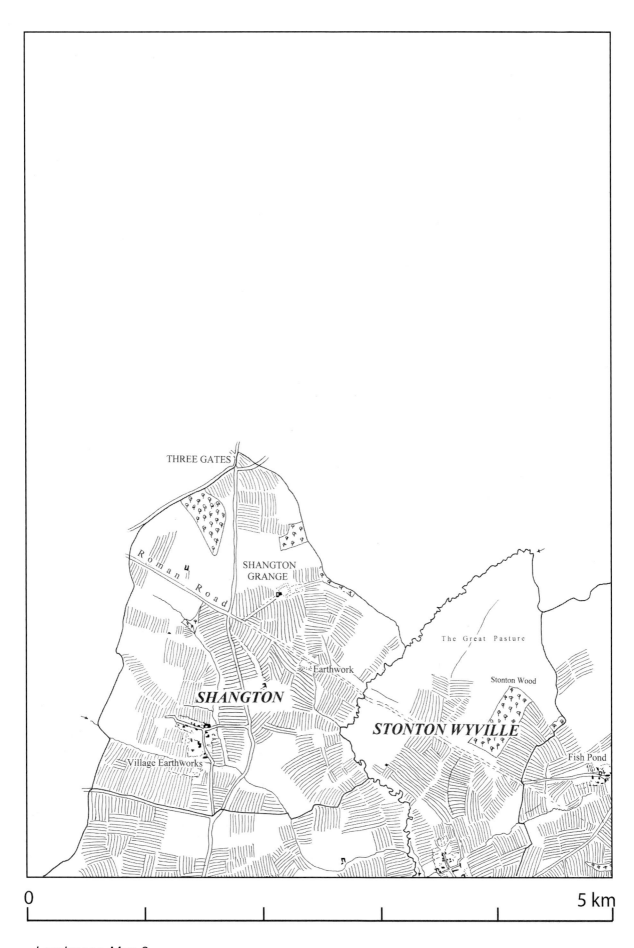

THREE GATES

SHANGTON
GRANGE

Roman Road

Earthwork

SHANGTON

The Great Pasture

Stonton Wood

STONTON WYVILLE

Village Earthworks

Fish Pond

0   5 km

Landscape Map 2

GLOOSTON

Hallaton Wood

Glooston Wood

CRANOE

OTHORPE

Earthwork

Motte & Bailey

Hare Pie Bank

Mound

HALLATON

Railway

0   5 km

Landscape Map 3

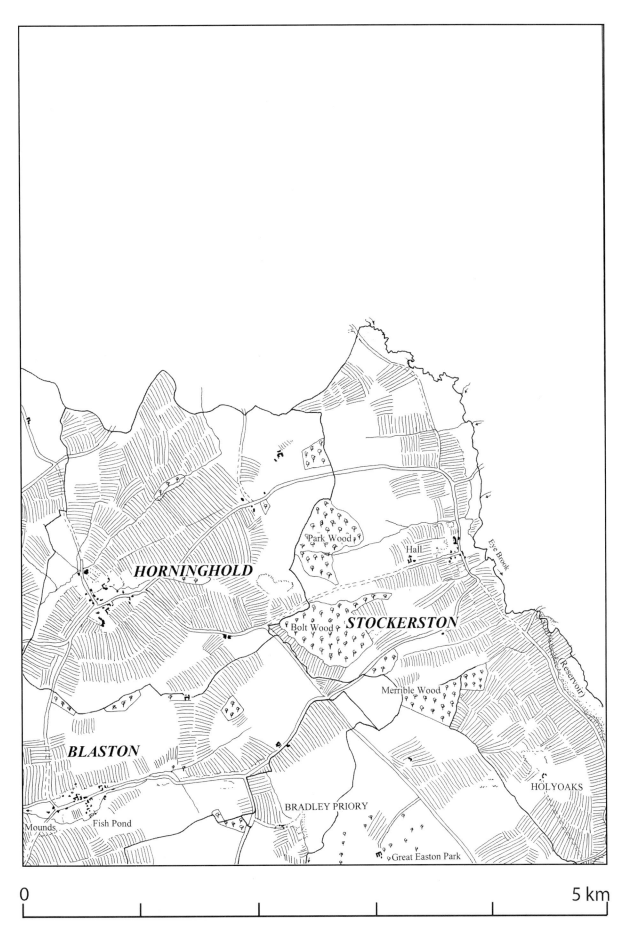

HORNINGHOLD

STOCKERSTON

Park Wood

Hall

Eye Brook

Bolt Wood

Merrible Wood

(Reservoir)

BLASTON

HOLYOAKS

Mounds

Fish Pond

BRADLEY PRIORY

Great Easton Park

0   5 km

Landscape Map 4

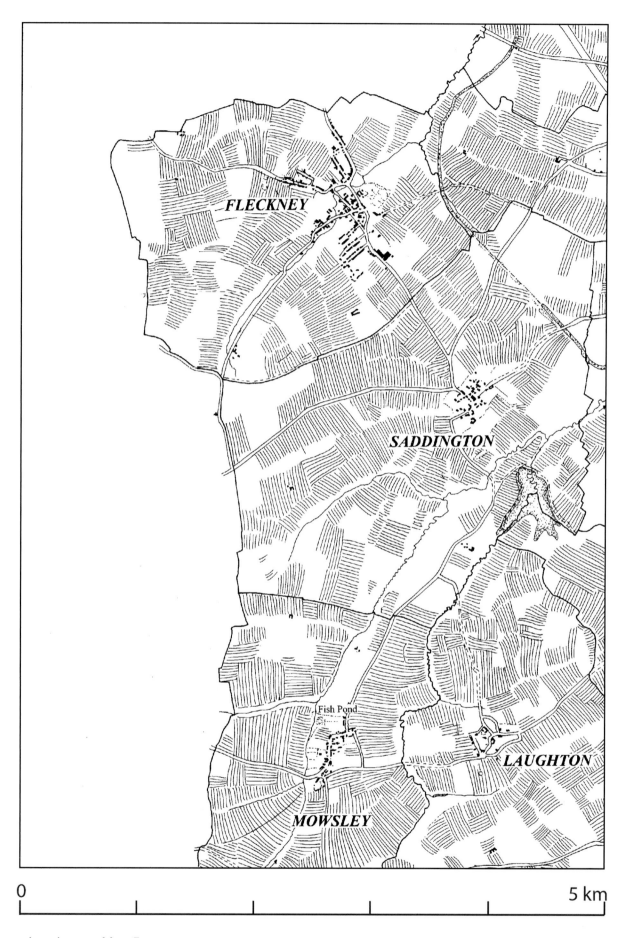

FLECKNEY

SADDINGTON

LAUGHTON

Fish Pond

MOWSLEY

0   5 km

Landscape Map 5

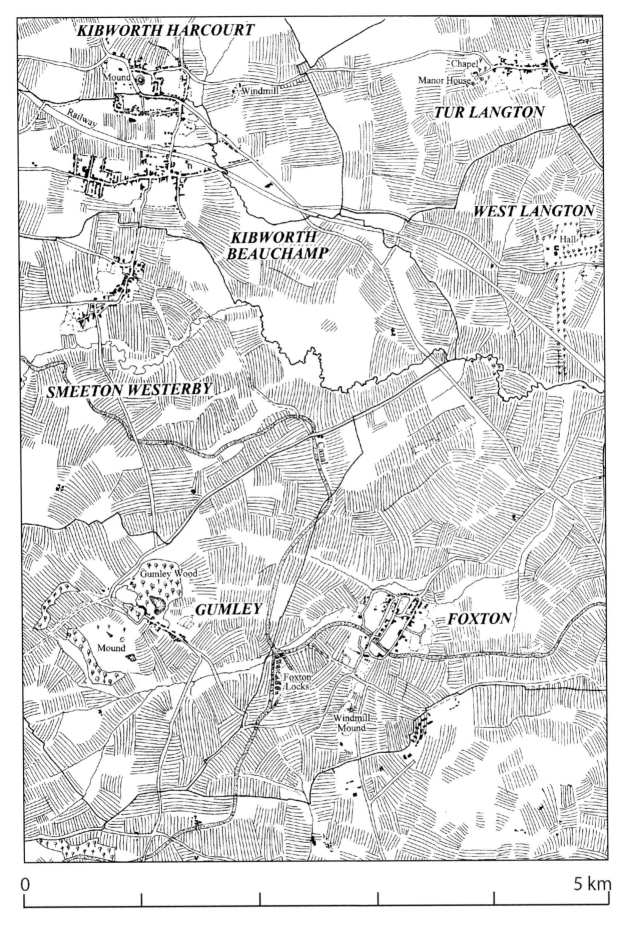

KIBWORTH HARCOURT

Mound

Railway

Windmill

Chapel
Manor House

TUR LANGTON

WEST LANGTON

Hall

KIBWORTH
BEAUCHAMP

SMEETON WESTERBY

Canal

Gumley Wood

GUMLEY

FOXTON

Mound

Foxton
Locks

Windmill
Mound

0   5 km

Landscape Map 6

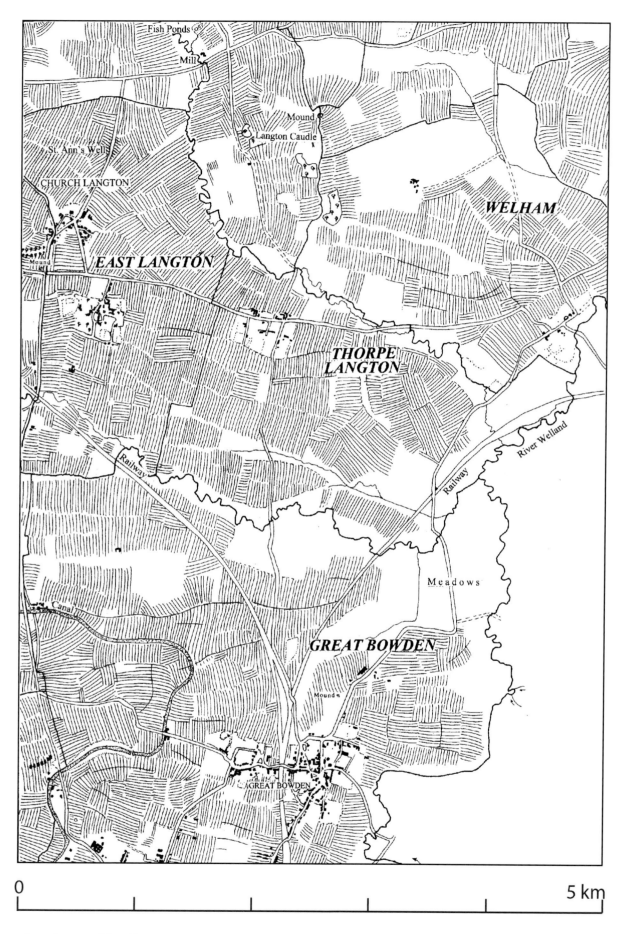

Fish Ponds

Mill

Mound

Langton Caudle

St. Ann's Wells

CHURCH LANGTON

Mound

EAST LANGTON

WELHAM

THORPE LANGTON

Railway

River Welland

Railway

Meadows

Canal

GREAT BOWDEN

Mound

GREAT BOWDEN

0   5 km

Landscape Map 7

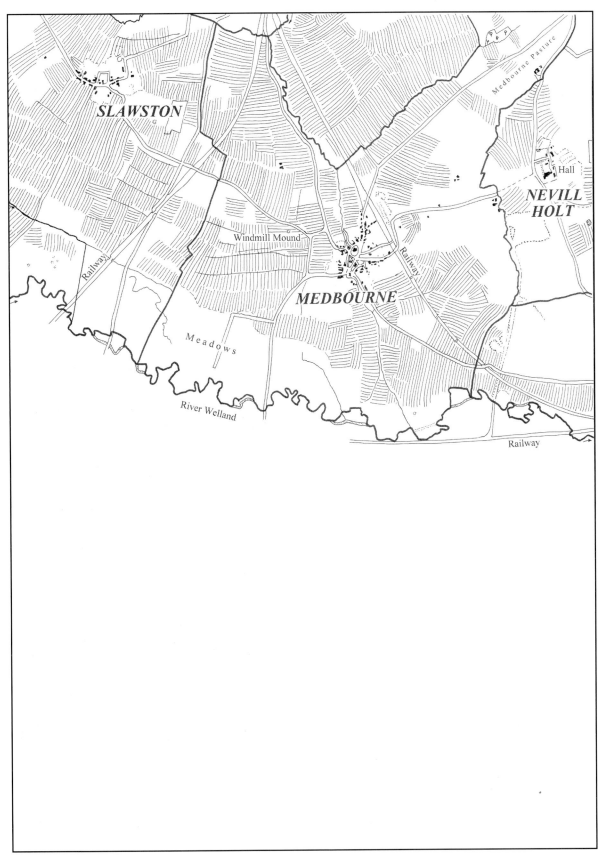

SLAWSTON

NEVILL
HOLT

Hall

Medbourne Pasture

Windmill Mound

Railway

Railway

MEDBOURNE

M e a d o w s

River Welland

Railway

0   5 km

Landscape Map 8

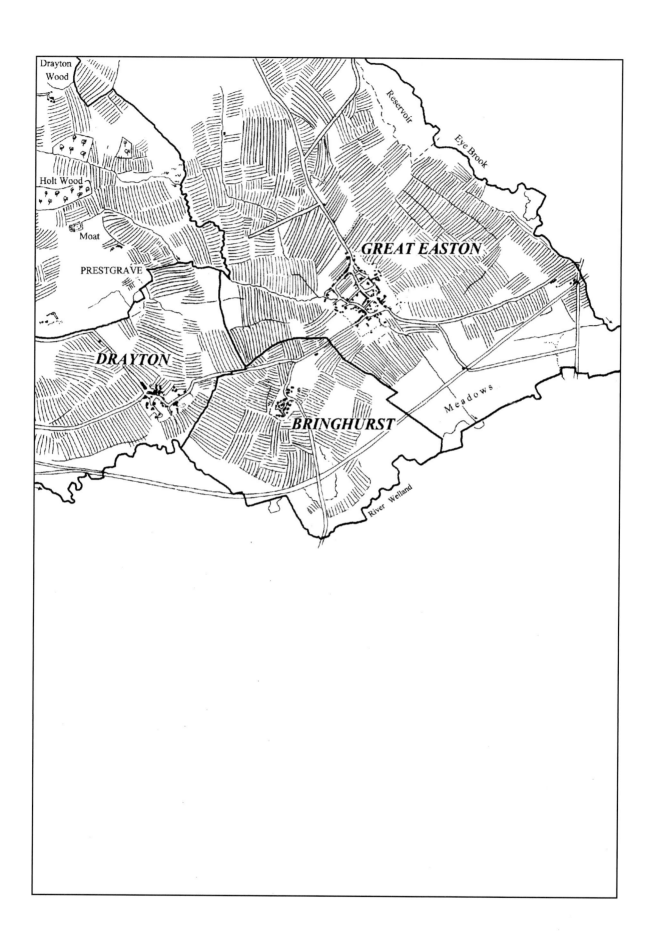

0   5 km

Landscape Map 9

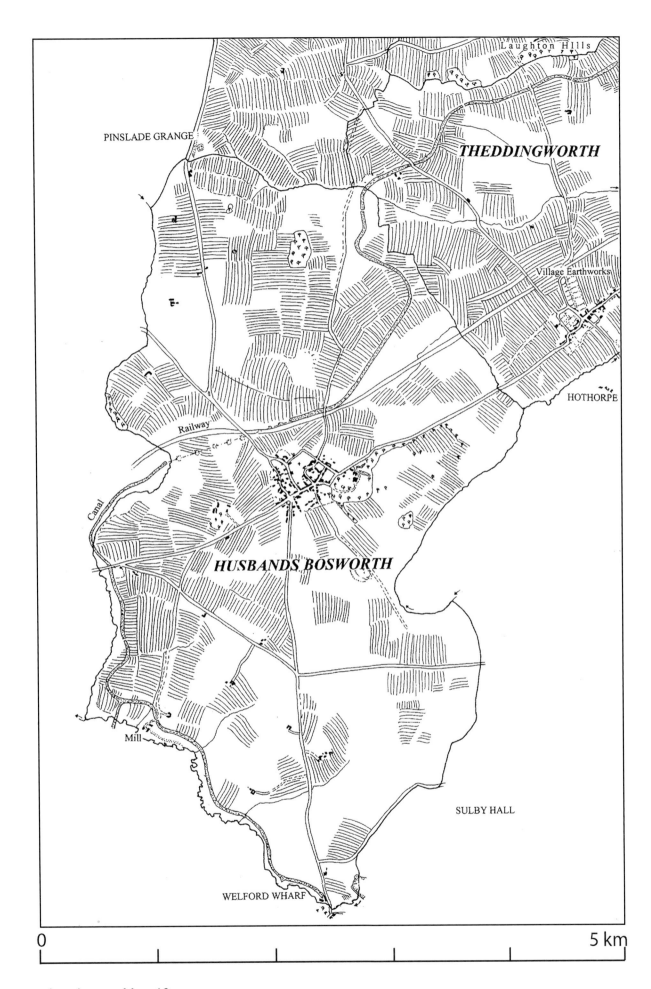

PINSLADE GRANGE

Laughton Hills

THEDDINGWORTH

Village Earthworks

HOTHORPE

Railway

Canal

HUSBANDS BOSWORTH

Mill

SULBY HALL

WELFORD WHARF

0   5 km

Landscape Map 10

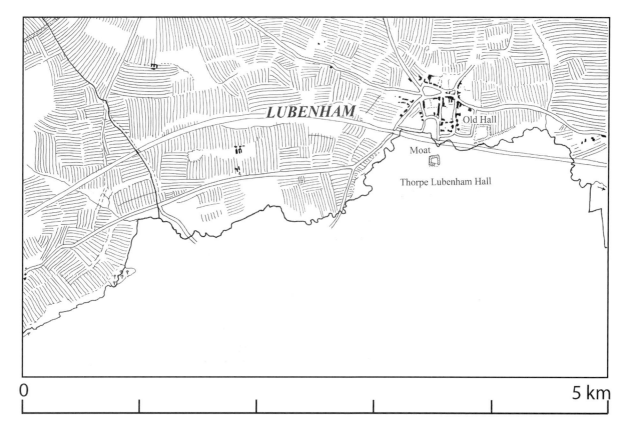

Landscape Map 11

Thorpe Lubenham farmhouse (Nichols 1798, V2, pt2, 701) see entry for Lubenham p87.

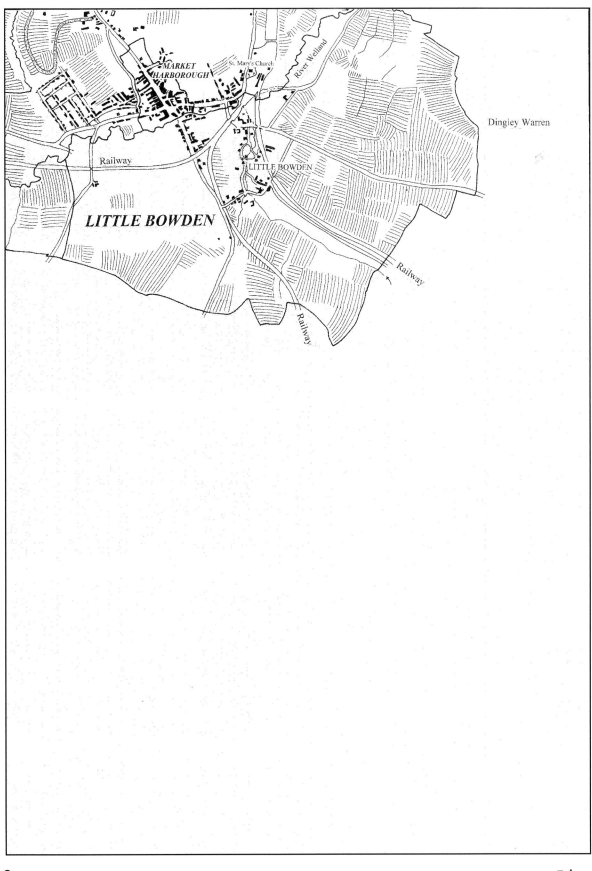

MARKET HARBOROUGH

St. Mary's Church

River Welland

Dingley Warren

Railway

LITTLE BOWDEN

LITTLE BOWDEN

Railway

Railway

0   5 km

Landscape Map 12

The Medieval Earthworks of South & South-East Leicestershire
Part 3

Billesdon Area

This volume is dedicated to the memory of

John Nichols

whose magnificent volumes on the History of Leicestershire
have been a constant inspiration

JOHN NICHOLS, PRINTER,
F.S.A. of Lon: Edin: & Perth.
Born Feb. 2 1744-5; living 1812.

The eight-volume History and Antiquities of the Town and County of Leicester was completed by John Nichols in 1815. This grand work remains a key text for researchers investigating the county, its parishes, churches, great families and objects of antiquarian 'interest'. The content of the volumes can be confusing and perseverance is required in finding and identifying places which may not be located in the volume where the researcher thinks they should be. Nevertheless when putting together this Earthworks series they have been invaluable in bringing together in one place details of the landscape two hundred years ago and beyond so that we can correlate what we see today (or often do not), with what Nichols and his contributors saw then.

Image of John Nichols courtesy of Julian Pooley of the Nichols Archive Project.
http://www2.le.ac.uk/centres/elh/research/project/nichols/the-nichols-archive-project

Cover photo for Part 3 – Aerial view of the deserted village of Whatborough. Cambridge University Collection of Aerial Photography © copyright reserved

Frontispiece – opposite: Thomas Clerk's survey of the lands of Whatborough, 1586, showing the site of the deserted village. (Reproduced and © by kind permission of the Warden and Fellows of All Souls College, Oxford.)

INTRODUCTION TO THE BILLESDON AREA

The area covered by this report is the northern part of the present Harborough District. Prior to 1973 it was the Billesdon Rural District which originated in 1835 as the Poor Law Union, becoming a rural district in 1894. 1935 saw the rural district decreased by the annexing of Humberstone, most of Evington, and some of Thurnby civil parishes to Leicester (with some small parts going to Oadby in 1936). It was further reduced in 1966 by the annexation of part of Scraptoft, Stoughton and Thurnby parishes. In 1974 it became part of the Harborough non-metropolitan district, along with the Lutterworth Rural District, Market Harborough Rural District, and Market Harborough urban districts.

A comprehensive survey of the history of this area was published in 1964 as part of the Victoria County History (VCH) series (Lee and McKinley "A *History of the County of Leicester, Vol 5, Gartree Hundred*") hereafter referenced as VCH for this Part with page number to avoid multiple long repetitions.

This is the central part of an area referred to as "High Leicestershire", predominantly an area of heavy clay, with the villages generally sited on small areas of gravels. The area was intensively farmed in the early medieval period, and then subsequently it was much affected by depopulation, with the land converted to pasture. As a result it contains a remarkable amount of evidence of ridge and furrow arable fields and abandoned settlements. Some of the most celebrated deserted villages in England are here, such as Ingarsby, Cold Newton, North Marefield, Lowesby, Whatborough and Great Stretton.

The eastern part of the area, around Launde and Owston, seems always to have retained quite a lot of woodland, and in this secluded district there were two monastic houses – Owston Abbey and Launde Abbey, and also a motte and bailey castle at Sauvey (Withcote).

Billesdon was a small market town, traditionally a focal point for the area, and it continued to be a local market centre until the mid 20th century. Much of the Billesdon area still feels remarkably rural, but the suburbs of Leicester have recently spread out across Scraptoft, Thurnby, Bushby and Great Glen.

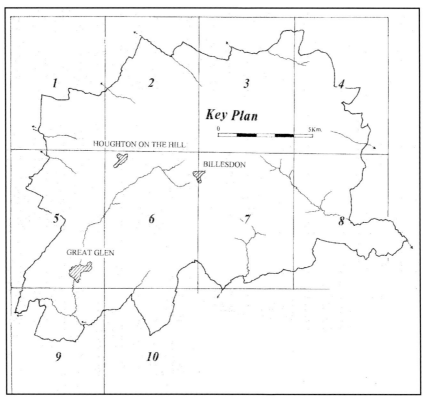

Outline of Billesdon rural district. Numbers 1 to 10 refer to the landscape maps at the end of this part.

ALLEXTON

Open Fields

Enclosure took place in 1555, according to a Terrier of 1635 (Beresford 1949, 102). The wood of "Fritheland" is mentioned in 1234 (Squires 1995, 90, quoting Farnham 1933).

Moated Site and Earthworks (fig 73)

SK817005

On the south side of the Eye Brook a narrow pond (a) and an "L" shaped pond (b) combine with the brook to enclose a level platform (c) which seems likely to be the site of a medieval manor house. The brook appears at some time to have flowed along the channel (d) south of its

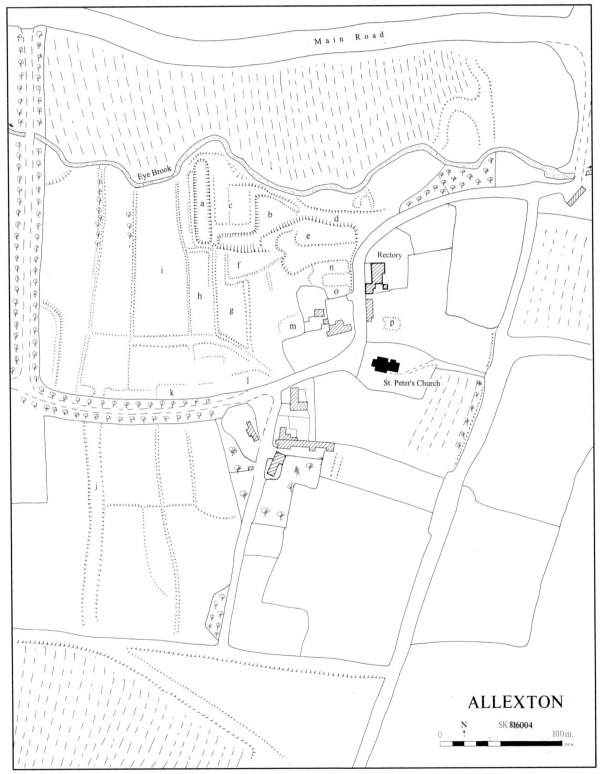

Figure 73: Allexton

present course. Outside the moat are two building platforms (e, f) and several old enclosures (g, h, i). South of these is an old street of the village, with house sites at (k) and (l) which have old crofts or enclosures behind them, and the line of a back lane. Across the road, to the south, are more old enclosures and a hollow way (j). To the east, near the Rectory, are several more house platforms (m, n, o, p). (Surveyed 3rd September 1980.)

BILLESDON

Open Fields
There were open fields prior to enclosure in 1764 – Stonepitt Field (north and east of the village), Portbridge Field (north and west of the village), and Mill Field to the south (VCH, 10).

Village Earthworks (Fig 74)   SK720032
The lane (a) leading north from the Market Place used to extend as a hollow way flanked by slight earthwork evidence of an abandoned area of the village. Some of this evidence was destroyed by the construction of the Billesdon by-pass. There were at least three house platforms (b, c, d), and a substantial enclosure (e). Across the lane are more areas with evidence of old enclosures at (f) and (g). To the north the field of old ridge and furrow has had a bank (h) dug at some time to divide off part of the field. The whole furlong of ridge and furrow was probably enclosed four or five centuries ago as it has a substantial bank (i) around the north and east sides. The east side is also flanked by another old hollow way (j). (Surveyed 26th September 1985.)

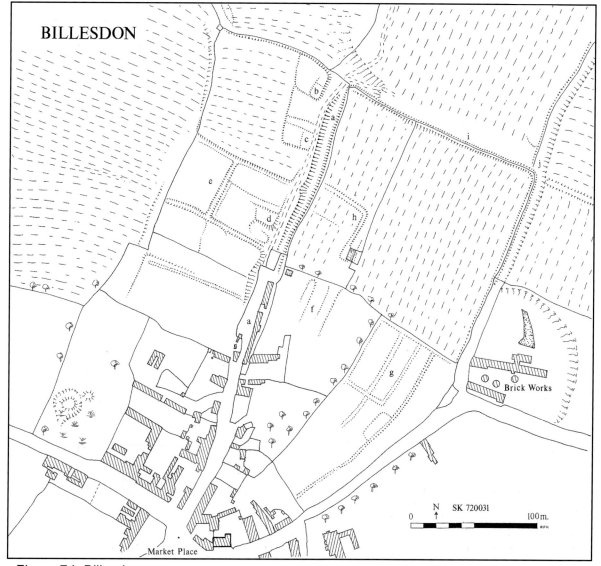

Figure 74: Billesdon

Billesdon had two annual fairs and a Friday market in the 17th century, but these had been discontinued by the end of the 18th century (VCH, 11).

BURTON OVERY

Open Fields
Three open fields are recorded in 1622; South Field, North Field, and Towards Carlton Field. In 1638 North Field is called Brook Field, and in 1674 Towards Carlton Field is called Mill Field. The enclosure act dates from 1765 and the award was made in 1766 (VCH, 72-3). After enclosure much of the land was used as pasture as a description in 1790 mentions the 'opulent graziers' living there (*op cit*).

Village Earthworks (figs 75.1, 75.2 both overleaf)   SK6797
The village of Burton Overy has considerable evidence of changing use, in and around the existing houses and gardens.

Figure 75.1, village north
The village street runs SSW - NNE and at its north end it continues as a hollow way, with two more hollow ways (a) and (b) diverging to left and right. Hollow way (b) curves back southwards, enclosing an area of old enclosures, while on its north side is a house platform (c), and to the east is another (f). Hollow way (a) is flanked on its north side by a complex of building platforms (d) and on the south side by another platform (e) in a field with more terraces which may contain the sites of old buildings.

North of the Rectory is an area of levelled terraces around (g), suggesting the former sites of buildings or gardens, while to the east across the main street are two more house platforms (h) and (i). South west of the Rectory is a field called "The Banks", which has been a Scheduled Monument for many years. This now seems most likely to be the remains of a medieval or early post-medieval garden, with long, narrow fishponds at (j) and (k) running along the slope and enclosing an area of hillside. It is possible that the features north of the Rectory at (g) may have been a continuation of the prominent banks at (k). A garden of this size would have been associated with a large manor house, probably in the area south of St. Andrew's Church, where there are foundations at (l) and building platforms at (m, n, o). The field to the south has two more small house platforms at (p) and (q).

Figure 75.2, village south
Fig. 3.2 shows yet more earthwork features. A substantial area of the medieval settlement at the south end of the village is now pasture land. Beginning at the west, there is a fishpond (a), and two large building platforms (b, c). There are three or four smaller platforms around (d), and further building foundations at (e) and (f). Further east there are more sites of buildings at (g, h, i, j, k). All of these building sites are surrounded by evidence of enclosures (crofts). Across the road is another, less well defined, area of village earthworks around (l).

Moving northwards along the west side of the village there are more sites of old buildings at (m, n) and possibly (o), also surrounded by evidence of old field boundaries. These features seem to be more recent than those marked at (a) - (k). (Sites surveyed 16th March 1984 - The Banks, and 1st March 1985 - remainder).

Water Mill
A mill is mentioned in 1440, probably sited on the stream west of the church (VCH, 73)

Windmill
A windmill is mentioned in 1646 (VCH, 73).

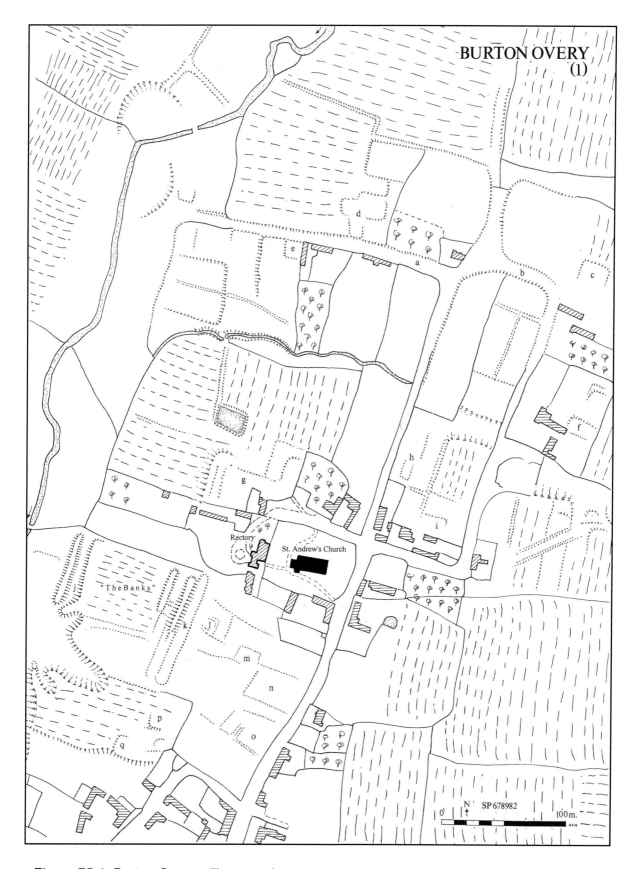

Figure 75.1: Burton Overy, village north

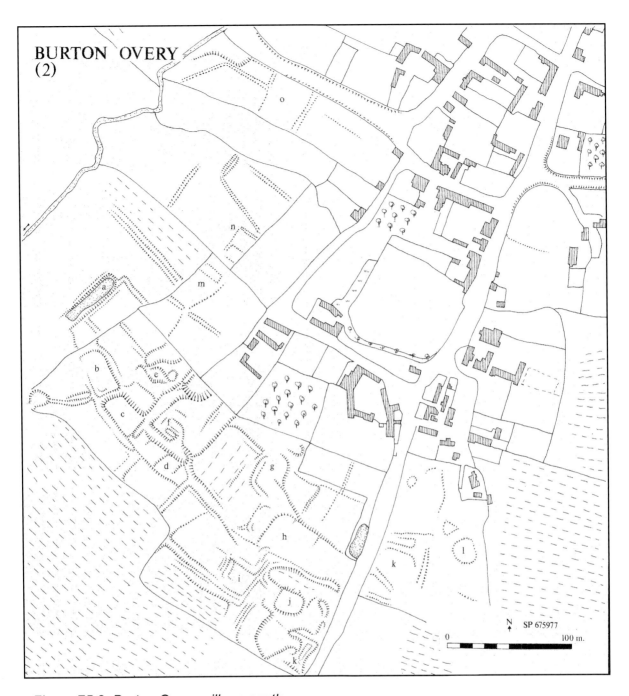

Figure 75.2: Burton Overy, village south

BUSHBY

Open Fields

Although Bushby, and its close neighbour Thurnby, have archaeological evidence of ridge and furrow, there seems to be little documentary evidence. Both Bushby and Thurnby are probably described under Stoughton in Domesday Book (VCH, 323). They may have shared their open fields which may have been common to both townships. Middle Field is mentioned in 1622 when there was a close in it. Bushby was probably enclosed before 1640 at the same time as Stoughton (*op cit*). (See also entry for Stoughton later in this section.)

CARLTON CURLIEU

Open Fields

Large-scale conversion of the open fields to inclosures was being pushed forward by the Bale family in 1599-1607, with a reduction of the arable land from 48 yardlands to 8, worked by three ploughs (VCH, 79).

Village Earthworks (figs 76.1, 76.2)   *SP694968*

Carlton Curlieu is a classic "deserted village", with the Hall, the Rectory, and one farm, surrounded by pasture fields packed with earthwork evidence. The gardens and parkland of the Hall were laid out over the hollow ways and house sites.

Starting with the north end of the village (fig 76.1) there is the hollow way (a) of a back lane, and an old enclosure (b). The pattern of village earthworks becomes clearer further south around (c) and is discussed below. The present Rectory lies to the west of the old Rectory, which is marked at (d) on an estate map of 1664 (NRO, Map/703). It was demolished before 1846 and replaced by the present building in the earlier garden. There are slight earthworks of the building platform. The Rectory still has an impressive walled garden (e), which is shown on the 1664 map, apparently containing an orchard. To the north are two quite large gravel pits (f, g) probably to provide material for building and road surfacing. This field was called "Gravel Pit Close" on the 1664 map. A platform (h) may indicate the site of another building.

Figure 76.2 opposite shows the main area of earthwork evidence. South-west of the Hall a hollow way (a) leads westwards through the field. This is marked on the 1646 map as "An old Street". At that time there were still two buildings alongside it, at (b) and at or near (g).

On the north side of the hollow way are numerous sites of buildings, most clearly north of (a) at

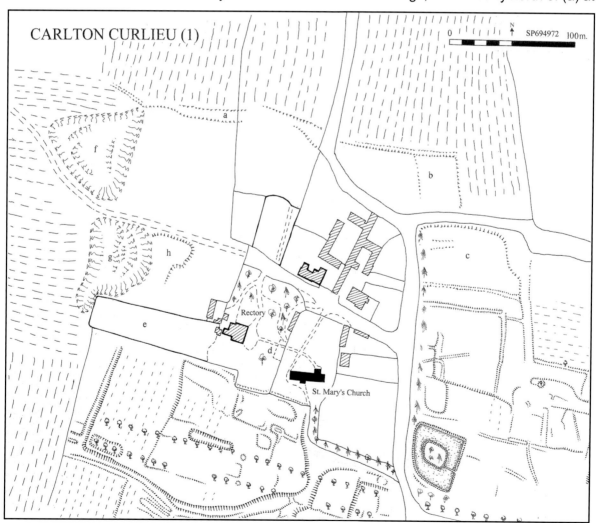

Figure 76.1: Carlton Curlieu, village north

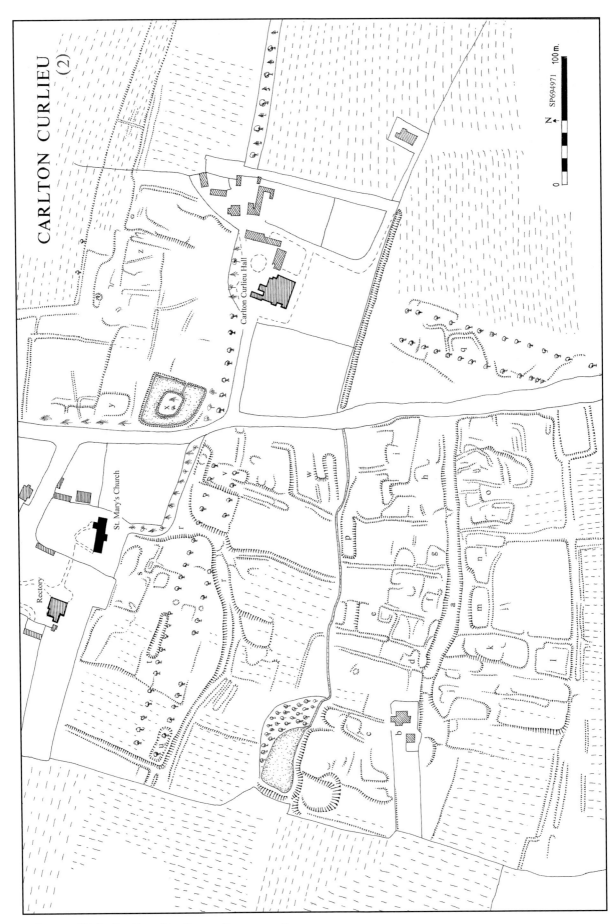

Figure 76.2: Carlton Curlieu, village south

(c, d, e, f, g, h, i). Similarly on the south side there are more sites of houses (j, k, l, m, n) and around (o). Returning to the north side again, there was a fishpond (p) alongside the stream. This was probably part of the gardens of the house shown in 1664 in the area of (g), which seems to have been quite substantial and may have been the village's second manor house. The area of village earthworks extends east across the road, with more building platforms around (q). To the north-west, across the stream, there is another hollow way (r), running roughly parallel to (a). North of it is an area of terraces and building platforms, including foundations of a small building at (s) and fish ponds at (t) and (u). These features could be associated with the vanished 17th/18th century avenue of trees, or could be the gardens of another vanished, high-status house, and it is noteworthy that this field is called Hall Close on the 1664 map.

To the east are more platforms around (v), where another large house existed in 1664. The area south of this, running down to the stream and including another terrace or platform (w) may be the site of gardens belonging to the house.

Across the road, to the east, is what seems to be an ornamental moat (x), the south arm of which is shown on an estate map of 1781 (ROLLR, DG4/55). As a moat, it may be an 18th/19th century feature, similar to the "decoy" in Galby, described below. To the north is a house platform (y), fronting onto the street, with indications of two or three more in a line extending northwards. Further east, the old terraces and field boundaries around (z) seem to relate to an outbuilding and walled orchard belonging to Carlton Curlieu Hall. The Hall itself is described by Pevsner as a building of c.1632 (Pevsner & Williamson 2003, 122), possibly built on foundations of early 16th century work. (Survey 1st-2nd March 1983, site visit 23rd August 2014)

Windmill SP695956
A windmill is mentioned in 1592 and 1661 (VCH, 79). It is marked on the 1664 map at a location on the hilltop at Carlton Clump.

COLD NEWTON

Open Fields
The fields had been enclosed by 1641 (Beresford 1949, 122, under Newton, Cold)

Village Earthworks (fig 77) SK716066
This village attracted the attention of W. G. Hoskins in the 1950s. Lying in an exposed position on a ridge it was distinguished as *Cold* Newton as early as 1428. It was a chapelry of Lowesby, and probably a daughter settlement, and so "cannot have come into existence much before the eleventh century or the late tenth" (Hoskins 1956, 40). In 1086 it had eleven households, and in 1377 thirty-eight taxpayers are listed, which in Hoskins' opinion represented a population of about sixty inhabitants. From the records, the community seems to have remained much the same size until the 19th century.

The village was served by two north-south lanes which survive as hollow ways (a) and (b), with a back lane (c) along the east side of the settlement. Alongside the back lane is a conical mound (d), possibly a mill mound, but as it is sited near the Manor House it could be a prospect mound associated with the gardens. There is a substantial terraced area north west of the mound, and an old fishpond just outside the present garden wall.

South of the Manor House are two building platforms (e), and further south again is an embanked hollow (f), perhaps a crew yard to shelter the cattle in winter. Southwards again is a well-preserved rectangular moated site, with a platform approximately 40m. square, likely to be the site of a medieval manor house, with an outer enclosure on the west side.

On the west side of hollow way (b) are more house sites (h, i, j, k), and yet more as we start to look north along hollow way (a), at (l, m, n, o). Further north again is an area of more clearly preserved remains, with a platform (p) at the north and four locations (q, r, s, t) where the foundations of stone buildings can be identified. It is possible that this area was abandoned at a later date, leaving evidence of post-medieval stone buildings, rather than their mud-walled

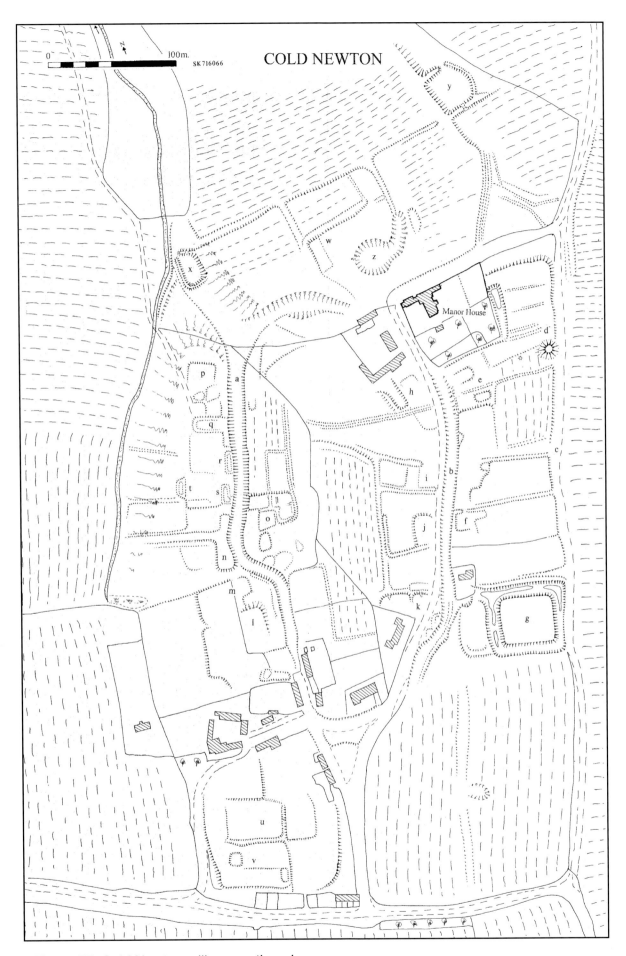

Figure 77: Cold Newton, village earthworks

medieval predecessors. At the south end of the village is another area of earthworks (u), with four or five levelled platforms where buildings probably stood. The area (v) has two small hollows, possibly old ponds or robbed-out foundations.

Moving to the north end of the village, there is a field called Chapel Hill Field. Within it, at (w) is a building platform, perhaps the site of the chapel. When Hoskins visited he noted several "blocks of weathered stone, apparently taken from the ruins of the chapel." (Hoskins 1956,40). To the west, near the stream, is a fishpond (x), while to the east, at the head of another shallow valley, is another embanked pond (y). These may have been part of the amenities of the surviving post-medieval Manor House. Perhaps the latest element in the earthwork remains is an old gravel pit (z), probably of 17th to 19th century date. (Survey 1992)

Earthworks, Cold Newton Lodge (The Grange) (fig 78)   SK717052

These rather mysterious earthworks extend up a steep hillside which has not been disturbed by modern agriculture. South-east of Cold Newton Lodge Farm is a straight ditch (a) enclosing one side of the site and marking the boundary of the ridge and furrow field to the east. Below the hillside are a defined terrace (b), with a rectangular platform (c) surrounded by a narrow moat and bank. Just around a spur of the hillside, and dug into the slope, are small terraced platforms (d) and (e), for buildings which no longer exist. At (f) is a marshy area with more slight earthworks, and around (g) are more building foundations. The hedge line (h), with a bank and ditch, seems to have been cut through this area at a later date, but seems to be related to the boundary ditch (a) and the moated platform (c). A possible interpretation is that an isolated medieval manor house or grange farm was created here, cutting through earlier earthworks in the process. At the crest of the hillside is the site of a post-medieval stone quarry (Q). There is slight evidence of several quarries along such escarpments in the area around Tilton on the Hill. (Survey 9th March and 23rd August 1983).

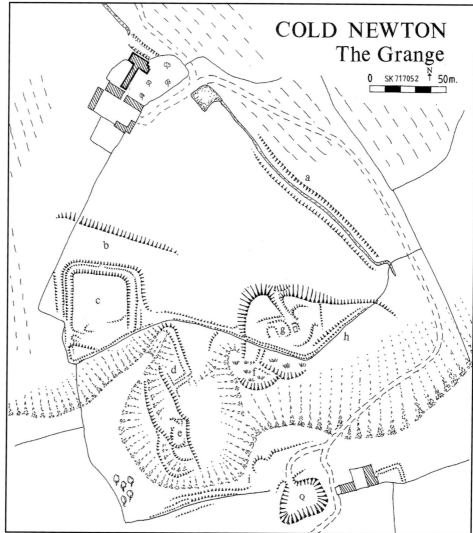

Figure 78: Cold Newton Lodge, (The Grange)

Earthworks at The Orchard (fig 79)

This roughly triangular area at the head of a shallow valley appears to be the site of a medieval monastic grange farm. A levelled terrace (a) appears to be a forecourt outside the likely area of the entrance. An almost continuous bank and ditch (b-b-b-b) encloses the sites of the buildings, including rectangular foundations of a substantial stone structure (c). This lies in an enclosed area (d) which retains evidence of ridge and furrow, and may be a later addition to the original site. Within the "core" area are two levelled terraces (e, f). Material has been quarried out at (g), either to form a pond or to supply building stone. There are clear wall foundations of a small stone building at (h), and a confused pattern of diggings and foundations at (i), with another small quarry pit outside the site at (j). (Survey December 1980)

This site has been identified in a recent publication as a small 12th century leper hospital, granted to the Order of St Lazarus in 1184. In this case there would presumably have been housing for a number of victims of leprosy in a small community sustained by farming activities. (Marcombe 2003, 154-161).

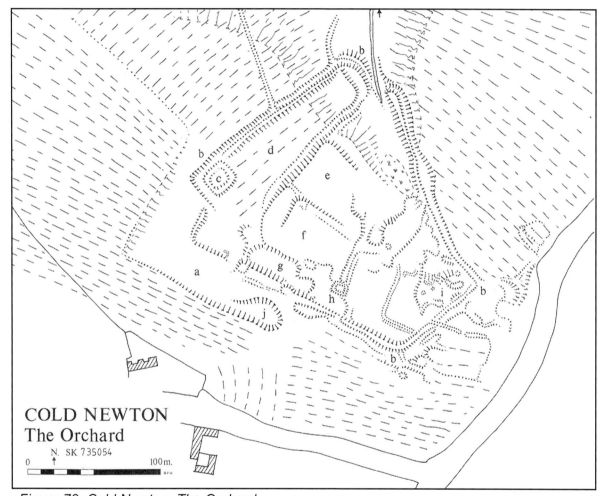

Figure 79: Cold Newton, The Orchard

EAST NORTON

Open Fields

Enclosure of the open fields here had been completed by 1632 (Beresford 1949, 122).

Village Earthworks (fig 80 overleaf)

Before the recent construction of a by-pass, the main road from Leicester to Peterborough ran through the village (a-a) partly in a hollow way. A lane runs south towards (b) where it also becomes a hollow way into the fields. The hollow way of another old lane (c) runs south of All Saints' Church, flanked by old enclosures (d) and (f), which probably contain house sites. There may have been a manor house in the area of (d) as there is an old fishpond (e) in a raised terrace next to the stream. Across the main road to the north is a large house platform (g), in another rectangular area of faint village earthworks (h). To the west of this a short hollow way (i) gave access to the fields, and there is an old gravel pit (k). At the east end of the village is another area of earthworks (I) with remains of three old closes bounded by a curving stretch of hollow way marking the old back lane and the edge of the ridge and furrow fields. (Site visit 2011)

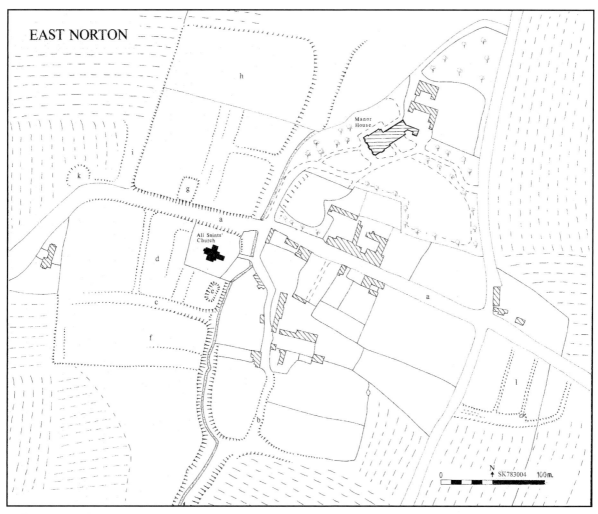

Figure 80: East Norton

FRISBY BY GALBY

Anyone interested in understanding the historical development of Frisby village should consult the fascinating essay "Galby and Frisby" by W. G. Hoskins (1950, 24-66).

Open Fields
The process of enclosure here was completed during the years 1638-79. There seem to have been three fields - East Towards Bilsdon, South Towards Ilston, and Town. Beresford suggests that Town Field lay on the north-west side of the parish, towards Galby and Houghton. (Beresford 1949, 106).

Village Earthworks (fig 81)   SK704015
There were about 39 families living here in 1086, and perhaps as many as 49 in 1381. By 1831 Frisby had just five remaining houses. A decline seems to have set in during the second half of the 15th century. The chapel of St James, served from the mother church in Galby, was in existence by 1220 but seems to have gone out of use in the 1540s, and Nichols reports that '*Mr Wyrley, who visited this chapel in 1591, found "nothing of any note there".*' (Nichols 1798, 573). Hoskins suggested it was located just south of Frisby House (Hoskins 1950, 48).

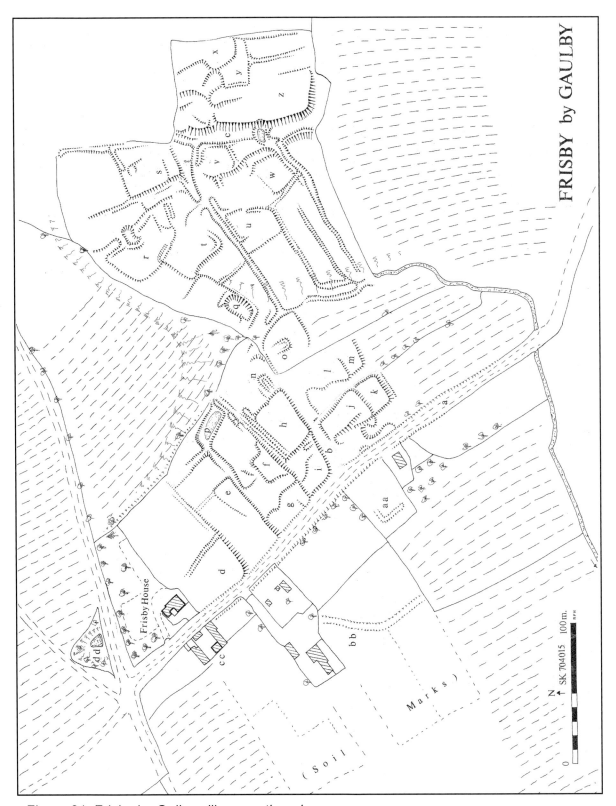

Figure 81: Frisby by Galby, village earthworks

The east end of this village is entirely deserted, but there are several occupied houses at the west end, reached by the lane in the hollow way (a). Half way down the hillside another hollow way (b) branches off to the east, and presumably there was a way through to another section of hollow way (c) cutting north-south through the east end of the village.

From Frisby House the land falls south-eastwards to the stream, with a large terrace (d), another containing a building platform (e), and more platforms at (f, g, h, i, j, k, l, m), all probably containing the sites of old houses or outbuildings. Just to the east, at (n) and (o) are the foundations of two small stone buildings. A fishpond (p) was probably part of the grounds of a large house at (g).

The eastern part of the village is on a facing slope across the small stream valley. There are two old fishponds (q, r) in an area of earthworks including two large building platforms (s) and (t). To the south across a narrow hollow way are at least three more building platforms (u, v, w), and the boundaries of three long, narrow old enclosures, stretching down to the stream. Across the old lane (c) are more earthworks, with levelled sites of at least two buildings (x, y) and a large levelled platform (z) which probably contains the foundations of more buildings. To the west of the hollow way (a) the land has largely been ploughed or redeveloped. Old aerial photographs record old building foundations (aa), and a length of ditch (bb). Just to the west of this feature, soil marks have revealed the former extent of the village. There is a fragment of a 16th century building (cc), probably the remnant of a manor house belonging to the Dand family. North of Frisby House, across the lane, is an old gravel pit (dd). (Site surveyed Easter 1981, additional field visit August 2014)

GALBY (or GAULBY)

Anyone interested in understanding the historical development of Galby village should consult the fascinating essay "Galby and Frisby" by W. G.Hoskins (1950, 24-66).

Open Fields
Mill Field is mentioned in the 16th century, east of the village and north of the road to Frisby. (VCH, 99). There were probably three fields, enclosed by private agreement between the freeholders in the early 17th century (Hoskins 1950, 43).

Village Earthworks (fig 82)   SK698010
The village is clearly less populated than it once was. There were about 32 families in 1086 and 1381, but then there was a striking fall in the numbers to about 14 families in 1563. (*op cit* 35).
Earthworks at the east end of this village were surveyed in September 1980 in advance of planned ploughing. The survey recorded an outlying block of village earthworks, with a building platform (a) on a terrace, more terraces at (b) and (c), and building platforms at (d) and (e) on two further terraces. The field next to Tamborough Farm had three more more platforms (f), (g) and (h).Ten or more houses have clearly existed in this area at various times in the past.
The village has not been enlarged in recent times, but there has been considerable redevelopment within existing plots along the west side. The fields in the centre of the village still contain building platforms (i, j, k,and probably l). There is an old enclosure west of St. Peter's Church, possibly the site of the medieval rectory,and quite a deep gravel pit (m), to the south of the churchyard.

Moat (fig 83)   SK696004
This small moat, with a platform 25m by 10m, lies by the stream south of the village. Although once thought to be a "homestead moat" it is clearly identified on the Galby Tithe Map as being a decoy, presumably to attract wild ducks to land and allow them to be shot. The site was surveyed on October 22nd 1980.

Water Mill   SK693003?
There was a mill valued at 2 shillings in 1086, and in 1429 a new mill was to be built on the Milne Holme by Roger Bache, a miller from Scraptoft (VCH, 99). The most likely site would seem to be about 400m west of the moat above, in a field called "Dams" on the Tithe Map. It had been replaced by the windmill (below) by 1610 (Hoskins 1950, 30).

Windmill
A windmill is mentioned in the 16th century (VCH, 99).

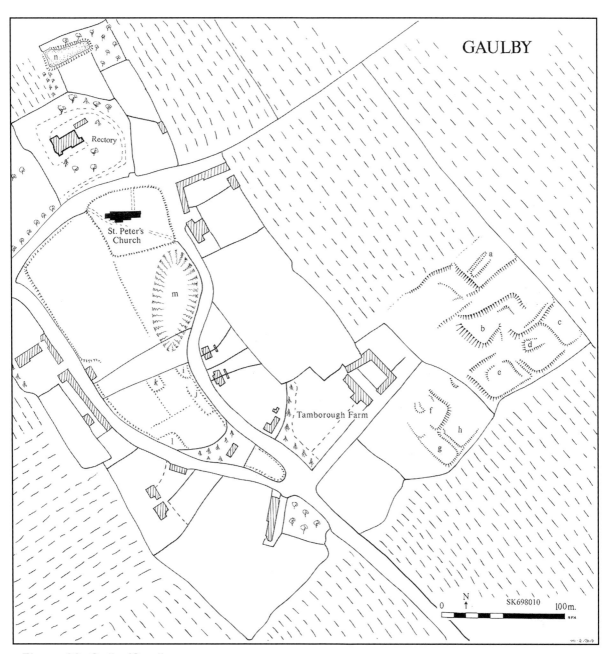

Figure 82: Galby/Gaulby

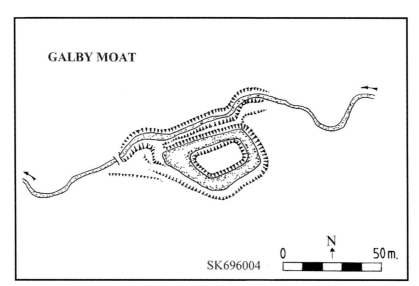

Figure 83: Galby/Gaulby Moat

GOADBY

Open Fields

The fields were partially enclosed by 1515 by Thomas Hazlerigg of Noseley, with the process being completed in 1677. In 1601 there were North Field, East Field (later Towards Keythorpe Field) and West Field (later Towards Noseley Field). In 1677 there were four fields;- North, Keythorpe, Rolleston, and South or Nether (VCH, 17).

Village Earthworks   SP750987

There are slight earthworks in the grounds of The Laurels and the two properties just to the east. The chapel of St. John was founded as a manorial chapel in the late 12th or early 13th century.

Ponds   SP761979

Peek & Parsons noted a series of ponds made along the bottom of a narrow valley here (Peek & Parsons 1972)

Mound   SP758981

"A small mound which ancient ploughing has accentuated." (op cit).

GREAT GLEN

Open Fields

In 1674 there were three fields: Stackley Field, Middle Field and Highway Field. The north end of the parish was enclosed in 1758, and the south end in 1759 (VCH,104).

Village Earthworks South (fig 84)   SP656972

At the south end of the village is a raised rectangular area (a) with traces of building foundations, and a building platform (b) just to the north. To the west are at least two more building platforms (d, e), and a slightly raised area, probably building foundations (f). The street continues southwards into the fields as a hollow way (g). (Survey, Summer 1990)

Village Earthworks North (fig 85)   SP653978

At the northern end of the medieval village is a sub-circular block of land enclosed by a bank

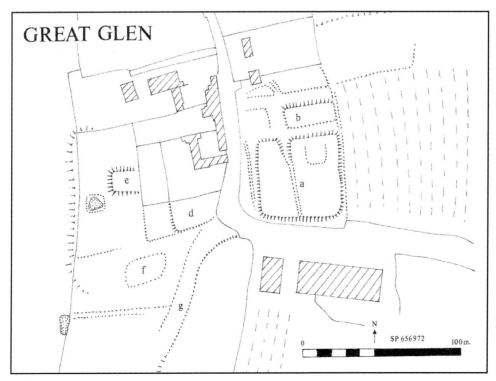

GREAT GLEN

SP 656972   100 m.

Figure 84:
Great Glen,
South

and ditch (a-a). To the south is a more rectilinear area, with St. Cuthbert's Church at the west end, then the Vicarage, then an area of earthwork remains, including a substantial building platform (b), with four or five more platforms around it. Further east is an area of old closes (c). To the south, across the stream, are more earthworks including an irregular building platform (d). Great Glen was granted a Monday market in 1272 and a yearly fair of three days embracing St. Cuthbert's Day. The markets and fair had been abandoned by 1792 (VCH, 105).

Water Mill and Windmill

A water mill is mentioned in 1086, 1265 and 1521. A windmill is mentioned in 1352 and 1563 (VCH, 105).

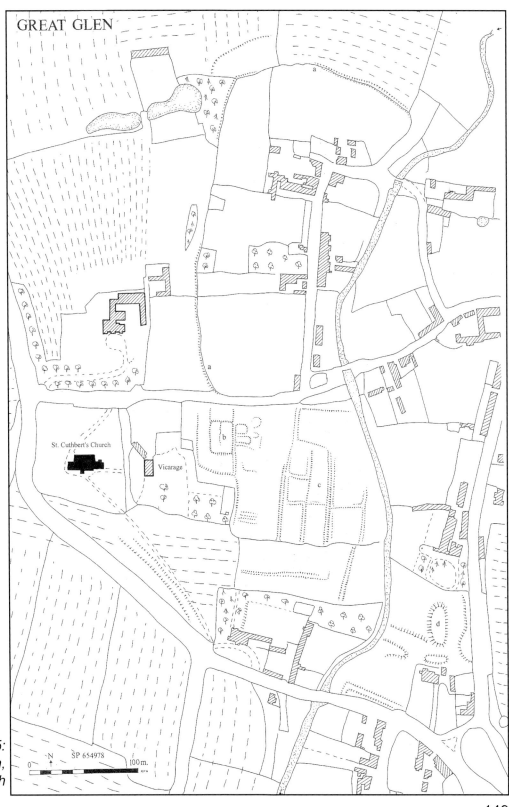

Figure 85: Great Glen, North

GREAT STRETTON

Open Fields

Some enclosure was carried out shortly before 1500. *"The open fields which remained seem to have been enclosed between 1640 and 1670, and the parish register shows a marked fall of population during the same period."* (Hoskins 1956, 42).

Village Earthworks (fig 86)   SK657003

One farm and the Church of St. Giles survive at this remarkably evocative site, less than five miles from Leicester Station. It lies alongside the Roman Gartree Road, which cuts past in a deep (and with modern traffic, hazardous) hollow way. The records of its history are few, and in places combined with those for Little Stretton. Hoskins considered that there were ten families in 1381, almost certainly a reduction from its population forty years previously (*op cit*). By 1563 there were 15 households, but only five in 1670, since when it has remained practically depopulated.

The lane to the church is visible as a hollow way (a) and at the church yard it turns eastwards (b), before taking another turn towards the south (c).

The whole south end of the village is a roughly rectangular manorial site, with an approach lane (d) to a forecourt area (e) which is surrounded by terraces and the sites of outbuildings. There must have been some sort of gatehouse and bridge (of which no trace is visible) onto the north side of the moated platform (f) which is packed with building foundations. There are old enclosures, probably gardens to the east of the moat and an orchard to the west , and two fishponds, (g) and (h). A mound (i) on the corner of the moat is probably a 16th/17th century prospect mound to give views over the gardens although Everson (2010, 58) considers it could also be a dovecot. For additional discussion and simplified plan see Everson (*op cit*).

Returning to the Gartree Road, a rectangular block of complex earthwork remains extends alongside it, with sites of buildings at (j, k, l, m, n, o, p, q, r, s, t, u, v, w, x, y), and probably elsewhere. Just south of the churchyard there appears to be another building platform (z) which underlies the ridge and furrow, suggesting it was abandoned at a very early date. There are more earthworks on the north side of the Gartree Road around the site of another building (aa). (Site surveyed 29th & 30th March, 1984).

HALSTEAD

Open Fields

Halstead's open fields have left evidence in the form of ridge and furrow but documentary sources are not in evidence.

Village earthworks (fig 87 overleaf)   SK750056

Halstead looks today like a part of Tilton on the Hill, but it is a completely separate village and parish. An access lane (a-a) off the Tilton-Oakham road leads to a sub-circular area of village earthworks, around (b), with probable sites of buildings (c) and (d). This area is on the summit of a hill. The remainder of the village is rectilinear in layout and extends along the road (e-e) which is in a hollow way in places, and which follows the crest of a ridge to Halstead House Farm before descending in a north-easterly direction towards Owston.

Starting at the west of Halstead village, there is an old enclosure (f) and another (g) on the east side of the lane (a). Going east, there are two old enclosures (h, i) with ridge and furrow evident within them, then two more enclosures on the north side of the lane (j, k), and several more on the south side (l, m, n, o, p, q). There are two hollows in area (m), suggesting that former buildings may have been removed, and a small terrace by (n) may also have been the site of a building. Another old enclosure (r) lies in the angle of the road junction, and buildings and enclosures (tofts and crofts) extend westwards from there to another abandoned croft at (s). There is another terrace, probably a building platform, east of the gravel pit at (t) and another levelled area, perhaps relatively recent. (Plan from aerial photos and site visit, August 2014.)

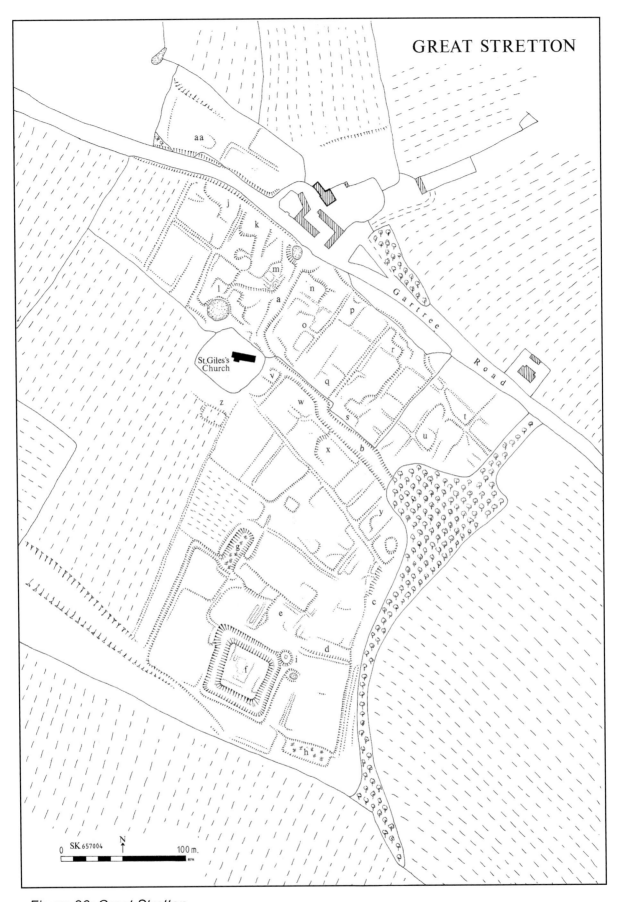

Figure 86: Great Stretton

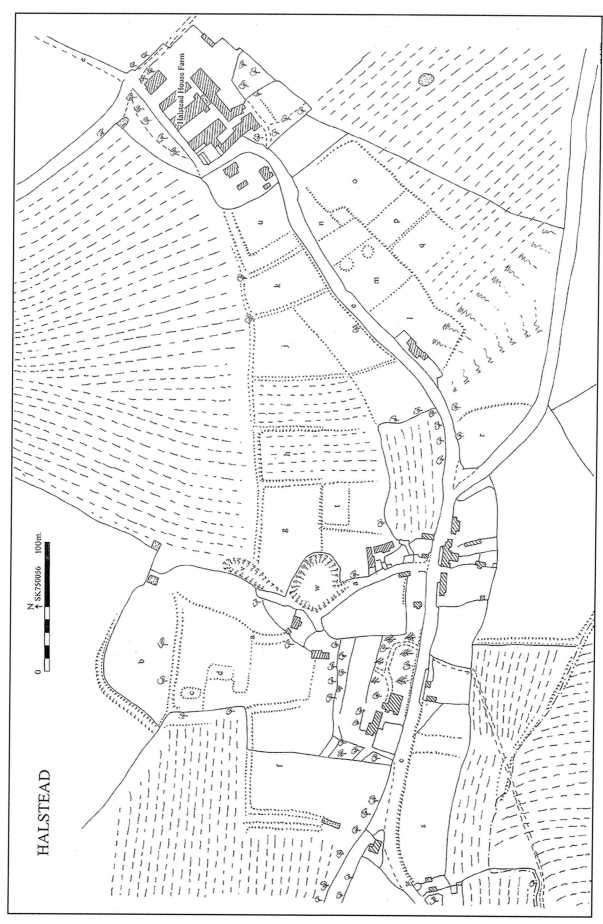

HALSTEAD

Figure 87: Halstead

HOUGHTON ON THE HILL

Open Fields

Much of the open field system remained in use until the 18th century, when the three fields, Brook Field, Mill Field and Middle Field were inclosed in 1765 (VCH, 159-160).

Fish Pond (fig 88)   SK 676032

The short lane alongside Houghton Rectory continues as a hollow way (a-a) down to the stream which has been partly straightened (b-b) and partly culverted (c-c). A short distance downstream there is a substantial earthen dam (d), which would have retained a pool of water extending approximately to the dotted line (e). The pond had a by-pass channel (f) allowing it to be drained when required, and east of this is a rectangular embanked enclosure (g) with faint earthworks. Just downstream of the dam is a small area (h) enclosed by a ditch containing faint ridges. This seems to have been created to cultivate plants, possibly willow saplings to make baskets. Back near the village is a building platform (i), indicating the former edge of the village, and two more mounds, (j) and (k) possibly the sites of more buildings, and another mound (l), either foundations of a fairly recent building, or a spoil tip. The hollow way (a) was replaced, probably in the 19th century, by a track (m-m-m), apparently to allow the creation of a small sub-circular pond (n). The fish pond probably dates from the 15th-17th century period, while the small pond (m) seems to have been created in the 19th century, after the abandonment of the original large pond. (Sketch survey, 18th December 2014)

Pillow Mound   SK685024

A low mound reported by C.E. Allin

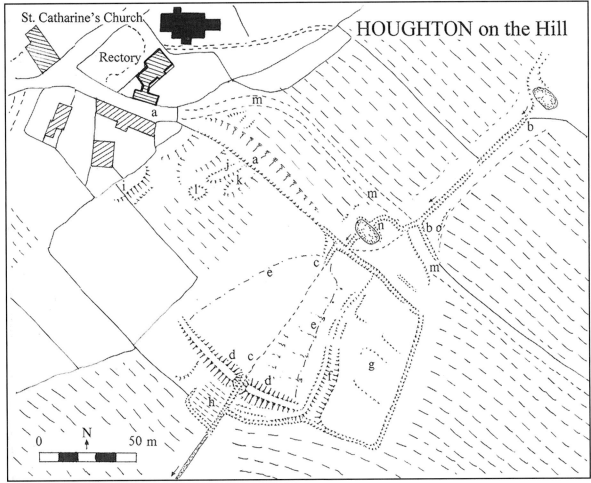

Figure 88: Houghton on the Hill

Windmill

A windmill is mentioned in 1308. One was demolished during the First World War and its stones used in the village war memorial. Houghton Windmill (Disused) is marked at this point alongside Ingarsby Lane on the 1st Edition OS 6" to 1 mile map. It was levelled by ploughing in the mid 20th century (VCH, 160).

HUNGERTON (or HUNGARTON)

Open Fields

There were three open fields in 1612: East, West and North. Baggrave, Ingarsby and Quenby were enclosed at early dates and there is little documentary evidence, but plentiful field evidence in the form of ridge and furrow.

Hungerton Village Earthworks (fig 89)

Hungarton is pleasingly sited on a tumbling hillside in a small stream valley. The Parish Church of St. John the Baptist is on a platform (a) high above the adjacent street. To the east are two old enclosures (b, d) together called "Dovecote Close" on an 18th century map and further east still is a small wood containing the site (c) where the map marks the dovecote, indicating a circular building. It is not known whether this would have belonged to the Vicarage or to a vanished manor house in this area.

To the north, alongside the street, are two house platforms (e) and (f). West of the church is another area of village earthworks, with old enclosures (g), (h) and (i), slightly terraced on the hillside. Across the stream, in a field of magnificent ridge and furrow, are two ditched enclosures, (j) and (k), perhaps post-medieval livestock pens.

The 18th century map shows several houses of which no trace remains. They were sited at (l, m, n. o, p) and (q), down the main street, (r) and (s) at the west end of the village (t, u) and (v), on the lane down to the stream, and in a row along the lane below the church (w, x, y, z). (Site visit 23rd August 2014)

Baggrave Village Earthworks (fig 90 overleaf)

Baggrave was a hamlet of Hungerton, and possessed a chapel of its own. In the year 1500 the Abbot of Leicester enclosed his lands in Baggrave. *"Five farmhouses and two cottages were pulled down or left to fall into ruin"* (Hoskins 1956, 38). There may have been more enclosing of land in 1502-3, but shortly afterwards the hamlet was described as "desolate and laid waste". (Hoskins 1950, 80-81)

The only building surviving at Baggrave village is the Hall. The main (south) front dates from 1752, but behind this is a core of Tudor building (Willatts 1991, 11-13). In its immediate vicinity any trace of the village has been removed by landscaping of the gardens, but in the parkland to the south remains of the village emerge.

The main street (a-a) is an impressive, straight hollow way. At the south end of the village more hollow ways show where lanes diverged to east and west (b-b). Just north of this junction is a moated manor house site, with a platform approximately 25m x 12m, on which are slight earthwork traces of buildings (c). On the north side of the moat is a probable forecourt area (d), with a platform (e) showing the site of outbuildings extending alongside the main street, while to the west is a small fishpond (f). There is another small fishpond further north at (g). From here northwards, building foundations extend continuously for over 200m along both sides of the hollow way. There are foundations of stone buildings at (h) and (j), and a substantial terrace at (k) with another small pond immediately to the north. The building platforms continue to (l). On the east side of the hollow way there is a house platform at (m), three small platforms at (n), and another at (o), with a further fishpond in the croft behind it at (p). There is a house platform at (q), and once more a fishpond in the croft behind it (r), this time extending along the eastern boundary of the plot. There are sites of two more buildings at (s) and (t), with yet another small pond (u). At the south-west corner of the site, and just outside the main block of the village, is another building platform (v). (Site surveyed 20th-22nd March 1989, note that this plan is not oriented with north at the top.)

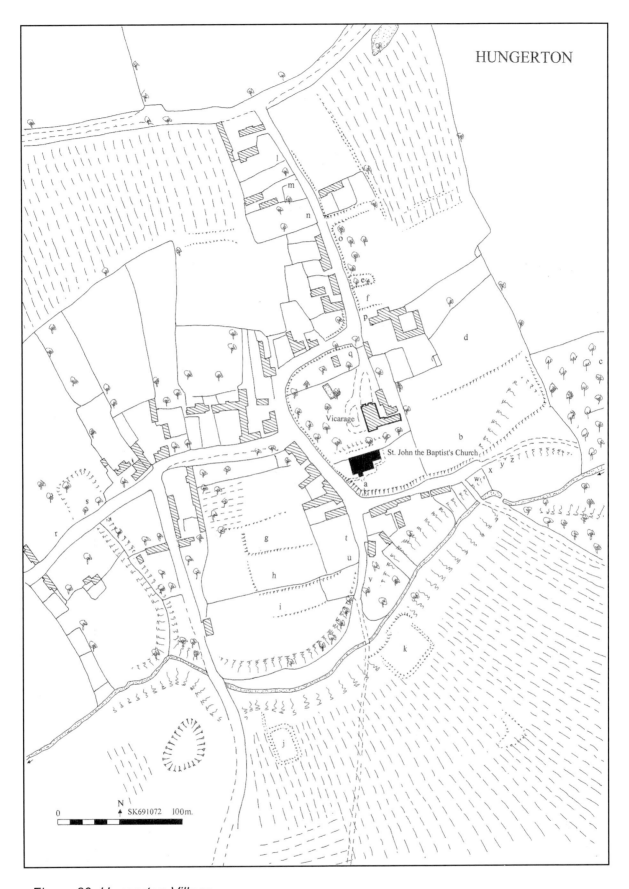

HUNGERTON

Vicarage

St. John the Baptist's Church

N
SK691072   100m.
0

Figure 89: Hungerton Village

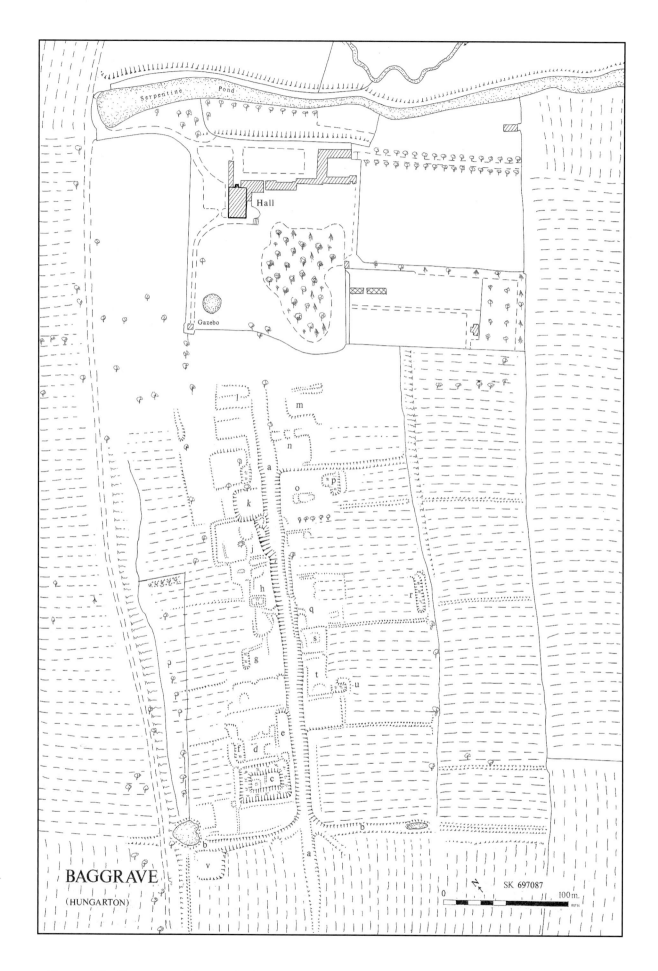

Figure 90: Baggrave (Hungerton)

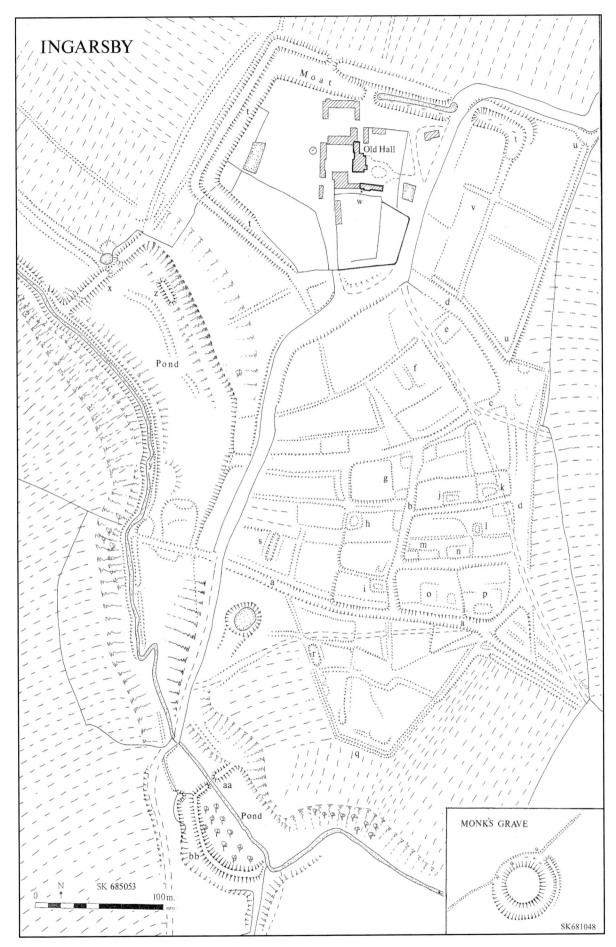

Figure 91: Ingarsby and Monks Grave, Hungerton

Ingarsby Village earthworks (fig 91 previous page)
SK685053

This is perhaps the most famous of Leicestershire's deserted villages, and somewhat unusual in that we know it was enclosed and depopulated by the canons of Leicester Abbey in the process of turning their Grange Farm into a modern and profitable sheep farm in the late 15th century. It was a large village in 1086, with a recorded population of 32. Leicester Abbey was granted the manor in 1352, and had purchased the rest of the land by 1458 or shortly afterwards. In 1469 they enclosed the whole lordship with hedges and ditches and converted most of it to sheep and cattle pastures. (Hoskins 1956, 46; 1950, 75-79). The village may have declined at an early date, as it had a very low poll tax quota in 1334. Ingarsby Old Hall site continued in occupation after the Reformation though how much building survival there was is open to question. Recent work by Everson indicates that there may be a post-medieval component of the landscape as garden design laid out over and around the medieval earthworks such as viewing mounds and driveways (Everson, 2010, 52-56).

The lane from Houghton on the Hill to Hungerton runs through the village from south to north. A hollow way (a) leads eastwards, with a branch off north (b) joining another east-west lane (c). Another old lane (d) extends along the eastern edge of the village.

The area between Ingarsby Lane and the hollow ways (a) and (d) is packed full of earthwork evidence of the village, with building platforms at (e), (f) and (g), the foundations of stone buildings at (h, i, j, k, l, m, n), and sites of more buildings at (o) and (p). An additional area of earthworks, south of hollow way (a), is surrounded by a bank and ditch (q), in three very straight lengths, which seems later than the village. There is a small pond just inside the bank at (r), and another small pond north of the hollow way at (s). See also National Monuments Register/English Heritage aerial view ref NMR 21907/23, 2003, in Emerson (*op cit*). (Site survey 5th December 1989)

Ingarsby Old Hall

Ingarsby Old Hall stands on the site of the Abbot of Leicester's grange farm, with an impressive surviving late 15th century building (w). Alongside to the north is the Old Hall itself, which has a core of late 16th century work and an early 18th century facade. These buildings are surrounded on three sides by a massive moat (t), presumably dating from the 15th century. On the east side the moat is not in evidence, and there is a broadly rectilinear area, enclosed by a bank (u). This would seem likely to be a garden associated with the post-medieval development of the old Hall. The moat in this area may have been filled in, and the area levelled to create a formal garden with a parterre centred on (v).

In the valley bottom to the west is a substantial earthen dam (x), which would when in use have retained a pool of water stretching nearly to Ingarsby Lane. There is a by-pass channel (y) cut into the hillside on the west side of the pond, and a small mound (z), which would have formed an island in the lake, probably to keep ducks. Upstream beyond the lane is the site of another pond, with a dam (aa) and a bypass channel (bb). The general layout of these ponds, with their bypass channels, is similar to the monastic ponds at Owston Abbey (also surveyed in this volume), and it seems quite likely that they provided fish to be eaten both at the Grange Farm and by the community at Leicester Abbey but were repurposed as part of the garden design after the Dissolution. (Ponds surveyed September 1994)

Mound, "Monks Grave" (fig 91 previous page, inset)
SK681048

Some 500m south-west of Ingarsby village is an isolated mound called the "Monk's Grave", with a central platform some 25m in diameter, surrounded by a ditch 10m wide. This has been variously interpreted as a small fortified site, and as a rabbit warren, but its purpose is not yet ascertained. It may also be a remote viewing mound for the landscape of the gardens (*op cit*).

Quenby Hall and Village Earthworks (fig 92, fig 93 overleaf)
SK701062

Quenby Hall is a classic Jacobean brick mansion, of "H" plan, built between 1618 and 1630/1 (Pevsner & Williamson 2003, 211). It is on the site of the small hilltop village of Quenby, and is surrounded by earthwork evidence, most of which seems to relate to gardens created around the Hall in the 17th century. The Hall stands in the middle of a levelled rectangular platform with parterres (a). To the south is a series of features extending down the hillside, with a big terrace (b) followed by an ornamental moat (c), then two successive terraces (d) and an elongated pond or "canal" (e). Beyond this is another ornamental moat (f). To the west of terrace (b) is another levelled garden terrace (g), overlooked by a prospect mound (h). Further down the hillside is another area of former gardens (i), containing a small pond (j), and beyond this is a larger enclosed area (k), perhaps once a plantation.

The main drive to the Hall is flanked on its north side by remains of two ornamental ponds (l, m), and two more on the south side (n, o). A sunken track and a bridge (p), allowed access (presumably for servants and livestock) from one side to the other without crossing the avenue. At some date, probably in the 18th or 19th century, the ponds were drained, and in the case of (o), partly removed by a gravel pit (q). There is another gravel pit to the south (q), which is marked as such (and therefore perhaps still in use) on the 1904 Ordnance Survey maps. South-west of the Hall is another area of earthworks (r), probably also part of the gardens.

Between the two gravel pits are some features which might relate to the medieval village, with a hollow way (s), flanked by platforms at (t) and (u). However even these could well be garden terraces, leaving us with no definite archaeological evidence that there was a village here at all! It seems to have been a small settlement, with perhaps eight to ten families in 1377 "*and it never seems to have been any larger than this*" (Hoskins 1956, 50). (Surveyed 10th August 1983)

A diagram taken from a map of 1810 (overleaf) shows the wider setting of the hall with field boundaries and ponds but provides no further detail of any extant earthworks apart from indications of the ponds at (e) and (f).

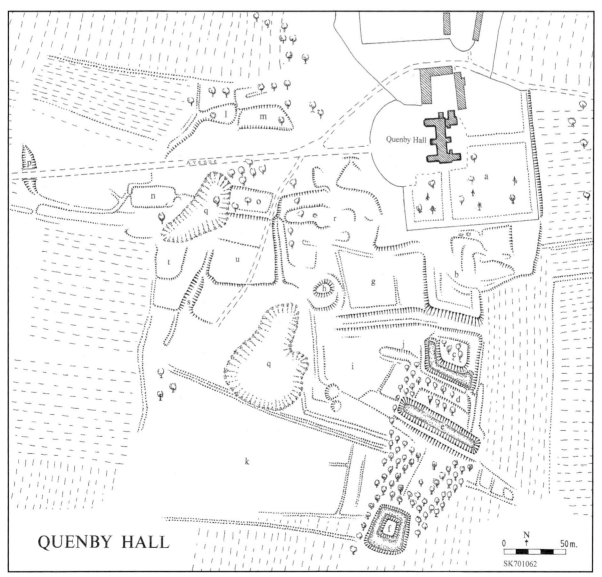

Figure 92: Quenby Hall Village Earthworks

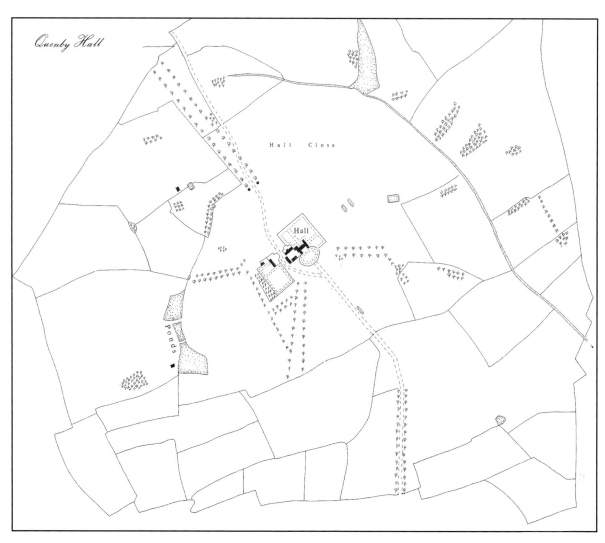

Figure 93: Quenby Hall grounds in 1810 taken from (poss ROLLR ref DE2687/71 Quenby Hall estate map) note orientation is different to Fig 92, north is to left.

Quenby Hall from Nichols 1800 (Vol 3, Pt 1, Pl XLIII, 297)

ILLSTON ON THE HILL

Open Fields
Illston was inclosed in 1788, without an Act (Beresford 1949, 121). Some enclosure took place in 1614. (VCH, 165)

Village Earthworks (fig 94 overleaf)

SP708994

The village extends along a street (a-a), which continues to the east as a hollow way (b). There is a well-defined back lane on the south side of the village (c-c), which follows the crest of the ridge, giving fine views across the south of the county. John Throsby (1790, 323) said, "*The village stands on a hill, in a fine air, over-looking a country stocked with excellent sheep and oxen. Here are about 30 dwellings.*" This is linked to the main street by a short hollow way (d), which extended further to the north-west as (e).

At the western tip of the village is very small moated site (f), with a platform only 15m by 5m, which has no evidence of building foundations. This seems too small to have enclosed a manor house, but may have been part of the gardens of such a house on the substantial building platform (g), just to the east. Throsby (*op cit,* 324) also reports "*The house which was occupied by the Needhams is nearly in ruin; a part of it is occupied by a farmer or grazier.*" On the west side of the "moat" is a fishpond (h). Around this on the west and north sides there used to be several building platforms (i, j, k, l, m), in a field which has been levelled by ploughing in recent years. If there were indeed a manor house at (g), the other features could perhaps be explained as gardens, ponds, farm and outbuildings.

Near St. Michael's Church are two building platforms (n) and (o), and to the south, opposite the Fox & Goose pub, is a field with slight terraces at (p) and (q), probably indicating the site of buildings. To the west is the current Manor House, with a walled garden (r). (Site visit 15th August 2014)

Illston on the Hill Church from Nichols 1798 (Vol 2, Pt 2 Pl XCV, 552)

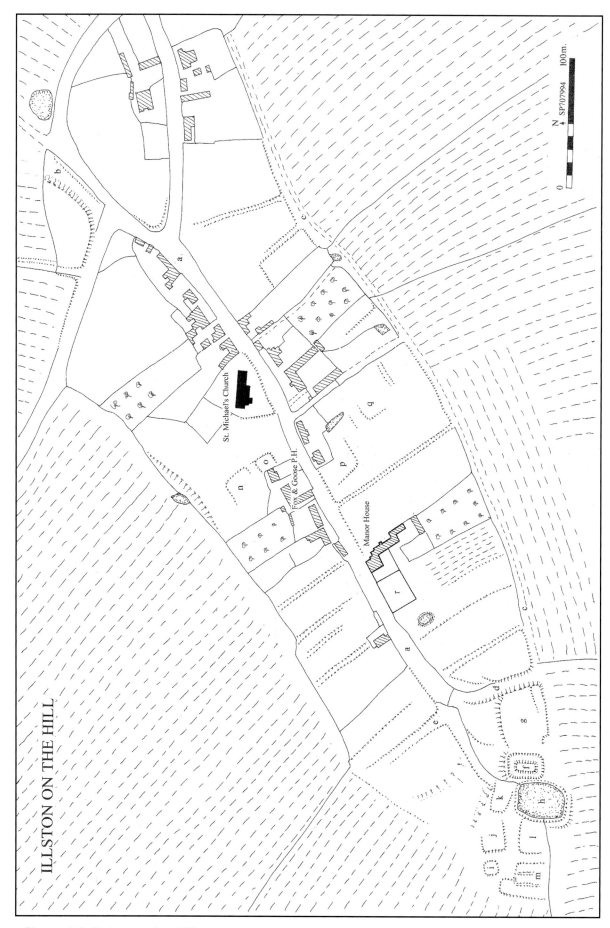

ILLSTON ON THE HILL

St. Michael's Church

Fox & Goose P.H.

Manor House

N SP707994

0 100 m.

Figure 94: Illston on the Hill

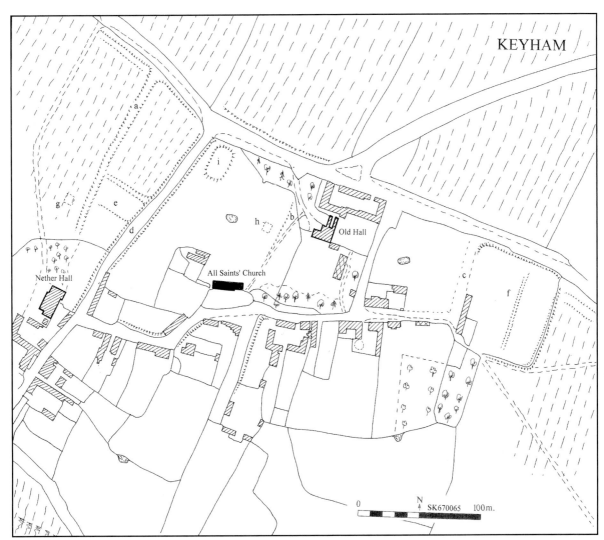

Figure 95: Keyham

KEYHAM

Open Fields
Keyham was enclosed during the period 1730 - 1850 (Beresford 1949, Plate 2).

Village Earthworks (fig 95)   **SK670065**
The layout of the village streets of Keyham shows evidence of being changed in the post-medieval period. Traffic now uses Snows Lane (d), rather than than the route at (a) which survives only as a hollow way. This may have been arranged to improve the privacy of the Nether Hall. Another old lane at (b) which is clearly shown on an 18th century map, (ROLLR 44'28/1359) has been closed off to improve the amenity of the gardens around the Old Hall. At the east end of the village there was another lane at (c), marked on the 18th century map, which had vanished by the end of the 19th century. The focus of the village seems to have moved away from the eastern end, and King's Lane, just east of the Old Hall, has sufficed to provide access for it. This decline is also indicated by the earthworks of an old close (f).
There is a slight platform at (e), possibly indicating the site of a croft.
The 18th century map marks the sites of two vanished dovecotes. One at (g) is the site of a dovecote belonging to the Nether Hall, and there used to be another at (h), by the Old Hall. A raised platform at (i) may be the site of another vanished building. (Site visit 23rd August 2014).

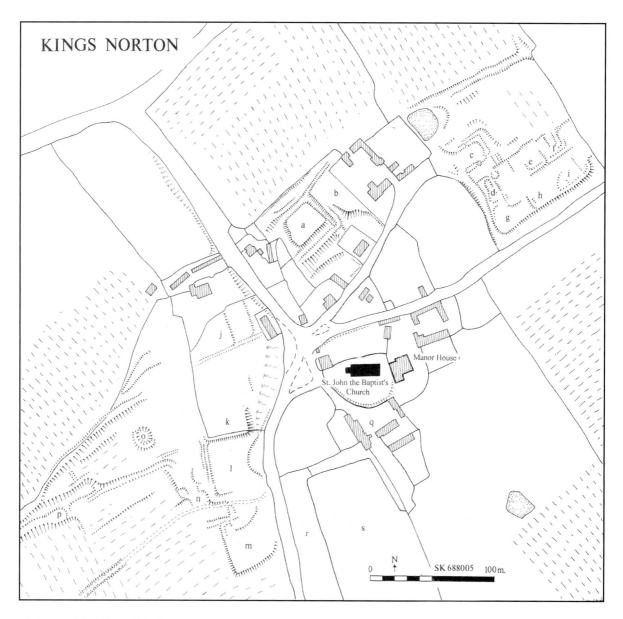

Figure 96: Kings Norton

KINGS NORTON

Open Fields

West, South and North Fields are recorded in 1360. In 1635 these had become Brig, Scockerhill and Middle Fields, and by 1638 Marr, Carlton Gate and Middle Fields (VCH, 258).

Village Earthworks (fig 96)   SK690007

Just north of the centre of the village is a large building platform (a), probably the site of a manor house, with a ditch, possibly a narrow moat, surrounding it. To the east at (b) is another platform, perhaps for outbuildings.

At the east end of the village is a rectangular close, more than half of which has earthwork evidence of demolished buildings. There are foundations of stone buildings at (c, d, e, f), and platforms at (g, h, i). There is evidence of several more vanished crofts on the west side of the village, with platforms at (j, k, l, m). An intriguing area of earthworks extends on to the west, with several small building platforms at (n), an embanked circular pond (o), and banks extending west from (p), probably plough headlands and an old track into the open fields.

The Manor House, which Pevsner describes as having a "*late 17th century parlour wing*" (Pevsner & Williamson 2003, 191), stands east of the church yard, which is considerably raised up above the surrounding land. William Fortrey (d.1722) is said to have demolished "*the old*

164

hall-house of Norton" with the intention of building a new one, but to have only completed the offices (presumably the outbuildings) before his death (VCH, 257, quoting Nichols, Vol II, Pt 2, 733, fn2). These buildings stood to the south of the church (q), and on the 1840s Tithe Map (ROLLR ref Ti/166/1), gardens are marked extending southwards from here, with a Yew Plantation alongside the road at (r) and a parterre with two ponds at (s). There is no obvious earthwork evidence of these features. (Surveys 26th Oct 1980 and additional site visit 15 August 2014)

Windmill
A windmill is mentioned in 1514 (VCH, 259).

LAUNDE

Open Fields
The parish was enclosed at an early date, before 1550 (Beresford 1949, Plate 1). Part of it is shown on the 1586 map of Whatborough (this volume, part 3, Frontispiece, bottom right hand side), with notes such as *"these lands do seem to have been arable"*, indicating that all of the northern part of the parish was entirely enclosed by that date. There is in fact good evidence of ridge and furrow across most of the parish.

Launde Abbey (fig 97)   SK797043
Launde was the site of an Augustinian Priory, founded by Richard and Maude Bassett before 1125, and converted to a mansion house in the 16th century (Liddle & O'Brien 1995, 2). At some date subsequently this house became known as Launde Abbey.

The north side of the present house incorporates the chancel and fragments of the transept arch of the monastic church. There are building foundations extending through (a), and geophysical surveys (Beavitt, 1995) have revealed the pattern of the claustral buildings to the west of the present house. There are earthwork remains, possibly of medieval buildings, around (b), while to the north at (c) is an old enclosure which is defined by the edge of the open fields and is therefore presumably medieval. (Evidence is from soil marks as this area has been ploughed). Most medieval monastic sites have fishponds to supply the community with fresh fish, and Launde is no exception. Only one, (d), of those near the house still contains water. There are earthwork remains of three more ponds (e, f, g) surrounding the north and east sides of the Abbey, and two (h) and (i) extending northwards down the valley bottom. All of these ponds could have been created for the monastery, but (f) and (g) have probably at least been modified to form part of the post-medieval garden scheme around the house (j).

There is much evidence of landscaping of the park, with an avenue (k) extending westwards from the front of the house, to an area of terraces, presumably gardens, around (m). A large park bank (n), probably post-medieval, extends southwards, cutting through an earlier (perhaps medieval) park bank at (o). East of the house is a wide garden terrace (p), and another one (q), flanking the pond (g). A broad, raised path (r) runs between these parterres to give access to the walled garden. These features were probably created during the 16th-18th century period. At the north of the site is a large pond (s), probably of 18th century date, built along the valley side. On the east side of pond (h) is an 18th century ice house. (Surveyed, 21st & 23rd March 1984)

Deer Park   SK804045
Launde Park Wood is thought to indicate the site of the medieval deer park, but its original shape is not yet clear. There is a bank extending east-west through the narrow point in the middle of the wood, and continuing westwards to form the southern boundary of the present parkland. Another bank extends along the southern edge of Launde Park Wood and continues westwards along the parish boundary. Launde Big Wood has earth banks on its north and south sides and also appears to be ancient woodland (Site visit 10th January 1985). The Park Wood is mentioned in documents from 1248, and the West Wood (or Big Wood) from 1540 (Squires 1995, 93). The park is also shown on Saxton's map of 1576 (Cantor 1970-1, 21).

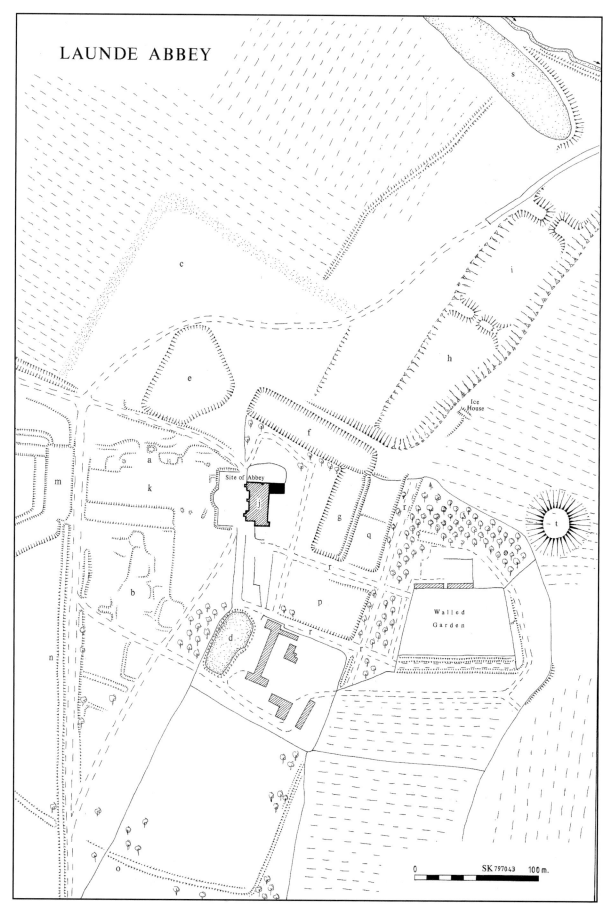

Figure 97: Launde Abbey

Mound (fig 97)

SK800044

A mound, (t) approx 2m high and 45-60m across, was recorded by the Ordnance Survey. This is an interesting feature, as it partially underlies the ridge and furrow, with the plough ridges extending up the slopes of the mound. This implies that the mound was created over 1000 years ago, and could in fact be of prehistoric origin.

Mound

SK791047

North-west of Launde Abbey, in a bend in the road, is a circular mound with a platform about 4m in diameter. This was surveyed by the O.S. (site ref SK70SE/3) and is probably a windmill mound.

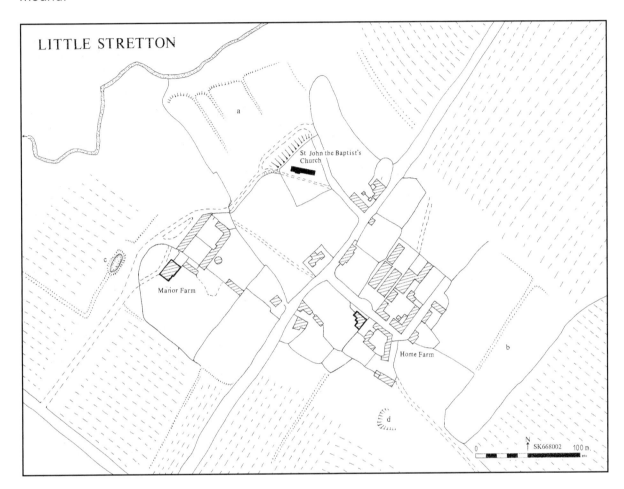

Figure 98: Little Stretton

LITTLE STRETTON

Open Fields

Little Stretton is mentioned in connection with the Nether Field of Great Stretton in 1674. Beresford suggests that the Nether Field may actually have lain in the parish of Little Stretton. (Beresford 1949, 113).

Village Earthworks (fig. 98)

Remains of old closes have been noted west of St. John's Church (a), and east of Home Farm (b). There is a small pond (c) west of Manor Farm, and an old quarry pit at (d).

Windmill

A windmill is noted in 1314 and 1446 (VCH, 263).

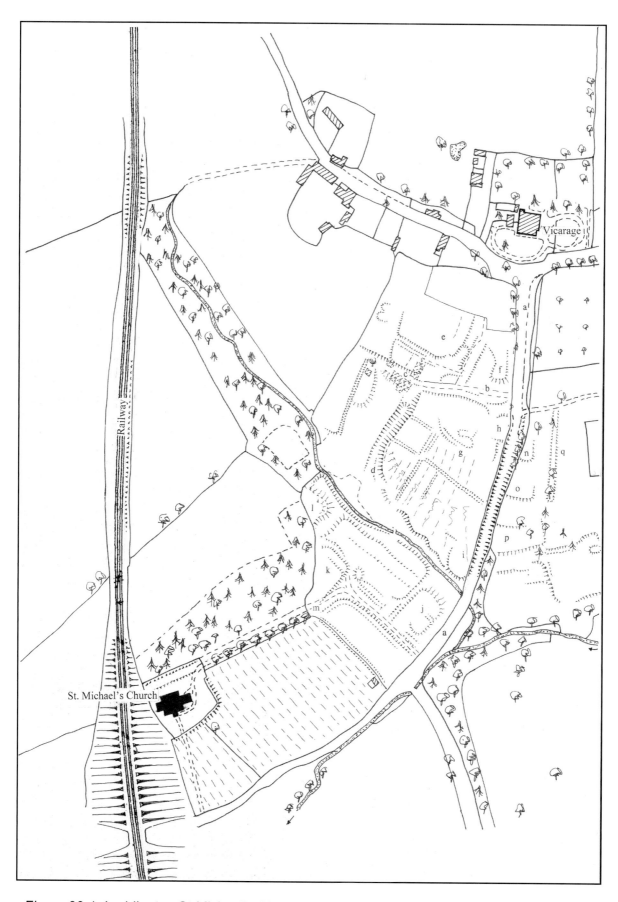

Figure 99.1: Loddington St Michael's Church

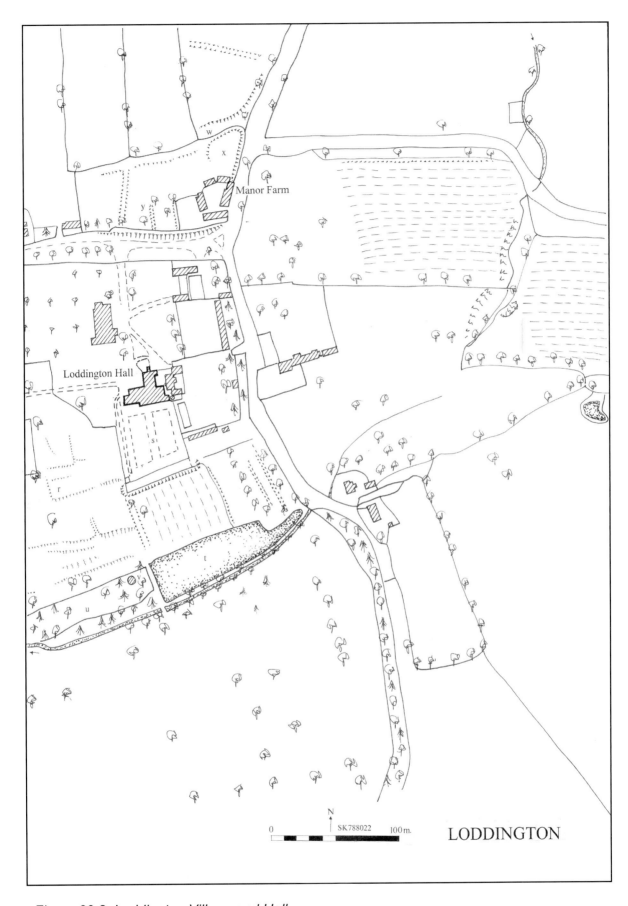

Manor Farm

Loddington Hall

N

0   SK788022   100 m.

LODDINGTON

Figure 99.2: Loddington Village and Hall

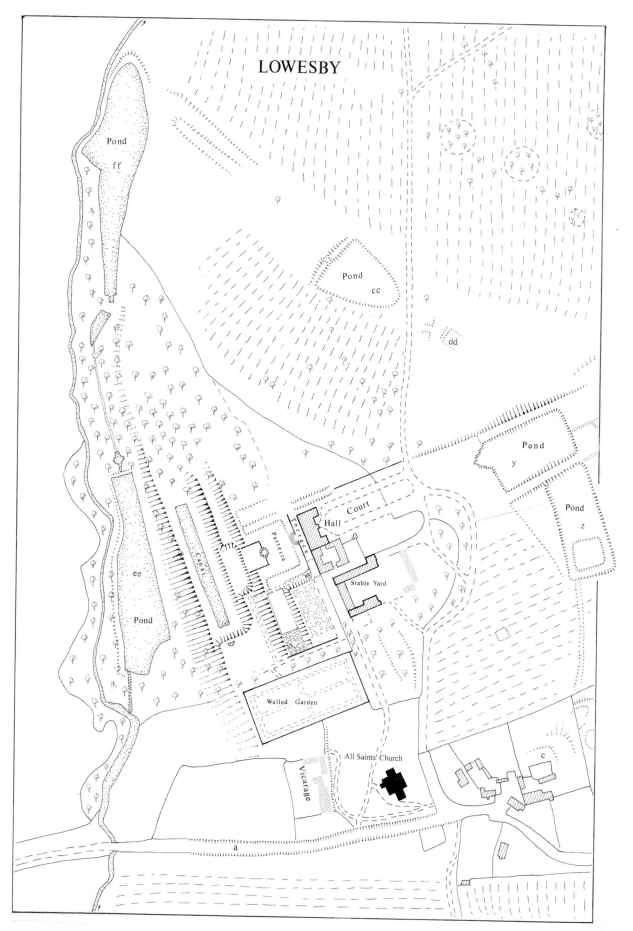

Figure 100.1: Lowesby Hall, gardens and church

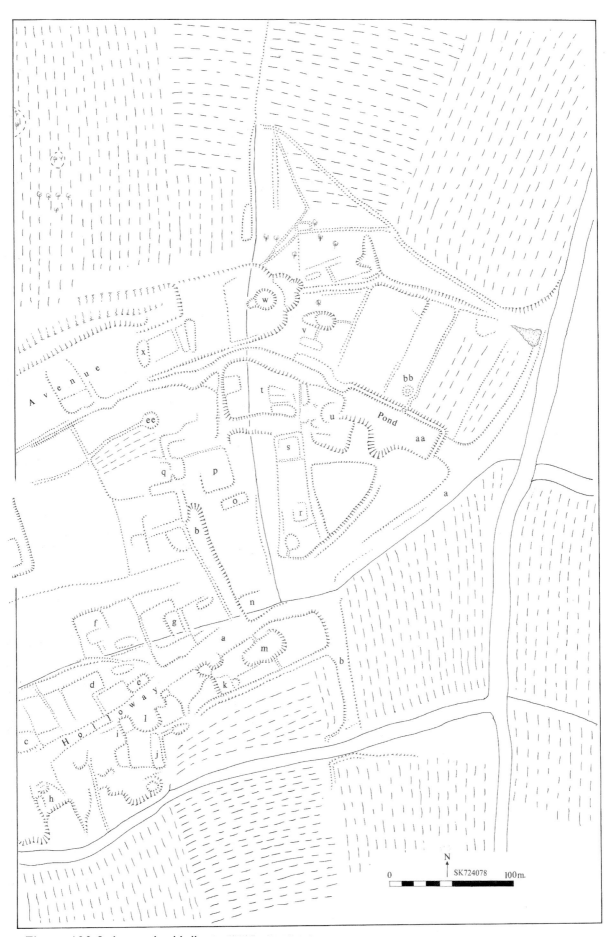

Figure 100.2: Lowesby Holloways

LODDINGTON

Open Fields
Final enclosure of the open fields here took place in 1625-46 (Beresford 1949, 121).

Village Earthworks, Hall Gardens and Fish Ponds (figs 99.1 & 99.2)   SK790021
A deep hollow way (a) extends southwards down the hillside from the vicarage on the present main street, towards the isolated site of St. Michael's Church (figure 99.1). The fields on either side have considerable earthwork evidence of the former extent of the village. A track (b) leads westwards to the site of a house and outbuildings (c) which were still in use in the 1880s. From there a hollow way (d) leads down to the stream, and the track probably used to continue across and lead directly to the church. The hollow way (d) seems once to have extended back northwards towards the vicarage, passing between an old close (e), and the site of a building platform (f). Further down the slope are more building foundations at (g), and below these the field has evidence both of early ridge and furrow and also of later subdivision into small closes. The present lane, in the hollow way (a), may be later than (d), but nevertheless is flanked by terraced platforms indicating former sites of buildings at (h. i, n, o, p).

Beyond the stream there is another, fairly large, building platform (j), and beyond it is the carriage drive (m) to St. Michael's Church. This was probably created in the 19th century to give an improved and more impressive approach to the church, which stands in a curious location in the corner of a furlong of ridge and furrow, encroached upon by the graveyard. There is no earthwork evidence north of the church to suggest any continuity of the village to this point, but back towards the east there are two substantial building platforms (k, l) above the stream.

To the east of hollow way (a) lie the grounds of Loddington Hall (fig. 99.2), with traces of former gardens extending down to the stream. Parallel to (a) is a tree-lined bank (q), probably once the western boundary of the Hall gardens, screening off the cottages at (n), (o) and (p). A garden terrace (r), extends west from the surviving walled garden (s). South of it are traces of at least two more terraces, which could indicate the sites of village buildings, or could be more post-medieval garden features. One of the two long ponds (or "canals") is drained (u), while the other (t) is still water-filled. There is a small garden-house at (v). Traces of a back lane at (w) behind Manor Farm run north of two probable house platforms at (x) and (y). Loddington Hall is a house of mainly late 17th century date (Pevsner & Williamson 2003, 278). (Sites surveyed 25th May and 8th June 2011)

LOWESBY

Open Fields
The village was enclosed in the late 15th century.

Village Earthworks (figs 100.1 & 100.2)   SK724078
The Domesday Survey of 1086 records 19 families in Lowesby, but it seems to have gone into decline not long afterwards, as there were only twelve farming households in 1309, and perhaps eight to ten families in 1377. "It was enclosed by the Ashbys about 1487 and immediately converted to pastures for sheep and cattle." (Hoskins 1956, 48). This means it would have ceased to exist as a village before 1500, but the earthworks are nevertheless impressive.

From near to the surviving All Saints Church the main street of the village can be traced eastwards as a hollow way (a), with more old lanes branching off to north and south (b-b). On either side of (a) for about 200 metres is a continuous area of earthwork remains, with the most obvious house sites at (c, d, e, f, g, h, i, j, k, n). There are also two hollowed-out areas (l) and (m) which could be crew-yards to house the livestock in winter. Another area of old buildings lies around the northern end of hollow way (b), with more building platforms (o, p, q). To the east are more sites of buildings at (r, s, t) and around (u). This area is flanked on the north side by another hollow way, largely remodelled by the creation of a post-medieval pond (aa). To the north, around (bb) is an area of rectilinear closes, probably also part of the village, with another hollow way along the north side.

Lowesby Hall was rebuilt both in the 17th and the early 18th centuries, including the creation of magnificent formal gardens. A grand avenue was laid out extending from the hall in a north-easterly direction, with a line of parterres and ponds, terminating at an elaborately-shaped area of parterre around a circular pond (w). This is on the crest of the slope with views to the east over a radiating pattern of features, with a long pond (aa, over the course of an earlier hollow way) extending eastwards, two small ponds, one shallow and one deep, at (v), and more features to the north.

The grand avenue was probably flanked by trees, which have long since gone, and consisted of a line of rectilinear garden plots or parterres, and ponds. Returning towards the Hall from the circular pond (w), there is an area of slight terraces or flower beds, then a small pond (x), a level parterre, some more slight terraces, another level parterre, and finally the large rectangular pond (y), which would have served to reflect (or "float") the vista, when seen from the first floor rooms of the Hall.

There was another large pond (z), containing an island, just south of pond (y). We have already noted another large rectilinear pond at (aa), and near to it are the foundations of a circular building (bb), perhaps a summer house or circular dovecote. North of the Hall is the site of another large ornamental pond (cc), and just to the south of it a small rectangular pond or tank (dd). In the valley bottom, extending alongside the stream, are two more large ponds (ee) and (ff), still water-filled.

The west front of the house has a terrace which extends southwards past a parterre and the walled gardens on the right, towards the church. Below this is another parterre, surrounded on three sides by a terrace walkway, then two more terraces, the bottom one of which contains a long pond or "canal".

After being given over to lawns and trees for many years, these terraces were restored and to some extent remodelled in the early 20th century under the supervision of the celebrated Edwardian garden designer Gertrude Jekyll. Two smaller terraces were created in the centre of the original ones, allowing visitors to descend from the Hall and the top terrace to the "canal" in easier stages. (Site surveyed 15th June 1989)

MAREFIELD

Open Fields
The fields were enclosed before 1550 (Beresford 1949, plate 1).

Village Earthworks (fig 101 overleaf)
In an area where so many villages have disappeared, Marefield, though always a tiny settlement, has been a stubborn survivor. The main street (a) is partly in a hollow way, and is crossed at right angles by another route, identified by hollow ways (b) and (c).

The east end of the village has gone out of use, with the site of a former building at (d), two substantial building terraces in the hillside at (e) and (f), and platforms of two more cottages at (g) and (h). Across the road at (i) is a linear bank. I am not sure if this is the site of more buildings, or the headland to the adjoining plough ridges.

Half way down the hillside between the village street and the stream must be a spring line, as there are three "perched ponds" cut into the slope; two long ones (j) and (k), and a smaller one (l) to the east. In each case a bank has been created on the down-slope side, to retain water in the pond. The village has also contracted from the west end, where there is evidence of a terrace at (m) within an old close. (Site visit 15th August 2014)

NOSELEY

Open Fields
In 1584 the names of the former open fields were recorded as Cotton's Field, Mill Field and Nether Field (VCH, 267).

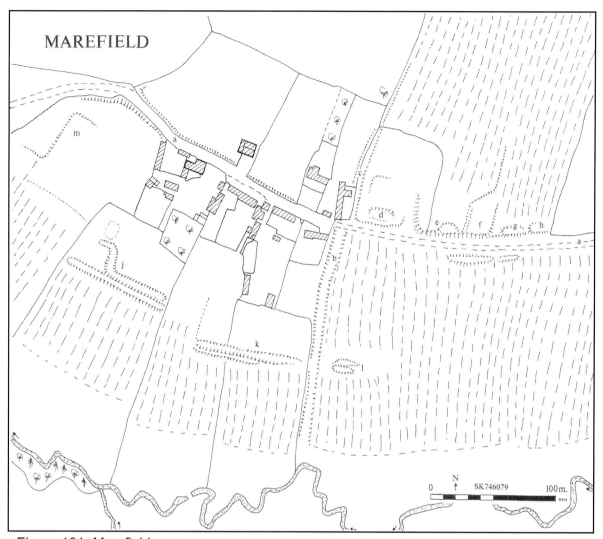

Figure 101: Marefield

Deserted Village and Landscaped Parkland (figs 102, 103) SP734986

Thomas Hazlerigg was accused in 1518 of having inclosed 11 farms and evicted most of the inhabitants in 1504-5 and 1508-9. Fifty-one people had been evicted and by 1517 the parish church was in ruins (Hoskins 1950, 86).

As noted above, the names of the open fields were still known in 1584, but by 1670 the Hall appears to have been the only house in the parish (VCH, 267). A later Hazlerigg, Sir Arthur (c1707-1763), went on a Grand Tour to Italy in 1723 and after his return set about rebuilding Noseley Hall and creating a formal garden and park around it (fig 103. plan of 1743 overleaf, Map viewed at Noseley Estate Office, 1990). The earthworks recorded around Noseley Hall (Fig. 102) are evidence both of the village and the park.

The old main street of Noseley is seen as a hollow way, curving down from the north-west towards St. Mary's Church and the Hall. Another hollow way (b) branches off west in the middle of the village. Along the east side of the main street (a) is a line of small closes, including identifiable sites of buildings at (c, d, e, f). On the west side of the street is a more typical block of medieval crofts, with probable sites of buildings at (g, h. i, j). There is a small fishpond (n) in one of the closes. South of the lane (b) are more building platforms, particularly at (k, l, m).

Turning now to the formal gardens, we have the assistance of the plan drawn up in 1743, which we can compare to the earthwork evidence. Along the south front of the Hall is a raised terrace, which still survives. South of this was a parterre (o), originally flanked by plantations, and beyond this a pond (p), now an irregular rectangle but shown in 1743 as cruciform in plan. To the south of it is another garden terrace (q). There is little trace of the avenue of trees leading south beyond this point, but the line of the parallel avenue just to the west is marked by the ridge (r-r) alongside the line of the original central path.

174

Figure 102: Noseley

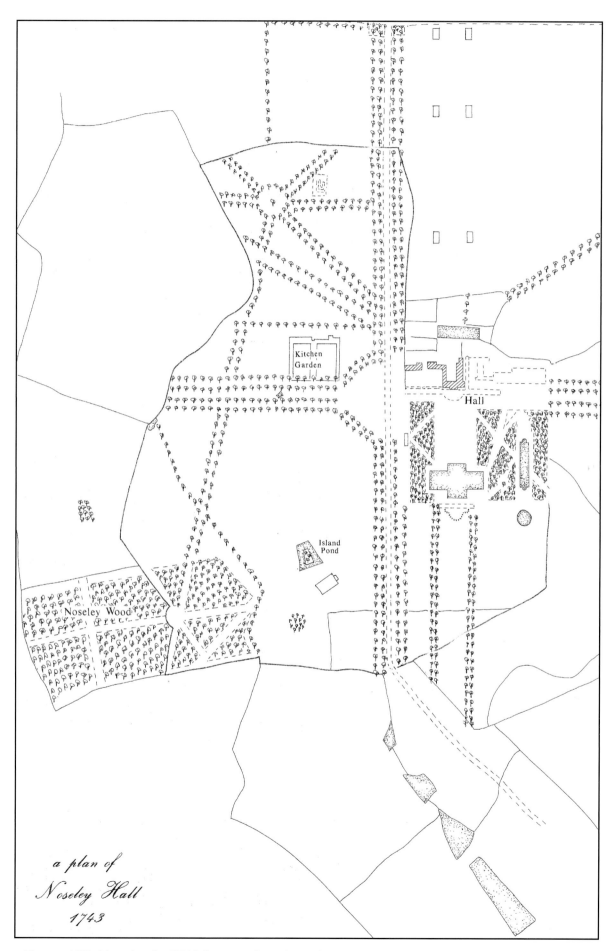

Kitchen
Garden

Hall

Island
Pond

Noseley Wood

a plan of
Noseley Hall
1743

Figure 103: Noseley in 1743 from a plan viewed at Noseley Estate Office, 1990.

The pattern of avenues as built must have differed somewhat from the plan, as more avenues survive as pairs of earthwork banks (s, t, u, v), where no avenues are indicated in 1743. However the Island Pond (w) still corresponds closely to the plan, and earthwork banks still mark the eastern boundary of Noseley Wood as it was in 1743. In the valley bottom further south the four ponds shown on the plan were all built, and remain water-filled apart from the bottom pond (x) which is a well-preserved earthwork.

There is no evidence for the double avenue heading west from the Hall, past the south side of the Kitchen Garden, but east of the Hall there is a rectangular terraced area at (z) where we would expect to have the starting point for the avenue towards the east. East of the cruciform pond, amongst the plantations, the 1743 plan shows a narrow ornamental pond or "canal". This survives to some extent as a less regularly-shaped pond, but the round pond marked further south on the plan appears today as a circular mound (y). (Survey c.1990, drawn here to a smaller scale than the other surveys)

Deer Park SP705983
A park was mentioned in an inquisition of 1278 when Anketin de Martivail '*died seized of a park and free warren at Noseley*' (Nichols 1798, 739). Cantor identifies this with the "Old Park" name on OS maps at the above reference (Cantor 1970-1, 23).

Windmill Mound SP729993
The mill is marked on Prior's map of Leicestershire, and there is a note in VCH, 267.

OWSTON

Open Fields
The fields were enclosed during the period 1550-1750 (Beresford 1949, plate 1).

Village Earthworks and Owston Abbey Site (fig 104 overleaf) SK774079
The Augustinian Priory of Owston was founded in 1161. St. Andrew's Church in Owston formed part of the original endowment and was modified to become the monastic church. In the early 18th century the gatehouse still stood just west of the church, at (a), and was drawn and engraved by Buck which was copied and reproduced in Nichols (below).

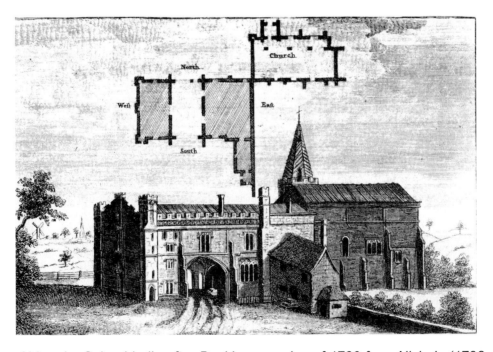

Owston Abbey by Schnebbelle after Buck's engraving of 1730 from Nichols (1798, Vol 2, Pt 2, pl CXXV, 761) showing a very useful record of the gatehouse and church, from the south, with a ground plan.

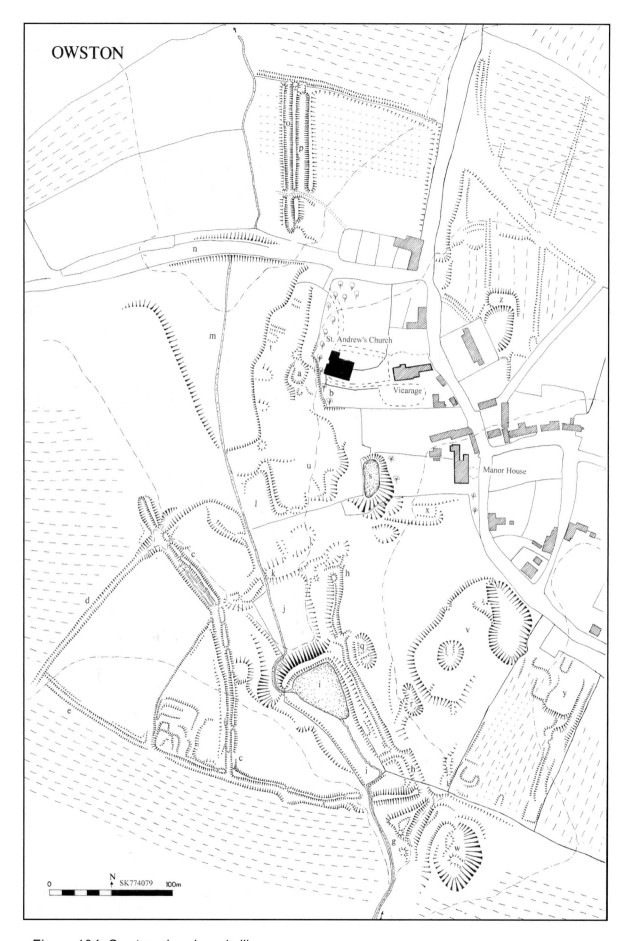

Figure 104: Owston church and village

A view of the north-east side of Owston church, done for Nichols by J. Pridden in 1793, after the demolition of the gatehouse. (Nichols 1798, Vol 2, Pt 2, Pl CXXVI, 763)

The cloister would have been on the south side of the church, at (b), and the blocked-up doorway of the "night stair" still remains at first floor level in the south wall of the church to witness this fact as can also be seen in the Buck engraving.

The monastic site was laid out in the bottom of a shallow valley. On the west side of the stream is a length of ditch and bank (c-c and continuing to the stream near (i).) which appears to be part of the original precinct boundary. Two more ditches (d) and (e) form a triangular annexe on the west side, and contain a rectangular area of terraced building foundations, perhaps a garden.

Water management was important in the construction of monasteries. At the south end of the plan is an arrangement of banks and channels (g), by which the stream was dammed to divert water from the valley bottom into a by-pass channel (h-h), from which it could be fed through a side channel into the first pond (i), or allowed to flow past it. The pond (i) is retained by a big earthen dam. Below it downstream is a shallower pond (j) retained by a low dam at (k), and another shallow pond (l). Below this is the largest pond in the series (m), where the water would have been retained by a large dam (n) which carries the road. Further north still are two long, narrow ponds (o) and (p), which must have played a part in the process of fish rearing and management. It has been suggested that they might have been divided up by nets or fences and used for different stages of the process of rearing small fish. They lie in an old close with a bank surrounding it.

To the east of the deep pond (i) are two more small ponds (q, r) in the hillside, probably on the spring line, and another (which has more of the appearance of a flooded quarry) at (s).

West of the church, near to the slight scarp formed around the pond (m) when it was full of water, are several small earthwork features (t), possibly part of the village, or early monastic buildings, abandoned when the pond was created. More earthworks around (u) are similarly difficult to interpret.

Returning towards the south of the site, a large irregular platform (v) seems to be composed of spoil from the adjacent stone quarry to the east. There is another old quarry further south at (w).

South west of the Manor House is a building platform (x), and further south again along the lane, the sites of several buildings are visible as terraces and a building platform at (y), with a hollow way down to the bottom of the close where there are more earthworks, including possibly another small pond.

North of the Manor House, behind a row of cottages, is another stone quarry and next to it is another building platform (z). North of this is evidence of more old closes and a hollow way forming a back lane to this part of the village. (Surveys 1980 and 9th May 1985)

Moated Site, "Oliver Cromwell's Castle" (fig 105)   SK788082

This isolated moated site was surveyed with the assistance of Mr R. P. Jarrett in the summer of 1980. The stream course was diverted slightly to the north in a channel (a), and a moat (b) 10-15m wide, dug out, isolating a sub-rectangular platform approximately 90m by 60m. There is a bank (c), probably the remains of a wall, along the east and south sides of the platform, widening out into a possible small building at the north end of the east side. The north-west corner of the platform has a projection and a recess. The projection (e) contains a building platform.

Much of the moat platform has faint traces of ridge and furrow, but there are indications of another building platform at (g). Outside the moat, to the south, are foundations of a stone building (h), possibly a gatehouse near the site of a bridge across the moat. This building stands in the westernmost of three embanked enclosures (i, j, k). To the north of (k) there is a shallow depression at (l), indicating the original course of the stream. Alongside this is a narrow pond (m), probably part of the supply channel which fed water from further upstream to fill the moat. There is a corresponding length of ditch or narrow pond on the west side of the moat (n).

The site has been identified as a possible secure granary belonging to Owston Abbey. It is known that the Abbey had a granary on their Knossington demesne farm, and Knossington is the next parish east from this site. The size of the site also indicates a wealthy owner, and there is little indication of buildings within the moat, implying that this is not a conventional manor house site.

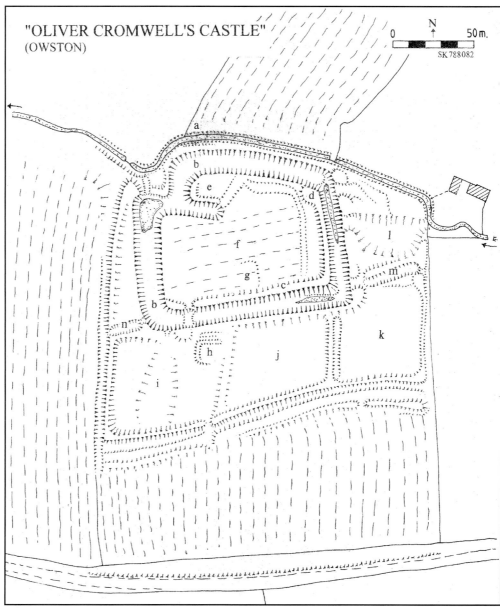

Figure 105: Owston - Oliver Cromwell's Castle

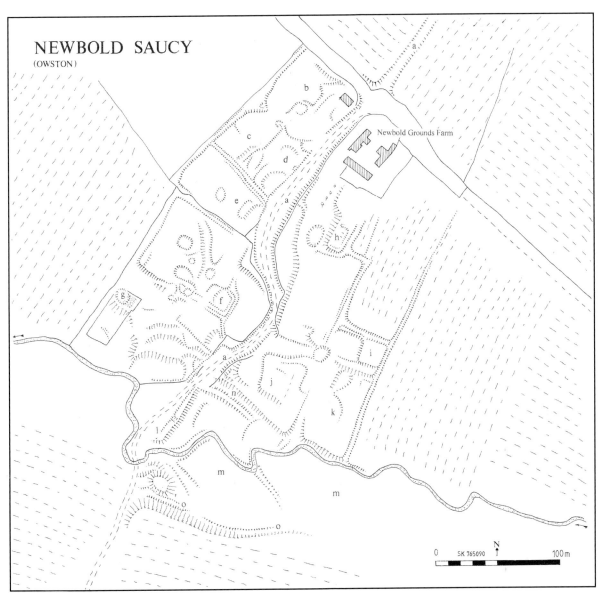

NEWBOLD SAUCY
(OWSTON)

Newbold Grounds Farm

0   SK 765090   N↑   100 m

Figure 106: Owston - Newbold Saucy village earthworks

Deer Park and Woods
A long-established deer park is recorded in 1279 probably in the south-east of the parish where the Owston Woods survive to this day. They are first mentioned in 1279 (Squires 2004, 149).

Newbold Saucy Village Earthworks (fig 106)   SK765090
The site of this deserted village lies south-west of Newbold Grounds Farm, alongside a hollow way (a-a-a). To the west is a complex of earthwork remains with building platforms around (b, c, d), and foundations of a building at (e). Somewhere in this area must be the foundations of the village chapel of St. Lawrence, built in the mid-12th century, when the inhabitants found it too dangerous to walk to the church in Owston (Hoskins 1950, 83). The field to the south has more remains of buildings in a rectangular close extending north and west from (f). Southwards again is a terrace with the site of a building (g), only abandoned in the 19th century. To the east of the hollow way there is a very well-preserved building platform at (h), another at (i), with indications of more around (j) and (k).

The lane following the hollow way crosses the stream just below the remains of an earthen dam (l) which would once have continued across the stream to retain a pond in the area m-m, flanked by ditches on either side, at (n) and (o). Both of these seem to be channels to allow water to flow past the pond. The southern channel (o) is the supply channel or leet for a water mill which stood at the southern end of the dam (l) and is now indicated by a mound of building foundations between (l) and (o). (Site surveyed 1980 with Mr R P Jarrett)

181

North Marefield Village Earthworks (fig 107)   SK749089

In 1086 North and South Marefield formed part of the soke of the royal manor of Rothley (Everson 1994, 23). A chapel was built here in the mid 12th century, but the village fields had probably been converted to pasture by the mid-15th century, and the settlement was entirely depopulated by 1540 (Hoskins 1950, 83-4). For further detail see Everson (1994, 22-4).

The site of the village lies east of the present farm, along an east-west hollow way (a-a-a). The centre of the village is at the confluence of two small streams. The west side was reached by a hollow way (b) and the east side by a hollow way (c). Another old lane (d) leads to the east, and north of this hollow way is a manorial site with a small moated platform (e) in the centre. Hoskins considered the island in the middle too small to have been the site of a manor house, and the moat therefore more likely to have been a fish pond. The size is about 10m. x 15m., which does not seem unduly small for a medieval house, if we assume all the service buildings lay outside the moat which Hoskins did not (*op cit*). Around the moat are building platforms (f, g) and a small fishpond (h) with a drainage channel to the main stream. The area around these features is divided up by various old enclosure boundaries.

To the west across the stream are more old closes, with building platforms at (i) and in a line along the street frontage at (j, k, l). In two places the foundations of the stone walls are visible. There is a hollowed-out area (m), perhaps a crew yard, and another building platform to the south at (n). South of the hollow way (a) are the foundations of another stone building (o) in an area with two crofts. To the east across the stream are foundations of three more buildings (p, q, r) and another building platform. There are more old closes to the north, in the angle between the two small streams, and in the piece of land between the streams and hollow way (b) including probable sites of three or four more buildings.

Between the stream and hollow way (c) is a plot with house foundations at (s, t, u). At (u) the wall footings are visible, and next to it are foundations of a small circular building (v), perhaps a dovecote. Finally, there is a rectangular block of village earthworks between the three hollow ways (a, c, d). Within this are building platforms around (w, x, y), and probably elsewhere. There is an old fishpond at (z). A more detailed assessment can be found in Everson (1994, 22-27).

ROLLESTON

Open Fields

The fields of Rolleston were open in 1658, by 1794 it was described as old enclosure (VCH, 20)

Village and Hall   SK731002

Rolleston Hall and its gardens are laid out over the site of a small village, but no clear earthwork remains have yet been identified. Plantations and fish ponds around the Hall may well have concealed or destroyed much of the evidence. The most likely place to find evidence is in the open area immediately south of the Hall, where parch marks of a possible hollow way have been observed from the air. Victoria County History noted that no early buildings survived, but "*they seem to have stood east of the church and garden*". The Hall of the 17th/18th century was demolished in 1955 and replaced by a new building (VCH 19).

Windmill Mound   SP736998

A windmill is mentioned in 1302 and existed until *c*1641 (VCH 21).

SCRAPTOFT

Open Fields

Scraptoft's open fields were enclosed by 1674 (Beresford 1949, 111).

Village Earthworks (fig 108)   SK645056

Although Scraptoft is on the edge of the Leicester suburbs, the village centre retains its ancient layout, and some open land. West of All Saints Church is a public open space, which despite landscaping in the mid-20th century still has evidence of building platforms at (a) and (b), and

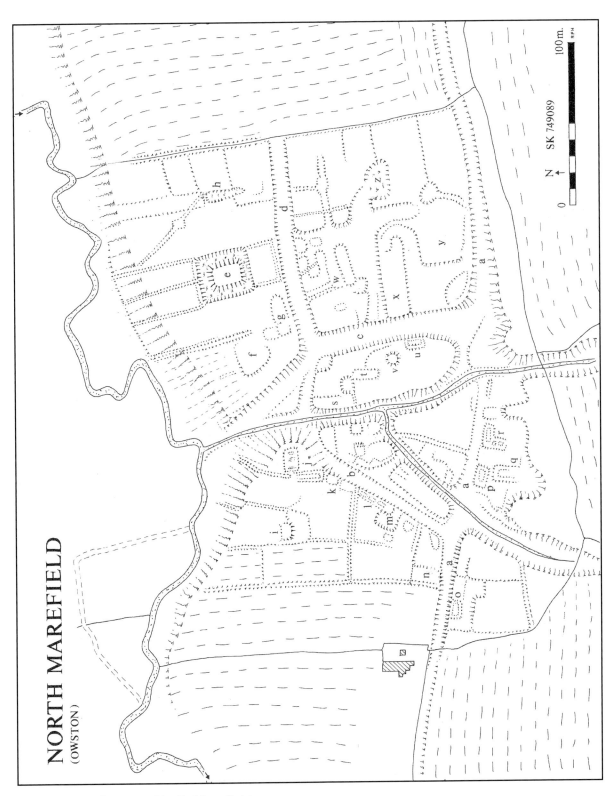

NORTH MAREFIELD
(OWSTON)

SK 749089

Figure 107: Owston, North Marefield

an old pond (c). Across the lane to the west is still (in 2014) a pasture field, with a hollow way (d), flanked by at least three old village crofts. There has been some quarrying in the north-east corner of the field.

To the north, old aerial photographs have recorded the line of the back lane (e) along the northern boundary of the village. This area is now built over.

Scraptoft Hall Gardens (fig 109)   SK648057

When the author visited to survey the grounds (29th March 1988, with a group of students) Scraptoft Hall was still, as Pevsner described it *"an impressive stone-fronted Early Georgian*

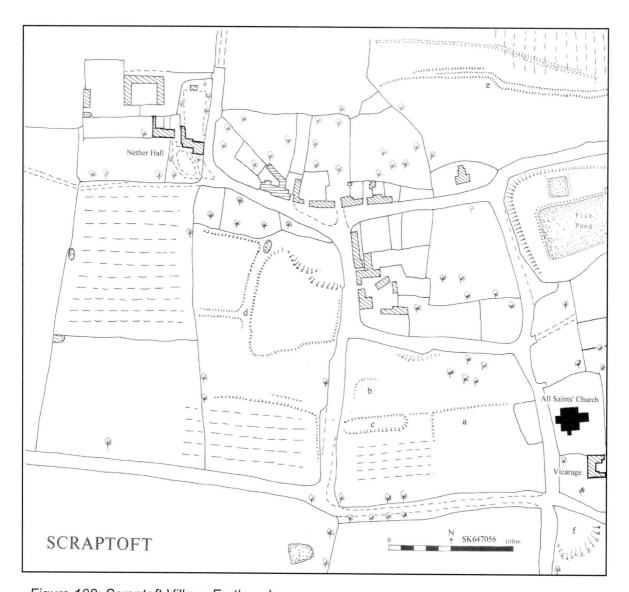

Figure 108: Scraptoft Village Earthworks

house lying behind a set of superb iron gates". Nichols states that the Hall was "*considerably enlarged about 1730, by Laetitia, the relict (widow) of Sir Edward Wigley*" (Nichols 1798, 784). Development of the outbuildings and area east of the Hall as a teacher training college after the Second World War had hardly spoiled its ambience. On the south side of the Hall were lawns with evidence of a levelled parterre, and extending south from here an avenue with remains of slight terraces. North-west of the Hall was a large embanked fish pond with another smaller pond alongside. To the east one could walk through the overgrown plantations to the artificial mound called "The Mount", with a shell-lined grotto in its base, and a spiral path up to the site at the summit where a summer house once stood.

These pleasure grounds at Scraptoft are described at length by John Throsby in his late18th century account of Leicestershire, because they were often opened for the people of Leicester to visit. These "*delightful groves*" extended over 100 acres, containing "*some attempts at temple forms, grottos, caves and water scenery...*" (Throsby 1789, 314 and 318).

Regarding The Mount, he notes "*At the extremity of the pleasure gardens, a mound of earth is raised, done at the expense of the late Mr. Wigley, which commands a rich and luxuriant prospect.*" "*On top of this mount, whose surface is clothed with shrubs and evergreens, is placed a kind of lanthorn, or summer house, in which you may sit secure from the cold blasts of winter, or favoured by summer's breeze under a canopy, surveying objects far and near.*" (*op cit, 318-9*).

On the occasion of a site visit in 2010 the Hall was a fire-gutted wreck, but it has now been restored and converted into apartments and the grounds are filled with high-density housing.

Figure 109: Scraptoft Hall Gardens

185

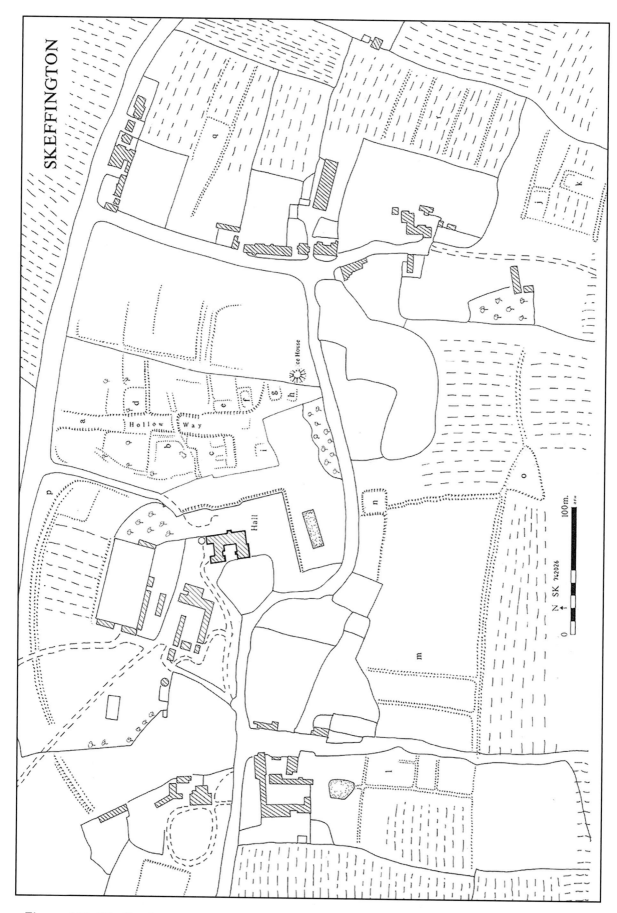

Figure 110: Skeffington

"Moat"   SK644064

The Scraptoft tithe map marks a small circular moat at this point, in the south-west angle of the cross roads (Nat Archives IR 30/19/123). The platform is shown as being about 20m in diameter, and the feature is described as "Garden and Moat". The fields to the north-west are called "Moat Close" and those to the north-east "Moat Meadow". This would seem to have been part of a landscape scheme associated with Nether Hall (top of fig 108) or Scraptoft Hall. The moat was filled in many years ago.

SKEFFINGTON

Open Fields
In 1674 there were three open fields: Wood, Mill and North Fields (Beresford 1949, 112).

Village Earthworks (fig 110)   SK750024
The landscaped grounds around the Hall have been laid out over a former area of the village. The Hall appears to have been rising in status during the 16th and 17th centuries. A hollow way (a) branches off the main Leicester to Peterborough road. It is flanked by old closes, with building sites at (b, c, d, e, f). There are distinct house platforms at (c) and (e), and foundations of a stone building at (f). Three more building platforms (g), (h) and (i), seem to be situated actually in the hollow way, with the mound of an 18th/19th century ice house nearby.

There are traces of more old buildings at the south-east corner of the village (j) and (k), and old closes at the south-east corner, around (l) and (m). Two drained ponds (n, o) may be part of a landscaping scheme extending south from the Hall. The northern boundary of the Hall gardens seems at one time to have been enclosed by a substantial bank and ditch (p).

Returning to the east end of the village, there is another building platform at (q), and to the south a field of ridge and furrow (r) has at some time been subdivided into narrow closes.

STOUGHTON

Open Fields
Three open fields are recorded in c1341 – Stoughton or East or Ladywong Field, Oadby or South Field, and Thurnby or North Field. The parish was inclosed piecemeal, partly by Leicester Abbey in the 15th and early 16th century, partly after the dissolution. The process of enclosure was probably complete by the 1630s (VCH, 328).

Village Earthworks (fig 111 overleaf)   SK639021
To the west of St. Mary's Church in Stoughton is a field of earthworks which appears to be the site of a vanished manor-house, or perhaps a grange farm. There is a large building platform (a), partially surrounded by two ponds (b, c) giving the suggestion of a moated site. The northern corner of the "moat" was probably filled in during construction of the tree-lined avenue to Stoughton Grange, in the 18th or 19th century. Between the moat and the church is an area packed with old foundations, with sites of buildings indicated at (d, e, f) and (g) (surveyed 18th November 1980). Nichols comments:- "*In the town of Stoughton the abbot and convent of Leicester built a most fair and beautiful chapel, with a high spire steeple, the window curiously wrought with stories expressing the benefactors' (coats of) arms.*" (Nichols 1798, 853). His engraved view of the church (left) shows in the background a thatched building standing in the area of the earthworks described above.

Stoughton Church (Nichols 1798, Vol 2/2, pl CXXXV, 848)

187

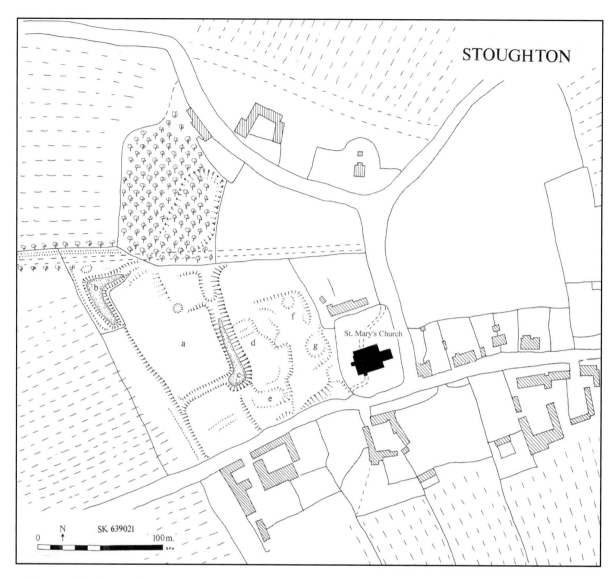

Figure 111: Stoughton

Stoughton Grange (fig 112)   **SK630021**

Stoughton Grange was one of the most valuable grange farms of Leicester Abbey, so we should expect to find some substantial earthwork remains. However it was also a grand 16th -19th century house, with landscaped gardens, and it is difficult to be sure what era the various earthwork features date from. It is also possible that the site (a) by Stoughton Church, is the original site of the grange farm.

The foundations of the post-medieval Stoughton Grange are still visible, and to the east of them is a garden terrace (b), with more traces of abandoned garden terraces to the north, and a long "canal" with a semi-circular pond. The canal looks to date from the 18th century, and is flanked on the north side by a raised avenue which curves northwards towards Stoughton village. This would presumably have been a carriage drive allowing the inhabitants of the Hall an elegant route to church. North of the canal is the site of a large sub-rectangular pond (c), with dams at each end. The eastern dam could have retained a pool of water extending to the avenue and perhaps beyond. The western dam is distinctly curved, and carries another driveway from the Hall, leading to the north lodge. Pond (c) appears to be a piece of 18th century landscaping. Nichols notes "the gardens are extensive, inclosed with brick walls. A large sheet of water runs by the side of a long walk, which extends from Stoughton hall nearly to Evington." (Nichols 1798, 852).

Downstream are two more functional-looking ponds, making good use of the topography. Pond (d) has a by-pass channel on the south side, traces of a small island, and a wave-cut notch which still marks the original extent of the water. There could have been a water mill sited on

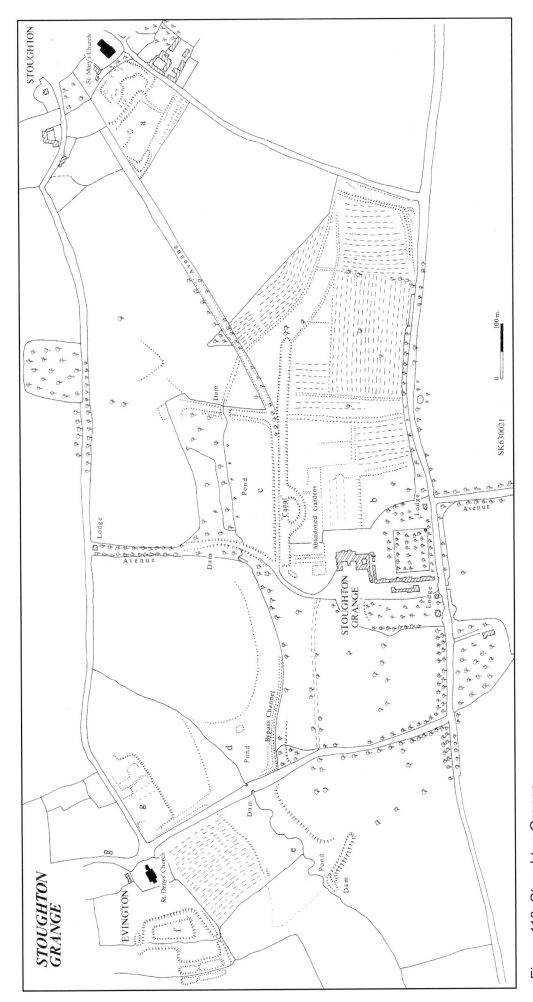

Figure 112: Stoughton Grange

the dam, which carries the lane from Evington to Oadby. To the west are the partial remains of another substantial earthen dam which would have retained a pond (e). Both (d) and (e) could be medieval or early post-medieval fish ponds. However they are actually in Evington parish, which argues against them being part of the medieval Stoughton Grange.

The mansion house of Stoughton Grange, rebuilt in the 18th century in a fashionable "Gothick" style, was extensively rebuilt in the late 19th century but only lasted in this form until just after the First World War, when the house, already empty and fire-damaged, was demolished by the new owners of the estate - the Co-operative Wholesale Society of Manchester, who farmed the land for the next ninety years or so. (Survey 19th November 1986)

Mills

In 1391 there is mention of a windmill and a water mill at Stoughton, and also a horse mill. (Nichols 1798, 851)

THURNBY

Open Fields

There is archaeological evidence of ridge and furrow fields around Thurnby, but apparently little documentary evidence. The open fields may have been shared with Bushby. Enclosure was before 1618. A Middle Field is mentioned in 1622 (VCH, 323).

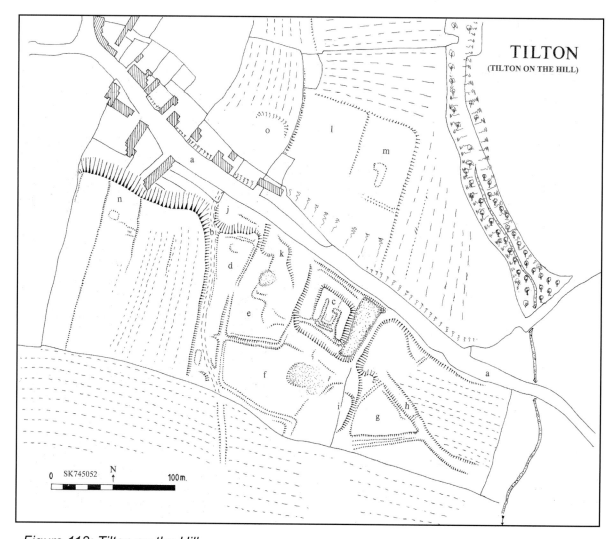

Figure 113: Tilton on the Hill

TILTON ON THE HILL

Open Fields

Final enclosure here took place in 1603 (Beresford 1949, 123).

Moated Site and Village Earthworks (fig 113)   SK745052

At the extreme south end of Tilton village are several pasture fields with earthworks, surveyed 27th October 1982. The lane (a) is in a hollow way as it leaves the village. and an old lane (b) branches off south along another, smaller hollow way into the fields. To the east of this lane is a complex of earthworks focused on a moated site. The moat platform (c) is approximately 30m square, and has evidence of building foundations, including the wall footings of a stone building in the centre. This appears to have been the location of a manor house, with old enclosures around it at (d, e, f, g) for gardens, orchards and outbuildings. There are building platforms at (e) and (i). East of the moat is a drainage channel (h), possibly widened for use as a fishpond. North-west of the moat are two house platforms (j) and (k) on the road frontage, possibly built after the moated manor house had been abandoned. Further west are foundations and a small building (n), perhaps a field barn.

Across the road to the north are two old closes, (l) and (m), with foundations of a building in (m). To the west of these is an old quarry pit (o), probably for stone.

Mound   SK743058

A mound, by the road, 200m north of St Peter's Church, is probably the site of an old windmill.

TUGBY

Open Fields

There were three open fields in 1674, Griff Field, Mile Field and Scrib Field (Beresford 1949, 113)

Village Earthworks (West) (fig 114 overleaf)   SK 760009

South west of the parish church is an area of earthworks, with two hollow ways (a) and (b), a small enclosure (c) with a pond, and small mounds, perhaps building sites (d). To the north a mound (e) has been suggested but not confirmed. The earthworks east of the church (f) are described below with the second part of the survey.

Village Earthworks (East)(fig 115)   SK762010

East of St Thomas a Becket's Church, flanking the main road, is an area of earthworks, with a cluster of rectilinear terraces, including building platforms, at (a), partly encircled on the north side by a ditch. To the east is a rectangular enclosure or yard, containing the foundations of another building (b). The field continues to slope gently towards the east, with the site of another building and a small pond at (c), and an elongated fishpond at (d). The earthworks suggest the existence of another, smaller pond just to the north of (d), and foundations of a small building just to the west of it. A possible interpretation of these features is that (a) is the site of a manor house and outbuildings, (b) the farm buildings, and (c) and (d) are features of the gardens.

The field to the south has evidence of a rectangular enclosure centred on (e). with a ditch along its northern sides and foundations of a small building in the north corner. There are remains of another elongated fishpond (f) on the south-east side of the enclosure, parallel to the stream. To the west is another building platform (g), and west again are two fields with evidence of old closes around (h) and (i). (Site surveyed 6th May 1992 with the assistance of Tugby Primary School)

Old Keythorpe (fig 116 overleaf)   SP765993

The hamlet of Keythorpe was depopulated about 1450-60 by Thomas Palmer of Holt. It is recorded that one house, probably the manor house from the moated site noted below, was

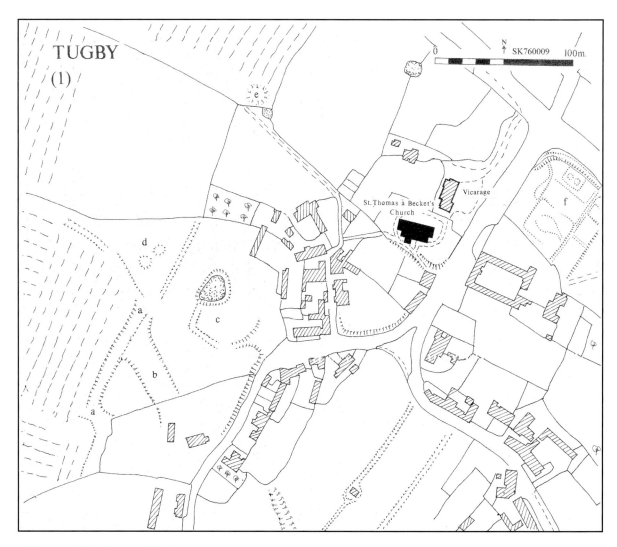

Figure 114: Tugby West

dismantled and re-erected at Skeffington (Hoskins 1950, 85-6). The area was landscaped with lakes and parkland in the 19th century, and partly levelled during the wartime "dig for Victory" in 1943. The site of a substantial rectangular moat remained faintly visible, and was photographed from the air as a soil mark. Fieldwalking in November 1981 produced a scatter of medieval pottery to confirm the identification of the site. The moated platform was approximately 40m square, and the fieldwalking produced medieval ridge tile from the manor house buildings.

WHATBOROUGH

Open Fields (frontispiece to Part 3, opp p130, Thomas Clerke's map of 1586)
The parish was enclosed before the end of the 15th century, but most of the ridge and furrow has been recorded on aerial photographs, and also drawn up on the 1586 map by Thomas Clerke on a basis of his study of ridge and furrow in what were then pasture fields.

Village Earthworks   SK771059
(aerial photographs front Part 3 and overleaf, fig 117 overleaf)

Whatborough exists today as an area of earthworks on a flat topped hill. Unlike most hills in the area this is topped with a layer of stone rather than heavy clay. In 1086 fifteen households are recorded, and in 1156 the land was granted to the Grandmontine Priory of Alberbury (Shropshire). In the early 15th century this was one of the "Alien Priories" which were suppressed by Henry V and in 1437 Whatborough was given to All Souls College, Oxford. The village had a chapel in 1220, served by the mother church at Tilton, but the population had probably

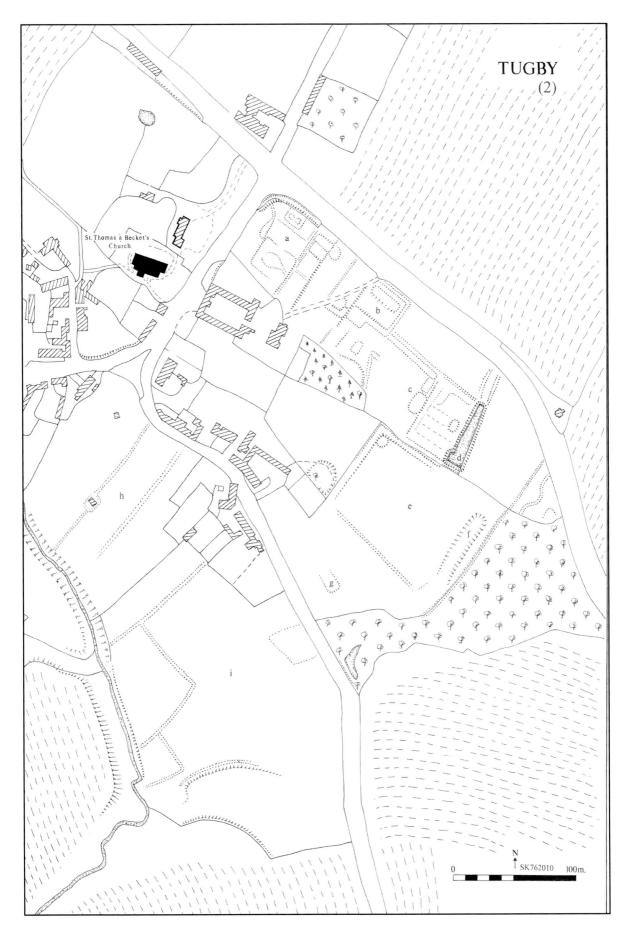

TUGBY
(2)

St.Thomas à Becket's
Church

N
SK762010

0   100m.

Figure 115: Tugby East

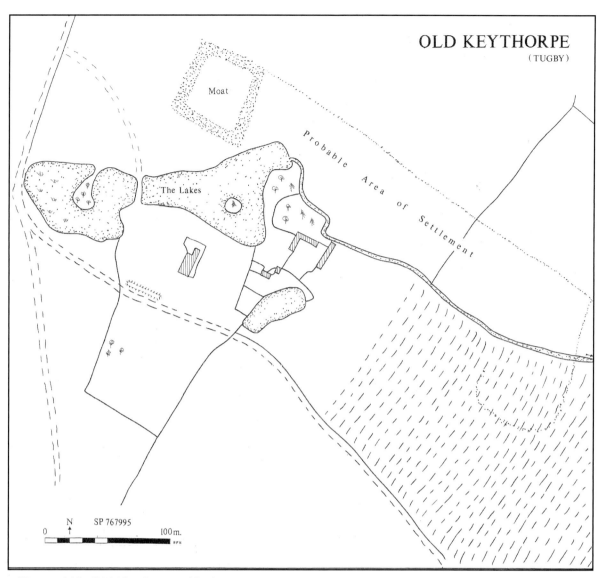

OLD KEYTHORPE
(TUGBY)

Moat

Probable Area of Settlement

The Lakes

N   SP 767995

0   100m.
RFH

Figure 116: Old Keythorpe, Tugby

declined to 7-10 households by the early 14th century, and this process continued. The College leased the lands to the nearby Launde Priory, who in 1495 inclosed the open fields and converted them to sheep pasture. Launde Priory was suppressed in 1539 and its lands appropriated by Thomas Cromwell. A dispute later arose about the extent of the lands owned by All Souls, and in 1586 the Warden of the College commissioned a map to record Whatborough parish in detail. This remains one of the earliest surviving maps of an English deserted village, although by the time it was made there existed only one house, the cottage of the shepherd, Christopher Tiptoft (Hoskins 1950, 96-8).

The earthwork remains were surveyed on the 23rd and 24th of February 1983. They comprised a west-east hollow way (a), with the main street of the village branching off

Aerial view of the deserted village of Whatborough looking south. By permission Cambridge University Collection of Aerial Photography © copyright reserved

194

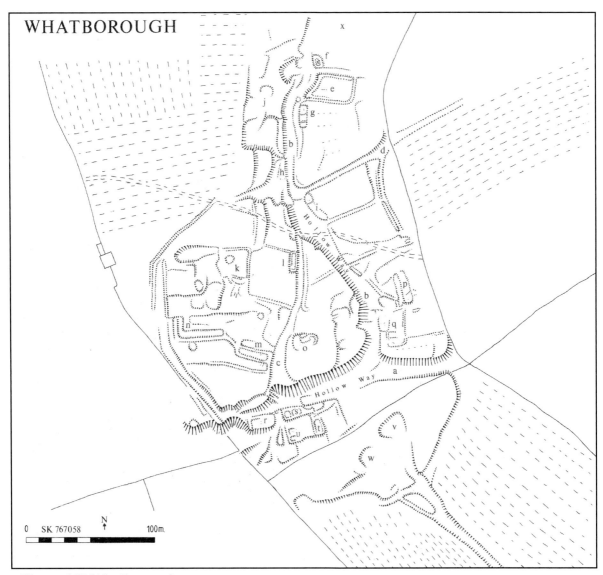

Figure 117 Whatborough

to the north as another hollow way (b). Another lane (c) cuts through the angle between (a) and (b) but is far less deeply incised, implying that it has had far less use. Another small hollow way leads from the centre of the village east to (d), where it crosses the line of the back lane along the east side of the village. The main street (b) is flanked by a mass of earthwork features, beginning at the north end of the village with an embanked enclosure (e) and foundations of two buildings (f) and (g). One of these may have been Christopher Tiptoft's house, marked on the 1586 map. Across the street are the sites of two more buildings (h) and (j). To the north and south of (j) are two hollowed out areas, possibly crew yards for livestock, which would have been in considerable need of shelter on this exposed site in the winter. To the south of hollow way (d) are two closes or crofts, with building foundations along the street frontage at (i).

To the south-west, across the street, is a sub-circular area of earthworks, cut through by the slight hollow way (c). The area to the west of (c) appears to have been one property, perhaps the monastic farm. There is a concentration of building foundations around (k), but the perimeter of the site is also marked by the tumbled walls of stone buildings at (l, m, n). There are additional walls evident between (l) and (k) and along much of the western perimeter of the area, where another slight hollow way leads around the outside of the walls.

Across the lane (c) to the east is a triangular block with evidence of more sites of buildings, especially at (o). To the east across the main street are remains of more stone buildings at (p) and (q). South of hollow way (a) is another block of earthworks with the wall foundations of at least four stone buildings at (r, s, t, u). Further down the slope are hollows (v, w) above the area where springs of water emerged from the hillside.

195

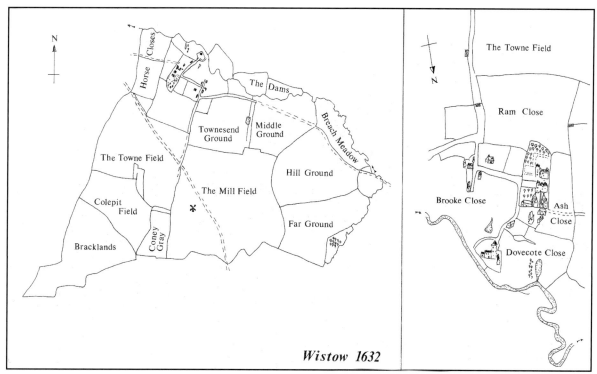

Figure 118: Wistow 1632 Map - Open Fields (taken from a photographic copy in ROLLR (P.P.101/2/3) from an original held at Wistow Hall. Catalogue ref via National Archives.) Note: Map right, North is at bottom.

There are several interesting features of Whatborough village. Firstly, the hilltop site immediately makes one suspect possible continuity back into the Iron Age, especially in the sub-circular area containing features (k, l, m, n, o). Secondly, for a small and seemingly poor village it has a lot of stone building foundations. Thirdly, it is the subject of the early map, which although drawn up years after the depopulation, records the ridge and furrow of the former open fields in great detail. This was the subject of a study by Naomi Hutchings (1989, 83-92).

WISTOW

Open Fields (fig 118)
In 1625 three open fields are recorded - Barleyhill Field, North Field and Lanver Field. The parish seems to have been mainly enclosed between 1609 and 1632 (VCH, 338). A map of 1632, surveyed for Sir Richard Halford, (photographic copy in ROLLR as above) records the names of The Mill Field, The Towne Field and Colepit Field. About half the parish appears to have been enclosed by the time of this map.

Village and Garden Earthworks (fig 119)   **SP642959**
The site of the village has been largely erased by later landscaping around Wistow Hall, or hidden under plantations of trees, but parts of the pattern can still be discerned. North of the Hall, across the road, is a hollow way (a). On the west side are two or three crofts, with the sites of buildings (d) and (e). There are two or three more old closes to the east alongside the road towards the church. South west of the Hall the village re-emerges, with a north-south hollow way (b) and a west-east one (c), which marks the edge of the settlement and the start of the open fields. On the west side of hollow way (b) are the sites of several buildings around (f) and (g), and on the east side at (h) and (i). Further east are more building platforms at (j) and (k). There are more building foundations to the south at (m). The map of 1632 shows the hollow ways (b) and (c) still in use as lanes, with four or five houses on either side of (b) in the area where I have recorded building remains.

The Hall was rebuilt on a large scale in early Jacobean times (Pevsner & Williamson 2003, 426) and surrounded with formal garden features. To the west of St. Wistan's Church is a field with more earthwork features, including two small ponds near the church yard, a building

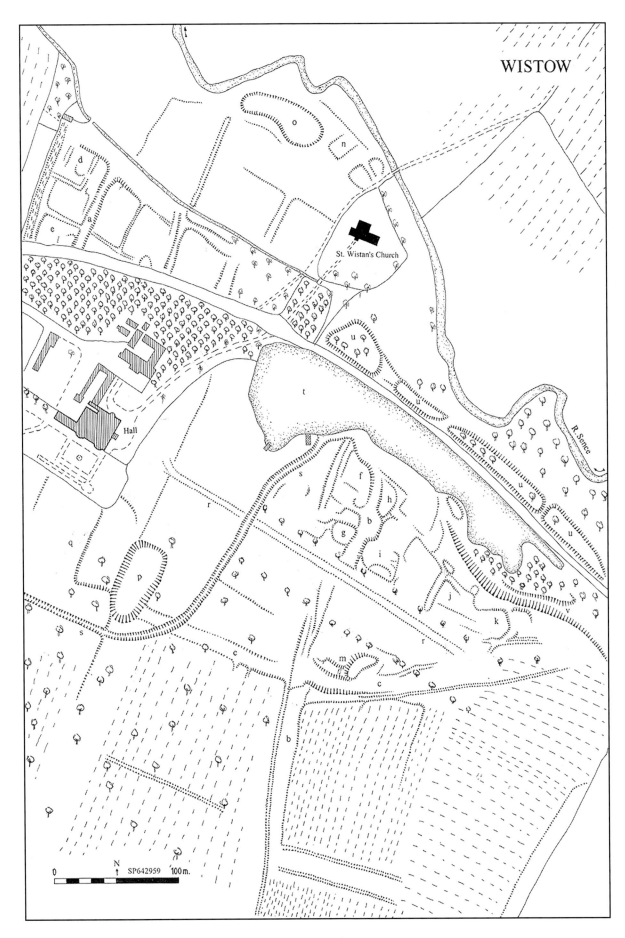

WISTOW

St. Wistan's Church

Hall

R. Sence

0   N↑ SP642959   100 m.

Figure 119: Wistow Village and Garden earthworks

platform (n), a large pond (o), a long straight bank and two slightly sunken rectangular plots. It is possible that all of these are features created in the post-medieval landscaping scheme. The field was called "Dovecote Close" in 1632 and (n) might be the site of the dovecote.

South of the Hall we can identify garden features including a fishpond (p), garden terraces (q) and a raised path (r) along the line of a great avenue of trees. The formal gardens were abandoned, probably in the late 18th or early 19th century in place of an informal landscaping scheme. A ha-ha ditch (s) provided an inconspicuous boundary between the lawns around the Hall and the grazed fields further away. A large, sinuous, lake (t) added a pleasing feature to the view from the south-east front of the Hall. The spoil dug out to make it was mounded up on the other side of the road (u-u) and planted with trees. The lake was supplied with water via a channel (v). This lake probably dates from about the period when the Hall was remodelled from its gabled Jacobean appearance to a more "Gothick" appearance, c.1810. (Surveys 26th and 28th July 1983)

Windmill   SK642946

A windmill is shown in this area on the map of 1632. It is not mentioned after 1675.

Water Mill

The map of 1632 shows a field south of St. Wistan's Church, called The Dams (Dames), possibly recording the site of an old mill dam.

Rabbit Warren   SK 640945

The 1632 map has a field named Coney Graye, indicating that this was a rabbit warren

NEWTON HARCOURT (Wistow)

VCH notes three open fields in Newton Harcourt - Mill Field, Common Field and Barley Hill Field. (VCH, 343-4).

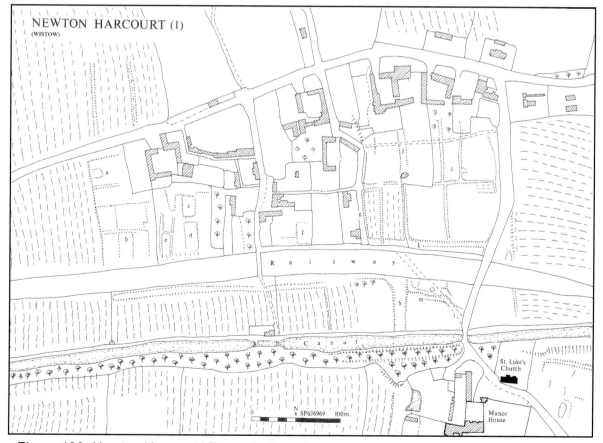

Figure 120: Newton Harcourt Village Earthworks

198

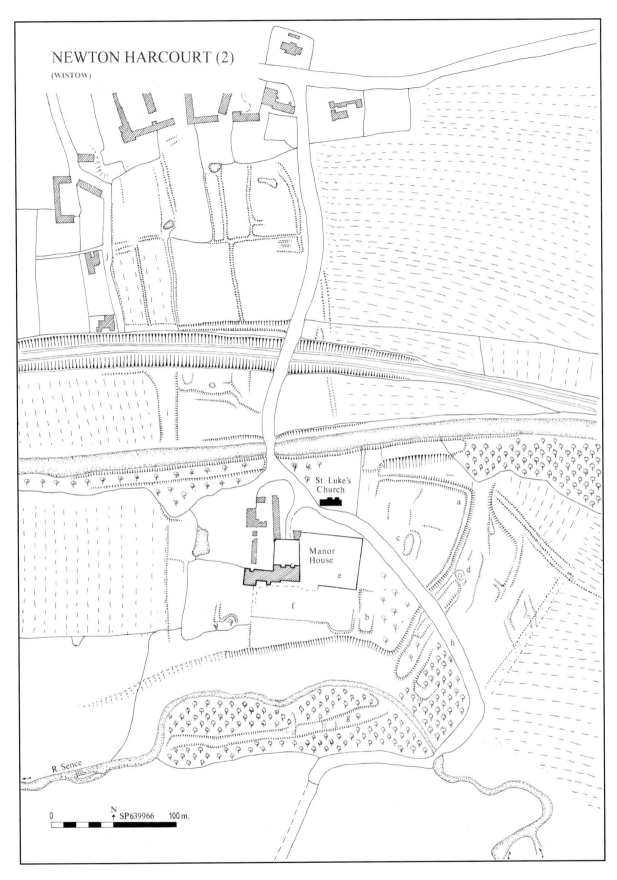

Figure 121: Newton Harcourt Manor Earthworks

Newton Harcourt Village Earthworks (fig 120)   **SP641967**

To the passing motorist, Newton Harcourt looks to be an almost entirely modern village, but if one explores on foot a different world unfolds, with 18th/19th century cottages set amid small pasture fields full of earthworks. An added interest is provided by the fact that the village was cut through by both the Grand Union Canal in the 1790s and the Midland Railway's Leicester to London line in the late1850s.

Several closes at the west end of the village have been ploughed in recent years, but old aerial photographs record sites of buildings at (a) and possibly at (b). The paddock to the east has traces of two more building platforms (c) and (d), and two narrow closes (e). Further east is another slight platform (f) and the hollow way of School Lane (g). Before the railway was cut through this seems to have zig-zagged south to join the hollow way (h). This is in line with a much smaller north-south hollow way (j). Another small lane (k) continued towards the east. This is now replaced by the path which follows the edge of the railway cutting, replacing a path (i) which existed in the mid-19th century and headed directly to the St. Luke's Church.

There are more old closes between School Lane and the hollow way (j), and east of (j) around (l). South of this point, on the south side of the railway, are foundations of more buildings (m). (Site visit 15th August 2014)

Newton Harcourt Manor House Earthworks (fig 121 previous page)   SP639966

The railway and canal seem to have caused some rearrangement of this area, with the road (h) now passing between St Luke's Church and the Manor House. In doing so it passes through an embanked enclosure, whereas it seems that in the past it would have been diverted around this area either to the east or the west. The enclosure (a) seems to have been part of the Manor House gardens, with a pond (c) near the centre, and a building platform (b), built into the sloping hillside. There are foundations of a small circular building, perhaps a dovecote, at (d). (Surveyed 19th July 1983)

Pevsner describes the Manor House as early 17th century, with a fine entrance arch into the courtyard, a walled garden (e) to the east, and a garden terrace (f) with views across the River Sence. There are indications of an old course of the river at (g). The west side of this area of earthworks is marked by the hollow way (i), beyond which is a fine sweep of ridge and furrow.

Mound

VCH notes a mound, probably a former windmill, "close to the north side of the road to Great Glen" (VCH, 344). It still existed in the 17th century and probably gave its name to Mill Field.

WITHCOTE

Open Fields

The parish had been enclosed by 1622 (Beresford 1949, 114) but as with many of the long-enclosed parishes in this volume, quite a lot of ridge and furrow survived to be recorded on mid-20th century air photographs.

Withcote Hall and Village   SK796057

Withcote Hall was rebuilt in the early 16th century and the early 18th century. It has some elements of a formal garden scheme still surrounding it, including a private chapel dating from about 1500. Leland noted "*Mr. Radcliffe builded here a right goodly house...I take this to be one of the fairest houses in Leircestershire, and to be the fairest orchardes and gardines of*

those quarters: but it standeth lowe and wete, and hath a pole (pool) afore it..." (Nichols 1795, 387 referencing Leland's Itineraries I). South of the Hall is a large pond, perhaps the one Leland mentioned.

To the west of the pond is a terrace which appears to have

Withcote Hall, from Nichols 1798, Vol 2, Pt 1, pl CXXI, 392 been part of an avenue extending south from the Hall, probably part of the 18th century gardens. There is a rectangular fishpond which may have been part of a 17th/18th century tree-lined avenue extending west from the house. Around the pond are traces of ridge and furrow and other slight earthworks.

The site of the medieval village is presumably hidden under the gardens of the Hall. At the time of the Domesday survey there was a total of three ploughlands, with one plough, four acres of meadow, and plentiful woodland. The village was rated at 17 shillings in the Lay Subsidy of 1445 (*op cit*).

Sauvey Castle (fig 122)   SK786052

This strongly fortified site lies at the junction of two stream valleys, where the natural topography has been used and enhanced. A substantial dam (a) would have created a pool (i-i-i) up the two valleys. The promontory between the two was cut through so that the water would have completely surrounding the castle site.

The main concentration of building foundations is in the motte at the east end of the promontory, with traces of a curtain wall (b), foundations of a possible tower (c), and traces of two rectangular buildings at (d) and (e). A steep-sided ditch (f) separates this from the bailey, which again has evidence of curtain walls, surrounding an open yard (g) which seems to have been subdivided into two parts along an east-west line. In the north-east corner of the bailey are foundations (h) of a stone building. The entrance to the site would have been over a fortified bridge at (j), where a mound of material now forms a causeway across the moat. From the bottom of the moat to the top of the bailey rampart in this area is a difference in height of over 20m. (Site visit *c*1980)

The castle was certainly in use in the 13th century. It has been described as a place of importance in the time of King John, and custody was usually granted to the King's Foresters in the Forest of Leighfield. It was allowed to fall into ruin after 1276 (VCH Vol 1, 249-250). Governors were appointed at various dates between 1215 and 1260. Nichols comments that *"in the Barons' wars, Sauvey Castle was reckoned a fort of great trust and importance. Soon after which wars, the said castle it may be presumed was demolished."*. (Nichols 1795 p394).

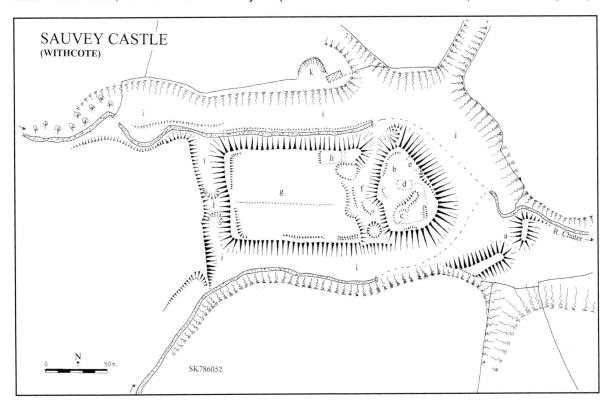

Figure 122: Sauvey Castle

201

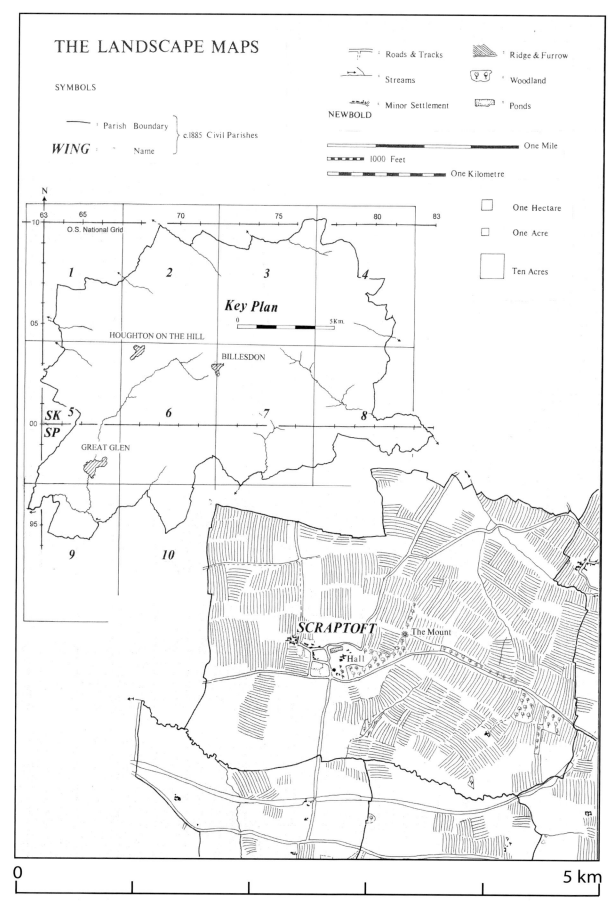

THE LANDSCAPE MAPS

SYMBOLS

⎯ : Parish Boundary ⎤
                      ⎬ c.1885 Civil Parishes
WING ⎯ : Name   ⎦

: Roads & Tracks   : Ridge & Furrow

: Streams   : Woodland

: Minor Settlement   : Ponds
NEWBOLD

One Mile

1000 Feet

One Kilometre

One Hectare

One Acre

Ten Acres

N

O.S. National Grid

63   65   70   75   80   83
10

1   2   3   4

Key Plan

05

HOUGHTON ON THE HILL

0   5Km.

BILLESDON

SK 5   6   7   8
SP
00

GREAT GLEN

95

9   10

SCRAPTOFT   ✳ The Mount

Hall

0   5 km

Landscape Map 1

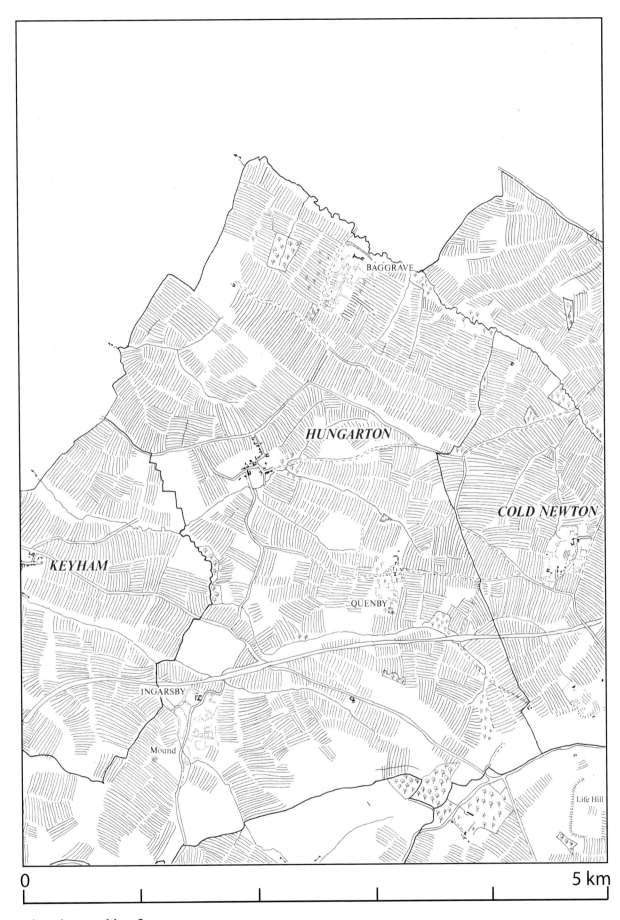

Landscape Map 2

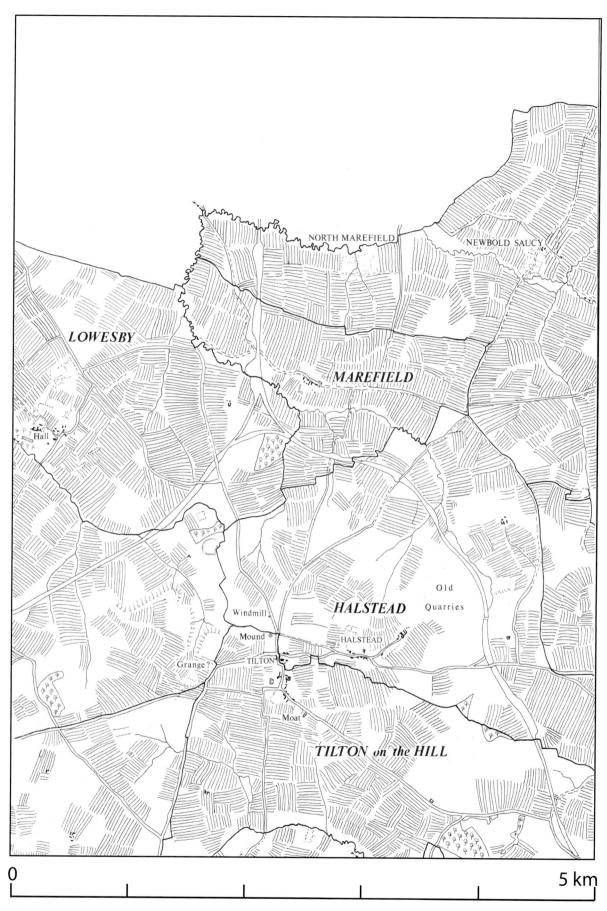

Landscape Map 3

0

5 km

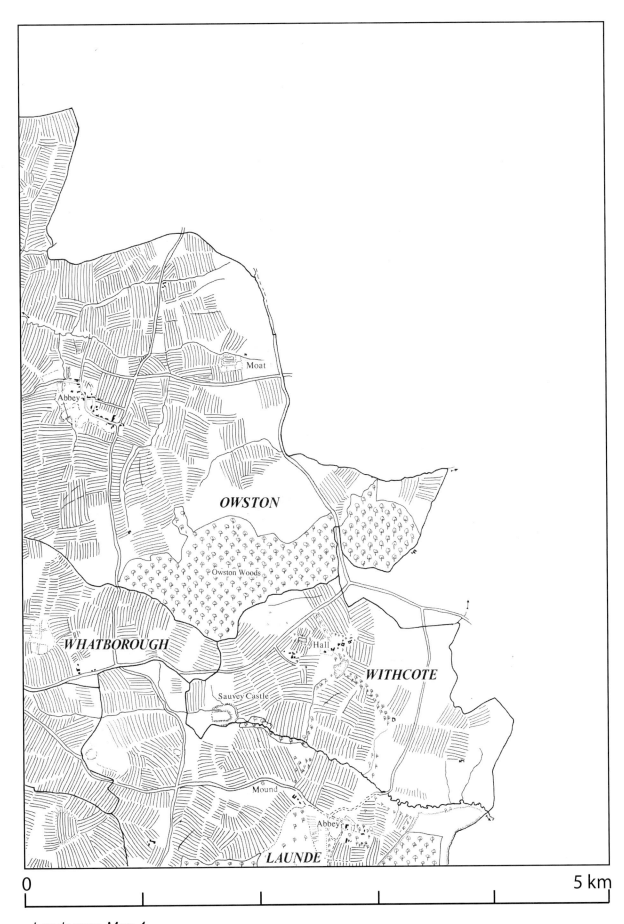

Moat

Abbey

OWSTON

Owston Woods

WHATBOROUGH

Hall

WITHCOTE

Sauvey Castle

Mound

Abbey

LAUNDE

0   5 km

Landscape Map 4

205

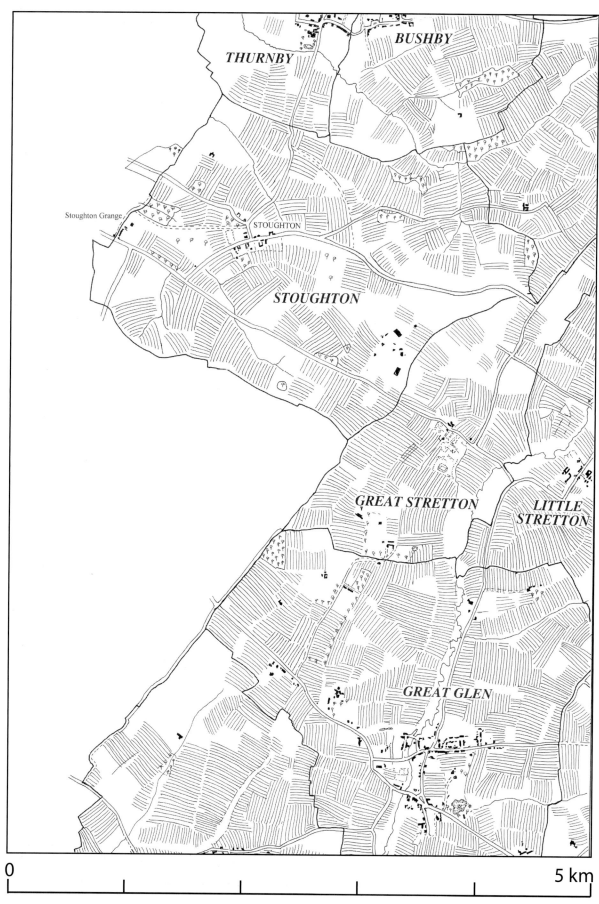

THURNBY

BUSHBY

Stoughton Grange

STOUGHTON

STOUGHTON

GREAT STRETTON

LITTLE STRETTON

GREAT GLEN

0   5 km

Landscape Map 5

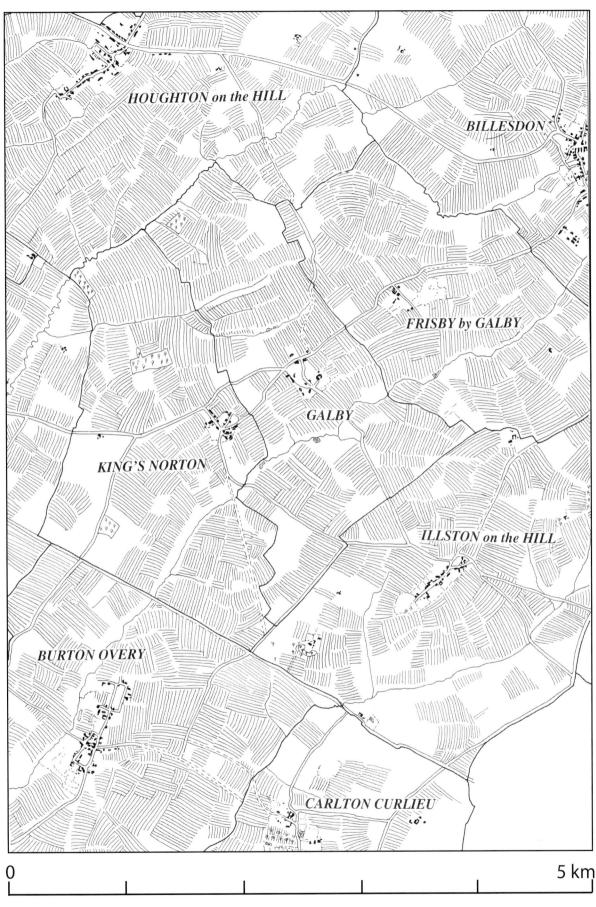

HOUGHTON on the HILL

BILLESDON

FRISBY by GALBY

GALBY

KING'S NORTON

ILLSTON on the HILL

BURTON OVERY

CARLTON CURLIEU

0   5 km

Landscape Map 6

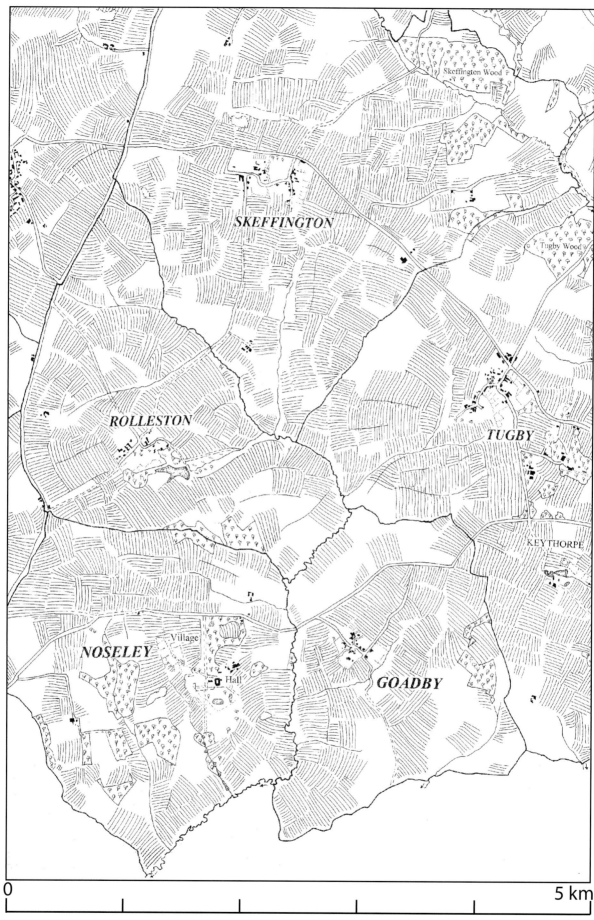

Landscape Map 7

LODDINGTON

Loddington Reddish

EAST NORTON

ALLEXTON

ALLEXTON

Eye Brook

0   5 km

Landscape Map 8

NEWTON HARCOURT

St. Wistan's Church

Hall

WISTOW

Canal

Coal Pit Lane

0   5 km

Landscape Map 9

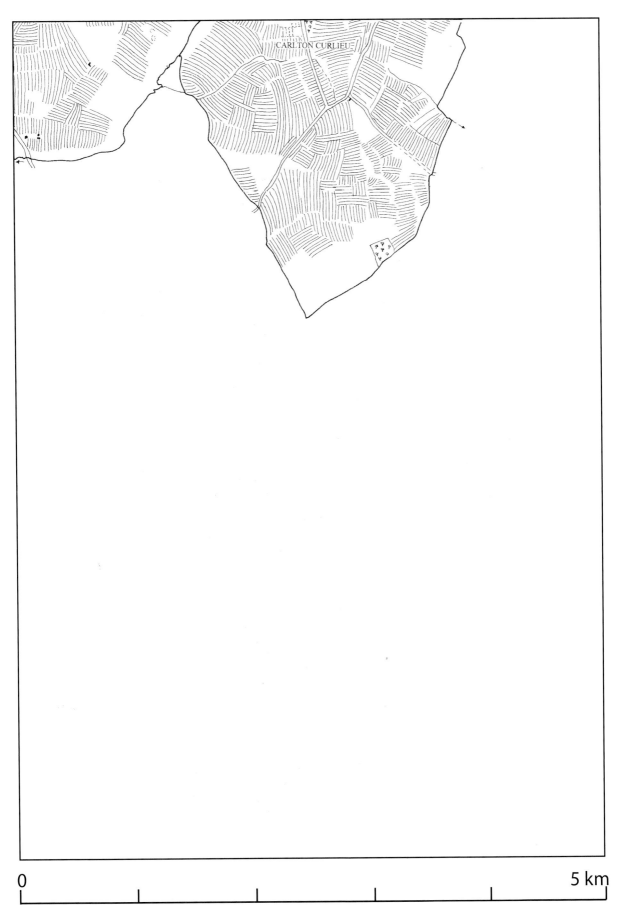

CARLTON CURLIEU

0   5 km

Landscape Map 10

REFERENCES AND ABBREVIATIONS

Baugh, G. C. et al, 1970. *History of the County of Staffordshire*, Vol 3. Victoria County History, London. Referenced online at http://www.british-history.ac.uk/vch/staffs/vol3/pp247-251

Beavitt, P., 1995. 'Geophysical and Building Survey of Launde Abbey'. *Transactions of the Leicestershire Archaeological and Historical Society*, 69, 22-30.

Beresford, M. 1949 'Glebe Terriers and Open-Field Leicestershire.' In: W. G. Hoskins, *Studies in Leicestershire Agrarian History. Leicestershire Archaeological Society Transactions* Vol 24 part 3 for 1948, 77-126: Leicester.

Brown, J., 2010. 'Report on Excavations in Market Harborough'. *Transactions of the Leicestershire Archaeological and Historical Society*, 84, 95-116.

Cantor, L. M., 1970-71. 'The Medieval Parks of Leicestershire'. *Transactions of the Leicestershire Archaeological and Historical Society*, 46, 9-24.

Cossons, A., 2003. *The Turnpike Roads of Leicestershire and Rutland*. Kairos Press: Newtown Linford.

Dyer, C. and Jones, R., (ed) 2010. *Deserted Villages Revisited*. Hertfordshire University Press: Hatfield.

Everson, P., 1994. 'The Deserted Village Remains of North Marefield, Leicestershire'. *Medieval Settlement Research Group Annual Report*, 9, 22-27.

Everson, P. & Brown, G., 2010. 'Dr Hoskins I Presume. Field Visits in the Footsteps of a Pioneer', in: C. Dyer and R Jones (ed.). *Deserted Villages Revisited*. Hertfordshire University Press: Hatfield. (surveys of Hamilton, Ingarsby and Knaptoft)

Farnham, G. F. 1933. *Leicestershire Medieval Village Notes*, 6 vols, Privately Printed. (Available at ROLLR)

Hartley, R. F., 1989. *The Medieval Earthworks of Central Leicestershire*. Leicestershire Museums, Arts and Records Service, Leicester.

Gray, H. L., 1915. *English Field Systems*. Cambridge, Mass.

Hall, D., 2014. *The Open Fields of England*. Oxford University Press: Oxford.

Hill, J. H., c1875. *History of the Hundred of Gartree*. Published for the subscribers, Leicester. (Largely a reworking of the Gartree volume of Nichols)

Hoskins, W. G., 1944-5. 'The Deserted Villages of Leicestershire'. *Transactions of the Leicestershire Archaeological and Historical Society*, 22, pt IV - 2, for 1941-2, 242-264.

Hoskins, W. G., 1950. *Essays in Leicestershire History*. Liverpool University: Liverpool. (Contains the essays 'Galby and Frisby', 24-66, and 'The deserted villages of Leicestershire', 67-107.)

Hoskins, W. G., 1956. 'Seven Deserted Village Sites in Leicestershire'. *Transactions of the Leicestershire Archaeological and Historical Society*. 32, 36-51.

Hutchings, N., 1992. 'The Plan of Whatborough - a study of a sixteenth century map of enclosure'. *Landscape History*, 1992, 83-92.

Jones, R., 2010. 'Contrasting patterns of village and hamlet desertion in England' in: C. Dyer and R. Jones (ed.). *Deserted Villages Revisited*. Hertfordshire University Press: Hatfield

Knox, R., 2015. 'The medieval fortified sites of Leicestershire and Rutland' in: *Medieval Leicestershire*. Leicestershire Fieldworkers: Leicester.

Lee, J. M. & McKinley, R. A., 1964. *The Victoria History of the County of Leicester, Volume 5, Gartree Hundred*. Published for the University of London Institute of Historial Research by Oxford University Press: London.

Liddle, P. and O'Brien, L., 1995. 'The Archaeology of the Abbeys and Priories of Leicestershire'. *Transactions of the Leicestershire Archaeological and Historical Society*. Vol 69, 1995, 1-21.

Marcombe, D., 2003. *Leper Knights: The Order of St Lazarus of Jerusalem in England, c1150-1554*. Boydell Press: Martlesham, Suffolk.

Morison, J. & Daisley, P. 2000. *Hallaton Hare Pie Scrambling & Bottle Kicking*. Hallaton Museum Press.

Nichols, J., 1795. *The History and Antiquities of the County of Leicester, Vol II, Part 1 Framland Hundred*. Nichols: London.

Nichols, J,. 1798. *The History and Antiquities of the County of Leicester, Vol II, Part 2 Gartree Hundred*. Nichols: London.

Nichols, J., 1800. *The History and Antiquities of the County of Leicester, Vol III, Part 1, The Hundred of East Goscote*. Nichols: London.

Nichols, J., 1810. *The History and Antiquities of the County of Leicester, Vol IV Part 1. Guthlaxton Hundred*. Revised version of the 1807 edition. John Nichols, London.
(All Nichols volumes were referenced in the republished edition of 1971 by Leicestershire Library Services in association with SR Publishers Ltd: Wakefield.)

NRO - Northamptonshire Record Office, Wootton Hall Park, Mereway, Northampton, NN4 8BQ

Page, W., ed., 1907. *The Victoria History of the County of Leicester, Volume 1*, (Natural History, Ancient man, Domesday, Ecclesiastical), Archibald Constable & Co Ltd: London.

Peek, R. A. P. & Parsons, D., 1972. *A provisional list of sites in Leicestershire recognised from aerial photographs*. Published as a duplicated list by University of Leicester Adult Education Department and CBA Group 6. (Copies held in Leicestershire Historical and Archaeological Society Library and in Leicestershire County Council HER.)

Pevsner, N. & Williamson, E. et al, 2003, rev 2nd edition. *The Buildings of England - Leicestershire & Rutland*. Yale University Press: New Haven and London.

ROLLR - Record Office for Leicester, Leicestershire and Rutland, 38 Long Street, Wigston, LE18 2AH

Royal Commission on the Historical Monuments of England (RCHME), 1981. *An Inventory of the Historical Monuments in the County of Northamptonshire, Volume 3, Archaeological Sites in North-West Northamptonshire*. Originally published by Her Majesty's Stationery Office, London. Referenced online at http://www.british-history.ac.uk/rchme/northants/vol3/pp175-178 (Stanford on Avon).

Score, V., 2010. 'Excavation of the Site of the Hospital of St. John the Baptist, Mill Farm, Lutterworth, Leicestershire'. *Transactions of the Leicestershire Archaeological and Historical Society*, 84, 165-187.

Score, V. & Morison, J., 2014. 'The Lost Chapel of St. Morrell, Hallaton'. *Transactions of the Leicestershire Archaeological and Historical Society*, 88, 55-74.

Squires, A. E., 1995. 'A Provisional List of the Medieval Woodlands of Leicestershire'. *Transactions of the Leicestershire Archaeological and Historical Society*, Vol 69, 86-96.

Squires, A. E., 2004. 'Parks and Woodland in Medieval Leicestershire' in: Bowman, P. & Liddle, P. *Leicestershire Landscapes*. Leicestershire Fieldworkers: Leicester.

Throsby, J., 1789. *Select Views in Leicestershire from Original Drawings containing seats of the nobility and gentry, town views and ruins, accompanied with descriptions and historical relations*. Published J. Throsby and sold by W. Richardson, Strand, London.

Throsby, J., 1790. *The Supplementary Volume to the Leicestershire Views containing A Series of Excursions in the year 1790, to the Villages and Places of Note in the County*. J. Nichols: London.

TLAHS: *Transactions of the Leicestershire Archaeological and Historical Society*, 1967-8. 43, 'Archaeology in Leicestershire and Rutland 1967-8, Report from Leicester Museums and Art Galleries, plus "Kibworth Harcourt",' 64.

Willatts, R., 1991 December. 'Baggrave Hall, Leicestershire'. *Context 32*, 11-13.

VCH = Victoria County History. Lee, J. M. & McKinley, R. A . 1964. *A History of the County of Leicester, Volume 5, Gartree Hundred*. Oxford University Press.

Wood, M., 2010. *The Story of England*. London: Viking.

Leicestershire Fieldworkers visiting Sauvey Castle earthworks

CIVIL PARISH AND SITE NAME INDEX

Site names are given only where the name differs from the civil parish name. Some places only appear on maps and this is indicated.